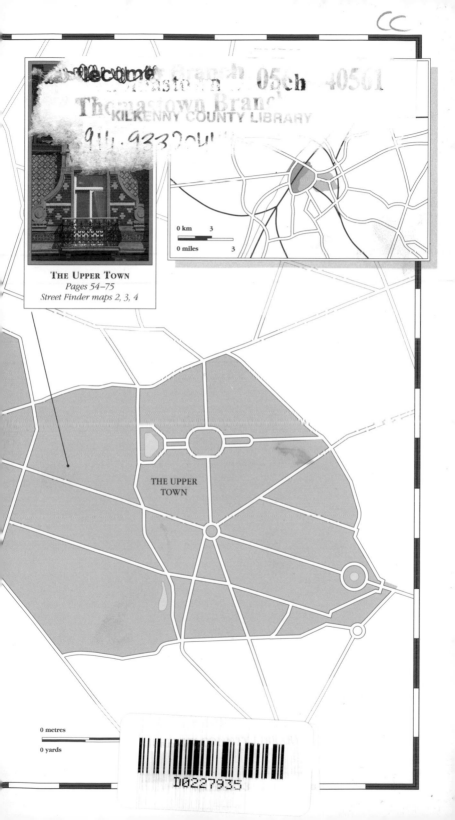

0 km   3

0 miles   3

**THE UPPER TOWN**
*Pages 54–75*
*Street Finder maps 2, 3, 4*

THE UPPER
TOWN

0 metres

0 yards

# EYEWITNESS TRAVEL GUIDES

# BRUSSELS
## BRUGES, GHENT & ANTWERP

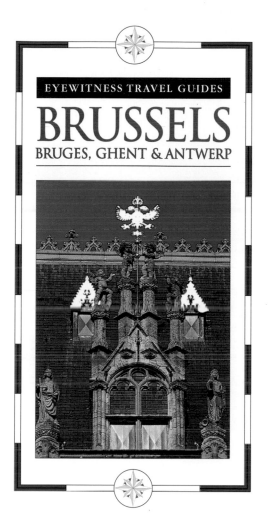

# EYEWITNESS TRAVEL GUIDES

# BRUSSELS

## BRUGES, GHENT & ANTWERP

DK

O M

LONDON, NEW YORK,
MELBOURNE, MUNICH AND DELHI
www.dk.com

Produced by Duncan Baird Publishers
London, England

MANAGING EDITOR Rebecca Miles
MANAGING ART EDITOR Vanessa Marsh
EDITORS Georgina Harris, Michelle de Larrabeiti
DESIGNERS Dawn Davies-Cook, Ian Midson
DESIGN ASSISTANTS Rosie Laing, Kelvin Mullins
VISUALIZER Gary Cross
PICTURE RESEARCH Victoria Peel, Ellen Root
DTP DESIGNER Sarah Williams

Dorling Kindersley Limited
PROJECT EDITOR Paul Hines
ART EDITOR Jane Ewart
MAP CO-ORDINATOR David Pugh

CONTRIBUTORS
Zoë Hewetson, Philip Lee, Zoë Ross,
Sarah Wolff, Timothy Wright, Julia Zyrianova

PHOTOGRAPHERS
Demetrio Carrasco, Paul Kenward

ILLUSTRATORS
Gary Cross, Richard Draper, Eugene Fleury,
Paul Guest, Claire Littlejohn, Robbie Polley,
Kevin Robinson, John Woodcock

Reproduced by Colourscan (Singapore)
Printed and bound by South China Printing Co. Ltd., China

First published in Great Britain in 2000
by Dorling Kindersley Limited
80 Strand, London WC2R 0RL

**Reprinted with revisions 2003, 2005**

**The information in this
Dorling Kindersley Travel Guide is checked regularly.**
Every effort has been made to ensure that this book is as
up-to-date as possible at the time of going to press. Some details,
however, such as telephone numbers, opening hours, prices,
gallery hanging arrangements and travel information are liable to
change. The publishers cannot accept responsibility for any consequences arising from the use of this book, nor for any material
on third party websites, and cannot guarantee that any website
address in this book will be a suitable source of travel information.
We value the views and suggestions of our readers very highly.
Please write to: Publisher, DK Eyewitness Travel Guides,
Dorling Kindersley, 80 Strand, London WC2R 0RL, Great Britain.

◁ The Grand Place, centre of the Lower Town, at night

# CONTENTS

## INTRODUCING BRUSSELS

Belgian heroes Tintin and Snowy

Revellers in colourful costume at a
festival in the Grand Place

Vista of a tree-lined path in the Parc du Cinquantenaire

Belgian oysters

Gilt statue on façade of a Guildhouse in Antwerp

Basilique National du Sacré-Coeur

Artist's impression of Cathédrale Sts Michel et Gudule in Brussels

# INTRODUCING
# BRUSSELS

# Putting Brussels on the Map

Brussels is the capital of Belgium and the centre of government for the European Union. Although Belgium is one of Europe's smallest countries, covering 30,500 sq km (11,580 sq miles), it has one of the continent's highest population densities, with 10 million inhabitants (300 people for every square kilometre). Belgium is a bilingual country (Flemish and French). Although Brussels falls geographically in the Flemish half, it is largely French-speaking. Belgium's largest city, with almost one million inhabitants, Brussels is also the most visited, receiving some six million visitors a year, although 70 per cent of these come for business. Today, Brussels' excellent communications make it an ideal place from which to explore historic Belgian cities such as Antwerp, Ghent and Bruges.

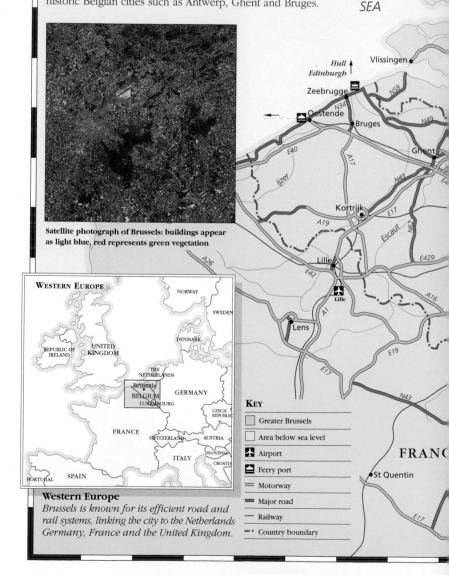

**Satellite photograph of Brussels: buildings appear as light blue, red represents green vegetation**

**WESTERN EUROPE**

NORWAY

SWEDEN

DENMARK

REPUBLIC OF IRELAND

UNITED KINGDOM

THE NETHERLANDS

Brussels

BELGIUM

GERMANY

LUXEMBOURG

CZECH REPUBLIC

FRANCE

SWITZERLAND

AUSTRIA

SLOVENIA

ITALY

CROATIA

PORTUGAL

SPAIN

## Western Europe
*Brussels is known for its efficient road and rail systems, linking the city to the Netherlands Germany, France and the United Kingdom.*

Hull

Harwich

NORTH SEA

Hull
Edinburgh

Vlissingen

Zeebrugge

N58

N34

Oostende

Bruges

N49

E40

A17

N43

Ghent

Ijzer

Kortrijk

A19

E17

N2

Escaut

Lille

E429

A26

E42

A16

Lille

A1

E19

Lens

E17

N43

FRANCE

St Quentin

E17

**KEY**

| | Greater Brussels |
| | Area below sea level |
| ✈ | Airport |
| ⚓ | Ferry port |
| ═ | Motorway |
| ▬ | Major road |
| — | Railway |
| ▬·▬ | Country boundary |

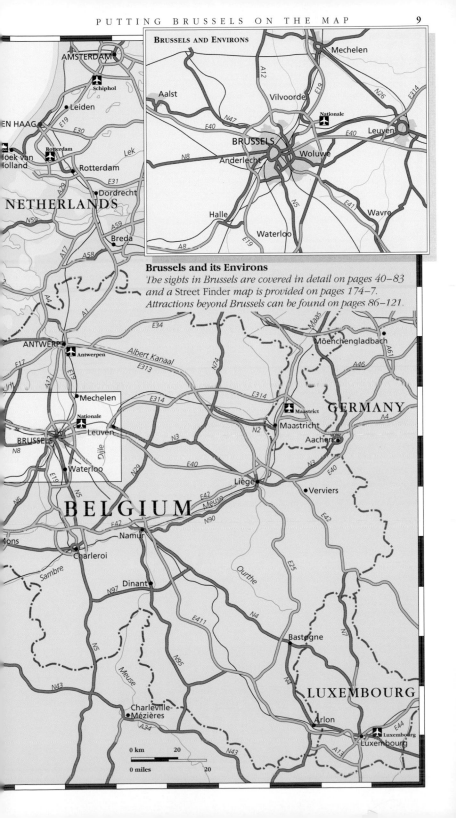

**BRUSSELS AND ENVIRONS**

Mechelen
A12
E19
N26
E314
Aalst
Vilvoorde
N47
Nationale
E40
E40
Leuven
BRUSSELS
N8
Anderlecht
Woluwe
N5
E411
Wavre
Halle
Waterloo
E19
A8

## Brussels and its Environs

*The sights in Brussels are covered in detail on pages 40–83 and a Street Finder map is provided on pages 174–7. Attractions beyond Brussels can be found on pages 86–121.*

# Central Brussels

CENTRAL BRUSSELS is divided into two main areas, each of which has its own chapter in the guide. Historically the poorer area where workers and immigrants lived, the Lower Town contains the exceptional 17th-century heart of the city, the Grand Place, as well as the cosmopolitan Place de Brouckère, and the historic workers' district, the Marolles. The Upper Town, traditional home of the aristocracy, is an elegant area which encircles the city's green oasis, the Parc de Bruxelles. Running up through the area is Rue Royale, which ends in the 18th-century Place Royale, home to the city's finest art museums.

**Hôtel de Ville**
*The focus of the Grand Place, Brussels' historic Town Hall dates from the early 15th century. Its Gothic tracery façade features the famous needle-like crooked spire (see pp44–5).*

## KEY

- Major sight
- Place of interest
- Other building
- **P** Parking
- Tourist information
- Police station
- Hospital
- Bus terminus
- Tram stop
- **R** Train station
- **M** Metro station
- Church

**La Bourse façade**
*Overlooking the city from busy Boulevard Anspach in the Lower Town, Brussels' Stock Exchange was built in 1873 in ornate style (see p47).*

**Place du Petit Sablon**
*This square is a jewel of the Upper Town. Originally a horse market, the central area became a flower garden in 1890, surrounded by wrought-iron railings decorated with stone statuettes. Each figure represents a medieval trade or craft that brought prosperity to the capital (see p68–9).*

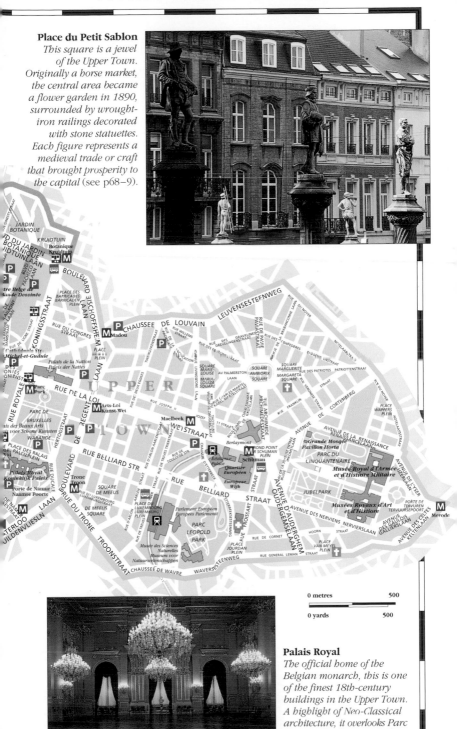

**Palais Royal**
*The official home of the Belgian monarch, this is one of the finest 18th-century buildings in the Upper Town. A highlight of Neo-Classical architecture, it overlooks Parc de Bruxelles (see pp58–9).*

0 metres 500
0 yards 500

# Brussels' Best: Architecture

REFLECTING Brussels' importance in the history of northern Europe, the city's architecture ranges from grand medieval towers to the glittering post-modern structures of European institutions. With a few examples of medieval Brabant Gothic still on show, the capital of Europe has the best Flemish Renaissance architecture in the world in the Baroque splendour of the Grand Place, as well as elegant Neo-Classical churches and houses. The quantity and quality of Art Nouveau *(see pp16–17)*, with its exquisite interiors and handmade features, are highlights of 19th- and 20th-century residential building. The cutting-edge designs in the Parliament Quarter, planned by committees of European architects, take the tour up to date.

**Basilique du Sacré-Coeur**
*Begun in 1904 and only completed in 1970, this huge Art Deco edifice is the world's fifth-largest church* (see p81).

BASILIQUE DU SACRÉ-COEUR

**Grand Place**
*Almost entirely rebuilt by merchants after French bombardment in 1695, this cobbled square is one of the world's best Baroque ensembles* (see pp42–3).

**Palais de Justice**
*Bigger in area than St Peter's in Rome, the city's law courts were built in Neo-Classical style using the profits of colonialism, and completed in 1883* (see p69).

Lower Town

**Porte de Hal**
*This imposing 14th-century tower is the only remaining trace of the city's solid, thick second perimeter wall. It owes its survival to its use as an 18th-century prison and latterly as a museum* (see p79).

| 0 metres | 500 |
| 0 yards | 500 |

**Cathédrale Sts Michel et Gudule**
*The white stone façade from 1250 is an outstanding example of Brabant Gothic style (see pp70–71).*

**Palais de la Nation**
*The home of the Belgian Parliament since the country's independence in 1830, this magnificent building was constructed in the late 18th century by the Neo-Classical architect Guimard, who also designed the expansive stone façade and many of the surrounding state buildings.*

Upper Town

**Palais d'Egmont**
*This 18th-century ducal mansion bears the name of a Flemish count executed for defending his countrymen's civil rights in 1568.*

**European Parliament**
*Named "Les Caprices des Dieux" ("The Whims of the Gods"), this postmodern building serves more than 700 politicians.*

# Belgian Artists

**B**ELGIAN ART ROSE to the fore when the region came under Burgundian rule in the 15th century. Renaissance painters produced strong works in oil, characterized by intricate detail and lifelike, unidealized portraiture. The quest for realism and clarity of light was heavily influenced by the new Dutch schools of art. Yet, in contrast, Belgium's second golden artistic age, in the 20th century, moved away from these goals, abandoning reality for surrealism in the challenging work of artists such as René Magritte.

Belgium is justifiably proud of its long artistic tradition. Rubenshuis in Antwerp *(see pp96–7)*, Brussels' Musée Wiertz *(see p72)* and Musées Royaux des Beaux-Arts *(see pp62–7)* are fine examples of the respect Belgium shows to its artists' homes and their works.

*Portrait of Laurent Froimont* by Rogier van der Weyden

## THE FLEMISH PRIMITIVES

**A**RT IN BRUSSELS and Flanders first attracted European attention at the end of the Middle Ages. **Jan van Eyck** (c.1400–41) is considered to be responsible for the major revolution in Flemish art. Widely credited as the creator of oil painting, van Eyck was the first artist to use the oil medium to fix longer-lasting glazes and to mix colour pigments for wood and canvas. As works could now be rendered more permanent, the innovation spread the Renaissance fashion for panel paintings. However, van Eyck was more than just a practical innovator, and can be seen as the forefather of the Flemish Primitive school

with his lively depictions of human existence in an animated manner. Van Eyck is also responsible, with his brother, for the striking polyptych altarpiece *Adoration of the Holy Lamb*, displayed in Ghent Cathedral *(see p110)*.

The trademarks of the Flemish Primitives are a lifelike vitality, enhanced by realism in portraiture, texture of clothes and furnishings and a clarity of light. The greatest interpreter of the style was Rogier de la Pasture (c.1400–64), better known as **Rogier van der Weyden**, the town painter of Brussels, who combined van Eyck's light and realism with work of religious intensity, as in *Lamentation (see p66)*.

Many in Belgium and across Europe were schooled and inspired by his work, continuing and expanding the new techniques. **Dieric Bouts** (1415–75) extended

the style. With his studies of bustling 15th-century Bruges, **Hans Memling** (c.1433–94) is considered the last Flemish Primitive. Moving towards the 16th century, landscape artist **Joachim Patinier** (c.1475–1524) produced the first European industrial scenes.

## THE BRUEGHEL DYNASTY

**I**N THE EARLY years of the 16th century, Belgian art was strongly influenced by the Italians. Trained in Rome, **Jan Gossaert** (c.1478–1533) brought mythological themes to the art commissioned by the ruling Dukes of Brabant.

But it was the prolific Brueghel family who had the most influence on Flemish art throughout the 16th and 17th centuries. **Pieter Brueghel the Elder** (c.1525–69), one of the greatest Flemish artists, settled in Brussels in 1563. His earthy rustic landscapes of village life, peopled with comic peasants, are a social study of medieval life and remain his best-known work. **Pieter Brueghel the Younger** (1564–1638) produced religious works such as *The Enrolment of Bethlehem* (1610). In contrast, **Jan Brueghel the Elder** (1568–1625) painted intricate floral still lifes with a draped velvet backdrop, becoming known as "Velvet Brueghel". His son, **Jan Brueghel the Younger** (1601–78) also became a court painter in Brussels and a fine landscape artist of note.

*The Fall of Icarus* by Pieter Brueghel the Elder

*Self-portrait* by Rubens, one of many from his lifetime

## THE ANTWERP ARTISTS

IN THE 17TH century, the main centre of Belgian art moved from the social capital, Brussels, to Antwerp, in the heart of Flanders. This move was largely influenced by **Pieter Paul Rubens** (1577–1640), who lived in Antwerp. He was one of the first Flemish artists to become known through Europe and Russia. A court painter, Rubens was also an accomplished landscape artist and interpreter of mythology, but is best known for his depiction of plump women, proud of their figures. Rubens was so popular in his own time that his bold and large-scale works were translated by Flemish weavers into series of tapestries.

**Anthony van Dyck** (1599–1641), a pupil of Rubens and court portraitist, was the second Antwerp artist to gain world renown. The Brueghel dynasty continued to produce notable figures: Jan Brueghel the Elder eventually settled in Antwerp to produce art with Rubens, while his son-in-law, **David Teniers II** (1610–90) founded the Antwerp Academy of Art in 1665.

## THE EUROPEAN INFLUENCE

THE INFLUENCE OF Rubens was so great that little innovation took place in the Flemish art scene in the 18th century. In the early years of

the 19th century, Belgian art was largely dominated by the influence of other European schools. **François-Joseph Navez** (1787–1869) introduced Neo-Classicism to Flemish art. Realism took off with **Constantin Meunier** (1831–1905) and Impressionism with **Guillaume Vogels** (1836–96). The Brussels-based **Antoine Wiertz** (1806–65) was considered a Romantic, but his distorted and occasionally disturbing works, such as *Inhumation précipitée* (c.1830) seem to have early surrealist leanings. **Fernand Khnopff** (1858–1921) was influenced by the German Romantic Gustav Klimt. An early exponent of Belgian Symbolism, Khnopff's work is notable for his portraits of menacing and ambiguous women. Also on a journey from naturalism to surrealism, **James Ensor** (1860–1949) often used eerie skeletons in his work, reminiscent of Bosch. Between 1884 and 1894, the artists' cooperative **Les XX (Les Vingt)** reinvigorated the Brussels art scene with exhibitions of famous foreign and avant garde painters.

**Sculpture by Rik Wouters**

## SURREALISM

THE 20TH CENTURY began with the emergence of Fauvism led by **Rik Wouters** (1882–1916), whose bright sun-filled landscapes show the influence of Cézanne.

Surrealism began in Brussels in the mid-1920s, dominated from the start by **René Magritte** (1898–1967). The movement had its roots back in the 16th century, with the phantasmagoria of Bosch and Pieter Brueghel the Elder. Fuelled by the chaos of World War I, much of which took place on Flemish battle-fields, Magritte defined his disorientating surrealism as "[restoring] the familiar to the strange". More ostentatious and emotional, **Paul Delvaux** (1897–1989) produced elegant, freakish interiors occupied by ghostly figures. In 1948 the **COBRA Movement** promoted abstract art, which gave way in the 1960s to conceptual art, led by installation-ist **Marcel Broodthaers** (1924–76), who used daily objects, such as a casserole dish full of mussels, for his own interpretation.

### UNDERGROUND ART

*Notre Temps* (1976) by Expressionist Roger Somville at Hankar station

Some 58 Brussels metro stations have been decorated with a combination of murals, sculptures and architecture by 54 Belgian artists. Although none but the most devoted visitor to the city is likely to see them all, there are several notable examples. **Annessens** was decorated by the Belgian COBRA artists, Dotremont and Alechinsky. In the **Bourse**, surrealist Paul Delvaux's *Nos Vieux Trams Bruxellois* is still on show with *Moving Ceiling*, a series of 75 tubes that move in the breeze by sculptor Pol Bury. At **Horta** station, Art Nouveau wrought ironwork from Victor Horta's now destroyed People's Palace is displayed, and **Stockel** is a tribute to Hergé and his boy hero, Tintin *(see pp18–19)*.

# Brussels' Best: Art Nouveau

A MONG EUROPE'S most important architectural movements at the start of the 20th century, Art Nouveau
in Belgium was led by Brussels architect Victor Horta
(1861–1947) and the Antwerp-born interior designer
Henry van de Velde (1863–1957). The style evolved
from the Arts and Crafts Movement in England and the
fashion for Japanese simplicity, and is characterized
by its sinuous decorative lines, stained glass, carved
stone curves, floral frescoes and elaborately curled
and twisted metalwork. As new suburbs rose up in
the 1890s, over 2,000 new houses were built in the
style. Although many were demolished, details can
still be seen in almost every Brussels street.

**Hôtel Métropole**
*The high-vaulted lobby and
bar of this luxurious 1894
hotel recall the city's fin-de-
siècle heyday (see p49).*

**Old England**
*This former department
store uses glass and steel
rather than brick, with
large windows and
twisted metal turrets
(see p60).*

*The Lower Town*

**Hôtel Ciamberlani**
*Architect Paul Hankar
designed this redbrick
house in rue Defacqz
for the sgraffiti artist
Albert Ciamberlani,
with whom he worked.*

**Musée Horta**
*Curved window frames
and elaborate metal
balconies mark this out
as the home and studio of
Art Nouveau's best-known
architect (see p78).*

**Hôtel Hannon**
*This stylish 1902 townhouse
was built by Jules Brunfaut
(1852–1942). One of its metal-
framed windows has striking
stained-glass panes (see p79).*

### Maison Cauchie
*Restored in 1989, architect Paul Cauchie's home in rue des Francs has examples of* sgraffiti, *a technique in which designs are incised onto wet plaster to reveal another colour beneath.*

### Maison Saint Cyr
*Horta's disciple Gustave Strauven was keen to out-do his mentor with this intricate façade, only 4 m (14 ft) wide (see p72).*

*The Upper Town*

### Hôtel Solvay
*An early Horta creation of 1894, this home was built for a wealthy family. Horta designed every element of the building, from the ochre and yellow cast-iron façade columns and glass front door to the decorative but functional doorknobs (see p79).*

| 0 metres | 500 |
| --- | --- |
| 0 yards | 500 |

# Belgian Comic Strip Art

**Tintin's dog Snowy**

BELGIAN COMIC STRIP art is as famous a part of Belgian culture as chocolates and beer. The seeds of this great passion were sown when the US comic strip Little Nemo was published in French in 1908 to huge popular acclaim in Belgium. The country's reputation for producing some of the best comic strip art in Europe was established after World War II. Before the war, Europe was awash with American comics, but the Nazis called a halt to the supply. Local artists took over, and found that there was a large audience who preferred homegrown comic heroes. This explosion in comic strip art was led by perhaps the most famous Belgian creation ever, Tintin, who, with his dog Snowy, is as recognizable across Europe as Mickey Mouse.

demonstrated by his work before and during the war, where he expressed a strong sense of justice in such stories as *King Ottakar's Sceptre*, where a fascist army attempts to seize control of a central European state. Hergé took great care in researching his stories; for *Le Lotus Bleu* in 1934, which was set in China, he wrote: "I started... showing a real interest in the people and countries I was sending Tintin off to, concerned by a sense of honesty to my readers."

**Spirou cover**

**Hergé at work in his studio**

## HERGÉ AND TINTIN

TINTIN'S CREATOR, Hergé, was born Georges Remi in Brussels in 1907. He began using his pen name (a phonetic spelling of his initials in reverse) in 1924. At the young age of 15, his drawings were published in the *Boy Scout Journal*. He became the protégé of a priest, Abbot Norbert Wallez, who also managed the Catholic journal *Le XXe Siècle*, and was swiftly given the

responsibility of the children's supplement, *Le petit Vingtième*. Eager to invent an original comic strip, Hergé came up with the character of Tintin the reporter, who first appeared in the story *Tintin au Pays des Soviets* on 10 January 1929. Over the next 10 years the character developed and grew in popularity. Book-length stories began to appear from 1930.

During the Nazi occupation in the 1940s *Tintin* continued to be published, with political references carefully omitted, in an approved paper *Le Soir*. This led to Hergé being accused of collaboration at the end of the war. He was called in for questioning but released later the same day without charge. Hergé's innocence was amply

**Statue of Tintin and Snowy**

## POST-WAR BOOM

BELGIUM'S OLDEST comic strip journal *Spirou* was launched in April 1938 and, alongside the weekly *Journal de Tintin* begun in 1946, became a hothouse for the artistic talent that was to flourish during the postwar years. Many of the country's best-loved characters were first seen in *Spirou*, and most of them are still in print. Artists such as Morris, Jijé, Peyo and Roba worked on the journal. Morris (b.1923) introduced the cowboy parody, *Lucky Luke* in *Spirou* in 1947, a character who went on to feature in several live-action films and many US television cartoons.

## COMIC STRIP CHARACTERS

Some of the world's best-loved comic strip characters originated in Belgium. *Tintin* is the most famous, but *Lucky Luke* the cowboy, the cheeky children *Suske en Wiske* and *The Smurfs* have also been published worldwide, while modern artists such as Schueten break new ground.

**Tintin by Hergé**

**Lucky Luke by Morris**

During the 1960s, the idea of the comic strip being the Ninth Art (after the seventh and eighth, film and television) expanded to include adult themes in the form of the comic-strip graphic novel.

## PEYO AND THE SMURFS

B EST KNOWN for *The Smurfs*, Peyo (1928–92) was also a member of the team behind the *Spirou* journal which published his poetic medieval series *Johan et Pirlouit*, in 1952. *The Smurfs* first appeared as characters here – tiny blue people whose humorous foibles soon eclipsed any interest in the strip's supposed main characters. Reacting to their popularity, Peyo created a strip solely about them. Set in the Smurf village, the stories were infused with satirical social comment. *The Smurfs* were a popular craze between 1983 and 1985, featuring in advertising and merchandising of every type. They spawned a feature-length film, TV cartoons and popular music, and had several hit records in the 1980s.

**Modern cover by Marvano**

## WILLY VANDERSTEEN

W HILE SPIROU and *Tintin* were French-language journals, Willy Vandersteen (1913–90) dominated the Flemish market. His popular creation, *Suske en Wiske* has

been translated into English and appears as *Bob and Bobette* in the UK, and *Willy and Wanda* in the US. The main characters are a pair of "ordinary" kids aged between 10 and 14 years who have extraordinary adventures all over the world, as well as travelling back and forth in time. Today, Vandersteen's books sell in their millions.

## COMIC STRIP ART TODAY

C OMIC STRIPS, known as *bandes dessinées* or *beeldverhaal*, continue to be published in Belgium in all their forms. In newspapers, children's comics and graphic novels the Ninth Art remains one of the country's biggest exports. The high standards and imaginative scope of a new generation of artists, such as Schueten and Marvano, have fed growing consumer demand for comic books. Both French and Flemish publishers issue

**Contemporary comic-strip artists at work in their studio**

over 22 million comic books each year. Today, Belgian cartoons are sold in more than 30 countries, including the US.

**Larger-than-life cartoon by Frank Pé adorns a Brussels building**

## STREET ART

T HERE ARE currently 18 large comic strip images decorating the sides of buildings around Brussels' city centre. This outdoor exhibition is known as the Comic Strip Route and is organized by the Centre Belge de la Bande Dessineé (the Belgian Centre for Comic Strip Art) *(see pp50–51)* and the city of Brussels. Begun in 1991 as a tribute to Belgium's talent for comic strip art, this street art project continues to grow. A free map of the route is available from tourist information offices, as well as from the comic museum itself.

*Suske en Wiske* by Vandersteen

*The Smurfs* by Peyo

**Contemporary cartoon strip by Schueten**

# Tapestry and Lace

**F**OR OVER SIX CENTURIES, Belgian lace and tapestry have been highly prized luxury crafts. Originating in Flanders in the 12th century, tapestry has since been handmade in the centres of Tournai, Brussels, Arras, Mechelen and Oudenaarde, while the lace trade was practised from the 1500s onwards in all the Belgian provinces, with Bruges and Brussels particularly renowned for their delicate work. The makers often had aristocratic patrons; intricate lace and fine tapestries were status symbols of the nobility and staple exports throughout Europe from the 15th to 18th centuries. Today Belgium remains home to the very best tapestry and lace studios in the world.

**Lacemaker's studio sign**

*Tapestry weavers numbered over 50,000 in Flanders from 1450–1550. With the ruling Dukes of Burgundy as patrons, weavers prospered, and hangings grew more elaborate.*

*Tapestry designs involve weaver and artist working closely together. Painters, including Rubens, produced drawings for a series of weavings of six or more on grand themes (detail shown).*

**The texture of the weave** was the finest ever achieved; often 12 threads to the inch (5 per cm).

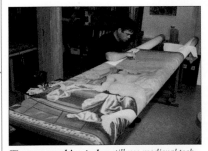

*Weavers working today still use medieval techniques to produce contemporary tapestry, woven in Mechelen and Tournai to modern designs.*

## TAPESTRY

By 1200, the Flemish towns of Arras (now in France) and Tournai were Europe-wide known centres of weaving. Prized by the nobility, tapestries were portable and could be moved with the court as rulers travelled their estates. As trade grew, techniques were refined; real gold and silver were threaded into the fine wool, again increasing the value. Blending Italian idealism with Flemish realism, Bernard van Orley (1492–1542) revolutionized tapestry designs, as seen above in *The Battle of Pavia 1525,* the first of a series. Flemish weavers were eventually lured across Europe, where ironically their skill led to the success of the Gobelins factory in Paris that finally stole Flanders' crown in the late 1700s.

*The lace trade* rose to the fore during the early Renaissance. Emperor Charles V decreed that lace-making should be a compulsory skill for girls in convents and béguinages (see p53) throughout Flanders. Lace became fashionable on collars and cuffs for both sexes. Trade reached a peak in the 18th century.

**Classical myths** were popular themes for tapestry series.

*Lace makers* are traditionally women. Although their numbers are dwindling, many craftswomen still work in Bruges and Brussels, centres of bobbin lace, creating intricate work by hand.

*Victorian Lace* heralded a revival of the craft after its decline in the austere Neo-Classical period. Although men no longer wore it, the growth of the status of lace as a ladies' accessory and its use in soft furnishing led to its renewed popularity.

**Belgian Lace** is bought today mainly as a souvenir, but despite the rise in machine-made lace from other countries, the quality here still remains as fine as it was in the Renaissance.

# Brussels: Political Capital of Europe

**Manneken Pis statue**

HOME TO MOST of the European Union's institutions and the headquarters of NATO, Brussels is one of Europe's most important political and business centres. Since the 1950s, the sense of Brussels as an international powerhouse has drawn an influx of people from around the world. The city has proved itself a fine host to the thousands of Eurocrats and business people that both visit and live here, with its celebrated hotels and restaurants, as well as with its cultural heritage, reflected in its historic buildings and museums. The people of Brussels are proud of their role in the new Europe. Despite the intricate and separatist-torn nature of Belgian politics, the country is unified in its support for a united Europe.

The UK, Denmark and Ireland joined the EC in 1973, increasing its population by 25 per cent. The expectation of a return to profitable trade was crushed by the world recession of the mid-1970s which brought economic hardship to each of the member states.

Nonetheless this decade saw two important innovations: the creation of the European Regional Development Fund, which offers aid to the poorest areas of the EC, including major beneficiary, Ireland, and the European Monetary System (EMS), established in 1979. Otherwise known as the Exchange Rate Mechanism or ERM, this system was designed to protect member states from the vicissitudes of world markets. The European Currency Unit or ECU, a forerunner to the single currency (the Euro), was also initiated, despite the problem of a budget deficit in the 1980s.

**The signing of the European Common Market Treaty, Rome, 1957**

## HISTORICAL BEGINNINGS

THE EUROPEAN Union has its origins in the aftermath of World War II. The spirit of postwar reconciliation led France and West Germany to join forces to create the European Coal and Steel Community (ECSC). The project to continue the consolidation of Europe as a single political and financial entity began with the signing of the Treaty of Rome in 1957. This inaugurated the creation of a common market, the European Economic Community (EEC). Initially, six countries joined the EEC *(see opposite)* and the organization came into being on January 1, 1958.

The EEC was made up of two bodies, the Council of Ministers and the Commission, and coexisted with the ECSC

and the atomic energy commission, Euratom. In 1967, however, these three groups merged, later becoming known as the European Community (EC). By this time the economic benefits of membership were evident, with intra-Community trade increasing by almost 30 per cent each year. The six founder members had also made an agreement on a common agricultural policy (CAP), which fixed prices and offered grants to EEC farmers. With economic improvement came calls for political union. As early as 1961, member states discussed the possibility of collaborative government. The larger states were less enthusiastic than smaller countries, and obstructed agreements over union.

**Euro coin**

## MAASTRICHT

AFTER THE BUDGET issue was resolved in 1988 by the then Commission President Frenchman Jacques Delors, the 12 member states began to discuss the creation of a single European currency. The foundations were laid by the Maastricht Treaty of 1992, which changed the EC into the European Union (EU) and which set out a detailed timetable for economic and monetary union (EMU). The treaty imposed stringent economic criteria on states which wanted to participate. At the 1992 summit held in Edinburgh, Brussels' position as the focus city of the EU was also confirmed.

Denmark and Britain were among those reluctant to commit themselves to the single currency, a situation reflecting Britain's great wariness of the far-reaching consequences of the idea and its ambivalence towards the European project in general. This was further illustrated by the fact that Britain is one of only two European Community countries (the other being Ireland) not to have signed up to the EU's Schengen Agreement, under which border controls between EU member states have been removed. This means that travellers can now journey around all of the other member states without once showing their passports.

## THE FUTURE

THE EU DEVELOPED throughout the 1990s with the arrival of Sweden, Finland and Austria in 1995 and, in 1999, the establishment of a single European currency in 11 of the EU's member states. During this time criticism of the EU escalated, and its bureaucracy was seen as a source of irritation by many of its citizens. The EU's executive body, the Commission has also been the focus of resentment. EU President Jacques Santer was forced to resign in 1999 after allegations of incompetence, mismanagement and fraud. He was replaced by former Italian Prime Minister Romano Prodi.

With the accession of 10 new states from eastern and southern Europe in 2004, the EU now has 450 million citizens. Debate continues about the long-term goal of increased political unity.

## THE EUROPEAN COMMISSION

THE COMMISSION is the EU's executive arm, responsible for formulating policies which are then ratified or rejected by the Council of Ministers. There are 25 Commissioners, including the President, each with a specific area of responsibility ranging from transport to technology. The Commission

is responsible for ensuring that policies are carried out, and that member states do not violate EC law.

Once based in the star-shaped Berlaymont building, the Commissioners have been rehoused while asbestos is removed from the building.

## THE COUNCIL OF MINISTERS

THE COUNCIL of Ministers is composed of representatives of each member state: each nation has a block of votes depending on its size. The Council must approve all legislation for the EU, often a difficult task given that most Europe-wide laws will seldom be to the liking of every state; most laws require a "qualified majority" (of around 70 per cent of the votes) before they are passed. The Council of Ministers meets behind closed doors, and its members are answerable only to their national governments, which has led to calls for reform.

## THE EUROPEAN PARLIAMENT

THE EUROPEAN Parliament is responsible for approving the EU's annual budget, as well as monitoring the Commission's performance.

The Parliament is the only European institution subject to election by the public. There are more than 700 MEPs, elected by proportional

representation. The Parliament sits in Brussels and Strasbourg. In Brussels, the glass-and-steel Parliament building on Rue Wiertz is nicknamed *Le Caprice des Dieux* (The Whims of the Gods) *(see p73)*.

## BRUSSELS' POLITICS

BELGIUM's system of government is complex as regional interests are powerful. The country is divided into three federal regions, Flanders Wallonia and Brussels, and conflict between separatist Walloon and Fleming factions threatens Belgian unity.

The Brussels' regional government oversees the city's 19 communes. Each one has its own powers, including a police force. Separate French and Flemish organizations rule on cultural matters.

**Contemporary geometric bridge in Brussels' Quartier Européen**

# BRUSSELS THROUGH THE YEAR

THE TEMPERATE climate of Brussels is typical of Northern Europe and means that a range of activities throughout the year take place both inside and out. Mild damp winters and gentle summers

Revellers at Ommegang

allow the city's strong artistic life to flourish in historic buildings and modern stadiums alike. The Belgians make the most of their seasonal changes. Theatre, dance and film start their season in January, with evening venues that range from ancient abbeys lit by the setting sun to drive-in cinemas. The city's flower festival launches the summer in highly colourful style, with the Grand Place literally carpeted in millions of blooms every other August. Through the year, festivals in Brussels range from energetic, exuberant historic processions that have taken place yearly since medieval times, to innovative European experimental art.

## SPRING

BRUSSELS' LIVELY cultural life takes off as the crisp spring days lengthen and visitors begin to arrive in the city. Music festivals take place in a wide variety of open-air venues. As the city's parks burst into bloom, the world-famous tropical greenhouses at Laeken are opened to the public and Brussels' chocolatiers produce delicious creations for Easter.

The Royal Glasshouse at Laeken, famed for its rare exotic orchids

## MARCH

**International Fantasy Film Festival** *(middle fortnight)*. Lovers of the weird and wonderful will find new and vintage work here in cinemas all over the city.
**Ars Musica** *(mid-Mar to early Apr)*. This celebration of modern music is one of Europe's finest festivals, boasting famous performers and beautiful venues, often the Musée d'art ancien *(see pp62–3)*. The festival is now a must for connoisseurs of the contemporary music world.
**Eurantica** *(last week)*. The Baudouin Stadium at Heysel plays host to hundreds of traders and members of the public anxious for bargains in the world of antiques.
**Easter** *(Easter Sunday)*. The annual Easter Egg hunt, with eggs allegedly hidden by the bells of churches in Rome. Over 1,000 brightly coloured

Easter eggs are hidden by adults in the Parc Royal, and Belgian children gather to forage among the flowerbeds.

## APRIL

**Sablon Baroque Spring** *(third week)*. The Place du Grand Sablon hosts new classical ensembles in a gathering of young Belgian talent performing 17th-century music.
**The Royal Greenhouses at Laeken** *(12 days, dates vary)*. The private greenhouses of the Belgian Royal family are opened to the public as their numerous exotic plants and cacti start to flower. Breathtaking 19th-century glass and wrought ironwork shelters hundreds of rare species *(see pp82–3)*.
**Flanders Festival** *(mid-Apr to October)*. A celebration of all things musical, this classical medley offers more than 120 performances by internationally renowned choirs and orchestras.
**Scenes d'Ecran** *(third weekend)*. Over 100 new European films draw crowds in cinemas across the city.

## MAY

**Europe Day Festivities** *(7–9 May)*. As the capital of Europe, Brussels celebrates its role in the European Union – even Manneken

Runners taking part in the Brussels twenty-kilometre race

AVERAGE DAILY HOURS OF SUNSHINE

Hours
10
8
6
4
2
0
Jan Feb Mar Apr May Jun Jul Aug Sep Oct Nov Dec

**Climate**
*Belgium has a fairly temperate Northern European climate. Although not often freezing, winters are chilly and a heavy coat is required. Summers are warmer and much brighter, though you will still need a jersey for the evenings. Rainwear is always a necessity.*

Pis is dressed as a Euro-supporter, in a suit of blue, decorated with yellow stars.
**Kunsten FESTIVAL des Arts** *(9–31 May)*. This innovative festival covers theatre and dance and is the forum for much exciting new talent.
**Queen Elisabeth Music Contest** *(May to mid-June)*. Classical fans will flock to the prestigious musical competition, now in its fifth decade. Young singers, violinists and pianists gather in front of well-known conductors and soloists to determine the champion among Europe's finest student players.
**Brussels Twenty-Kilometre Race** *(last Sunday)*. As many as 20,000 keen professional and amateur runners race round the city, taking in its major landmarks.
**Jazz Marathon** *(last weekend)*. Bistros and cafés are the venues for myriad small jazz bands, with some well-known artists playing anonymously.

on Belgian National Day. Families enjoy the Foire du Midi, the huge fairground over 2 km square (1 sq mile) covered with rides and stalls.

**JUNE**

**City of Brussels Summer Festival** *(early June to Sep)*. Classical concerts take place in some of the city's best-known ancient buildings.
**Festival of Wallonia** *(Jun–Oct)*. Covering Brussels and Flanders, this series of gala concerts showcases the best in young Belgian classical orchestral and soloist talent.
**Couleur Café Festival** *(last weekend)*. Spread over three summer evenings in the Tour et Taxis renovated warehouse, the fashionable and funky programme includes salsa, African drummers, acid jazz and multicultural music.
**Fête de la Musique** *(last weekend)*. Two days of concerts and recitals featuring world music take place in the halls and museums of the city.

**African drummer performing at the Couleur Café Festival**

**JULY**

**Ommegang** *(first weekend in July)*. This festival has been celebrated in Brussels since 1549, and now draws crowds from around the world. Translated as "a tour", the procession revolves around the Grand Place and the surrounding streets. Over 2,000 participants dress up and become members of a Renaissance town; jesters, courtiers, nobles and soldiers; they go on to parade before Belgian dignitaries. Tickets have to be booked months in advance.

## SUMMER

THE SEASON OF pageantry arrives with Ommegang in July, one of Europe's oldest and best-known processions, which takes place in the Grand Place and the surrounding streets. Multicultural music runs throughout the summer, with classical, jazz and avant-garde US and European performers playing in venues ranging from tiny beer cafés to the great King Baudouin stadium in Heysel. Independence is celebrated

**The Ommegang pausing in front of dignitaries in the Grand Place**

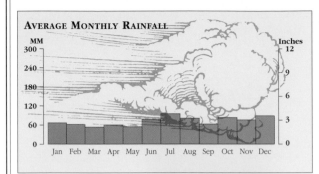

## AVERAGE MONTHLY RAINFALL

| MM | | | | | | | | | | | | Inches |
|---|---|---|---|---|---|---|---|---|---|---|---|---|
| 300 | | | | | | | | | | | | 12 |
| 240 | | | | | | | | | | | | 9 |
| 180 | | | | | | | | | | | | |
| 120 | | | | | | | | | | | | 6 |
| 60 | | | | | | | | | | | | 3 |
| 0 | | | | | | | | | | | | 0 |
| | Jan | Feb | Mar | Apr | May | Jun | Jul | Aug | Sep | Oct | Nov Dec | |

**Rainfall chart**
*On the whole Belgium is rather a rainy country, with Brussels experiencing constant low rainfall throughout the year. Spring is the driest season, but summers can be damp. In winter, rain may turn to snow and sleet.*

**Brosella Folk and Jazz Festival** *(second weekend)*. Musicians from all over Europe play informal gigs in the Parc d'Osseghem in the shadow of the Atomium.
**Festival d'Eté de Bruxelles** *(Jul–Aug)*. Classical concerts take place through the high summer in venues around the Upper and Lower Town.
**Foire du Midi** *(mid-Jul–mid-Aug)*. Brussels' main station, Gare du Midi, is host to this month-long funfair, which attracts people in their thousands. Especially popular with children, it is one of the biggest fairs in Europe, and includes an enormous Ferris wheel.
**Belgian National Day** *(21 Jul)*. The 1831 declaration of independence is commemorated annually with a military parade followed by a firework display in the Parc de Bruxelles.
**Palais Royal Open Days** *(last week in Jul–second week of Sep)*. The official residence of the Belgian Royal family, the opulent staterooms of the Palais Royal, including the huge throne room, are open to the public for six weeks during the summer *(see pp58–9)*.

## AUGUST

**Plantation du Meiboom** *(9 Aug)*. This traditional festival dates from 1213. Parading crowds dressed in huge puppet costumes parade around the Lower Town and finally reach the Grand Place where a maypole is planted as a celebration of summer.

**Costumed revellers at the Plantation of the Meiboom**

**Tapis des Fleurs** *(mid-Aug, biennially, for four days)*. Taking place on even-numbered years, this colourful celebration pays tribute to Brussels' long-established flower industry. The Grand Place is carpeted with millions of fresh flowers in patterns echoing historical scenes. The beautiful flower carpet measures 2,000 sq m (21,000 sq ft).

## AUTUMN

Fresh autumn days are the cue for many indoor events; innovative jazz is performed in the city's cafés and the French cultural centre in Le Botanique. Architecture is celebrated in the heritage weekend where the public can tour many private houses and personal art collections.

## SEPTEMBER

**The Birthday of Manneken Pis** *(last weekend )*. Brussels' celebrated mascot is clothed in a new suit by a chosen dignitary from abroad.
**Lucky Town Festival** *(first weekend)*. Sixty concerts take place in over 30 of some of Brussels' best-known and atmospheric cafés.
**Les Nuits Botaniques** *(last week)*. Held in the former greenhouses of the Botanical gardens, now the French cultural centre, this series of musical events is a delight.

**The Grand Place, carpeted in millions of fresh flowers**

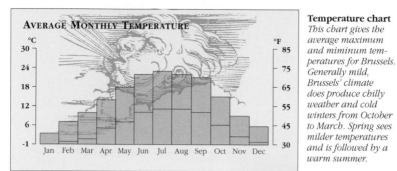

**AVERAGE MONTHLY TEMPERATURE**

**Temperature chart**
*This chart gives the average maximum and minimum temperatures for Brussels. Generally mild, Brussels' climate does produce chilly weather and cold winters from October to March. Spring sees milder temperatures and is followed by a warm summer.*

**Journées du Patrimoine/ Heritage Days** *(second or third weekend)*. Private homes, listed buildings and art collections are opened for a rare public viewing to celebrate the city's architecture.

## OCTOBER

**Audi Jazz Festival** *(mid-Oct–mid-Nov)* All over Belgium informal jazz concerts bring autumnal cheer to country towns and the capital. Performers are mainly local, but some European stars fly in for performances in Brussels' Palais des Beaux-Arts. Ray Charles and Herbie Hancock have appeared in past years.

## WINTER

SNOW AND RAIN typify Brussels' winter weather, and attractions move indoors. Art galleries launch world-class exhibitions and the Brussels Film Festival showcases new and established talent. As the festive season approaches, the ancient Lower Town is brightly lit and families gather for Christmas with traditional Belgian cuisine.

## NOVEMBER

**Nocturnes des Sablons** *(last weekend)*. Shops and galleries stay open until 11pm around the Place du Grand Sablon. Horse-drawn carriages transport shoppers around the area, with mulled wine on offer in the festively decorated main square.

## DECEMBER

**Fête de Saint Nicolas** *(6 Dec)*. The original Santa Claus, the patron saint of Christmas, is alleged to arrive in the city on this day. Children throughout the country are given their presents, sweetmeats and chocolate.
**Reveillon/Fête de Noel** *(24–25 Dec)*. In common with the rest of mainland Europe, Christmas is celebrated over a feast on the evening of 24 December. Gifts are given by adults on this day, and 25 December is traditionally for visiting extended family. The city's Christmas decorations provide a lively sight until 6 January.

## JANUARY

**Fête des Rois** *(6 Jan)*. Epiphany is celebrated with almond cake, the *galette des rois*, and the search for the bean inside that declares its finder king for the night.
**Brussels Film Festival** *(mid-late Jan)*. Premières and film stars are adding weight to this European film showcase.

## FEBRUARY

**Antiques Fair** *(middle fortnight)*. Brussels' crossroads location is useful here as international dealers

**Christmas market in the Grand Place around the traditional Christmas Pine**

gather in the historic Palais des Beaux-Arts *(see p60)*.
**International Comic strip and Cartoon Festival** *(middle fortnight)*. Artists and authors, both new and established, arrive for lectures and screenings in this city with its comic strip heritage.

### PUBLIC HOLIDAYS

**New Year's Day** (1 Jan)
**Easter Sunday** (variable)
**Easter Monday** (variable)
**Labour Day** (1 May)
**Ascension Day** (variable)
**Whit Sunday** (variable)
**Whit Monday** (variable)
**Belgian National Day** (21 July)
**Assumption Day** (15 Aug)
**All Saints' Day** (1 Nov)
**Armistice Day** (11 Nov)
**Christmas Day** (25 Dec)

# THE HISTORY OF BRUSSELS

As THE CULTURAL AND CIVIC *heart of Belgium since the Middle Ages, Brussels has been the focus of much political upheaval over the centuries. But, from the battles of the 17th century to the warfare of the 20th century, it has always managed to re-create itself with vigour. Now, at the start of a new millennium, Belgium's capital is prospering as the political and economic centre of Europe.*

When Julius Caesar set out to conquer the Gauls of northern Europe in 58 BC, he encountered a fierce tribe known as the Belgae (the origins of the 19th-century name "Belgium"). Roman victory led to the establishment of the region they called Gallia Belgica. The earliest mention of Brussels itself is as "Broucsella," or "settlement in the marshes" and dates from a 7th-century manuscript.

**15th-century Flemish tapestry showing the stars**

Following the collapse of the Roman Empire in the 5th century, a Germanic race known as the Franks came to rule the region and established the Merovingian dynasty of kings, based in their capital at Tournai. They were followed by the Carolingian dynasty, which produced one of the most important figures of the Middle Ages – Charlemagne (AD 768–814). His noted military expertise ensured that invaders such as the Northern Saxons and the Lombards of Italy were repelled. He was also credited with establishing Christianity as the major religion across western Europe. The pope rewarded him by crowning him Emperor of the West in AD 800; effectively he was the first Holy Roman Emperor, ruling a vast area extending from Denmark to Italy. By the 10th century, the inheritance laws of the Franks meant that the empire was divided up among Charlemagne's grandsons, Louis, Charles the Bald and Lothair. Lothair's fortress, founded in 979, marks the official founding of Brussels. The period had brought a measure of stability to the area's volatile feudal fiefdoms, leading to a trading boom in the new towns of the low countries.

## INDUSTRIAL BEGINNINGS

At the start of the 12th century, commerce became the guiding force in western Europe and the centres of trade quickly grew into powerful cities. Rivers and canals were the key to the growth of the area's trading towns. Ghent, Ypres, Antwerp and Bruges became the focus of the cloth trade plied across the North Sea between France, Germany, Italy and England. Brussels, with its skilled craftsmen, became a trade centre, and impressive buildings such as the Cathédrale Sts Michel et Gudule *(see pp 70–71)*, built in 1225, demonstrated its stature.

## TIMELINE

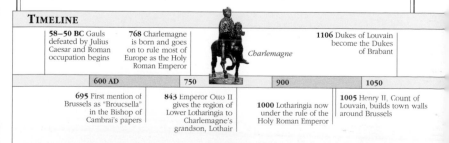

| **58–50 BC** Gauls defeated by Julius Caesar and Roman occupation begins | **768** Charlemagne is born and goes on to rule most of Europe as the Holy Roman Emperor | *Charlemagne* | **1106** Dukes of Louvain become the Dukes of Brabant |
|---|---|---|---|
| **600 AD** | **750** | **900** | **1050** |
| **695** First mention of Brussels as "Broucsella" in the Bishop of Cambrai's papers | **843** Emperor Otto II gives the region of Lower Lotharingia to Charlemagne's grandson, Lothair | **1000** Lotharingia now under the rule of the Holy Roman Emperor | **1005** Henry II, Count of Louvain, builds town walls around Brussels |

◁ *Philip the Good*, **Duke of Burgundy (c.1500) by Rogier van der Weyden**

Nineteenth-century painting of the Battle of the Golden Spurs

## THE CRAFTSMEN'S REBELLION

Over the next two hundred years Brussels became one of the foremost towns of the Duchy of Brabant. Trade here specialized in fine fabrics that were exported to lucrative markets in France, Italy and England. A handful of merchants became rich and exercised political power over the towns. However, conflict grew between the merchants, who wanted to maintain good relations with England, and their autocratic French rulers who relied upon tax revenue from the towns.

The 14th century witnessed a series of rebellions by the craftsmen of Bruges and Brussels against what they saw as the tyranny of the French lords. In May 1302, Flemish craftsmen, armed only with spears, defeated the French at the Battle of the Golden Spurs, named for the humiliating theft of the cavalry's spurs. Encouraged by this success, the Brussels craftsmen revolted against the aristocracy who controlled their trading economy in 1356. They were also angered by the Hundred Years' War between England and France, which began in 1337. The war threatened wool supplies from England which were crucial to their cloth-based

economy. The subsequent depression marked the beginning of decades of conflict between the craftsmen and merchant classes. In 1356, Jeanne, Duchess of Louvain, gained control over Brussels, and instituted the workers' Charter of Liberties. Craftsmen were finally given some political powers in the city. Trade resumed, attracting new people to Brussels. As the population grew, new streets were built outside the city walls to accommodate them. Between 1357 and 1379 a second town wall was constructed around these new districts.

## THE HOUSE OF BURGUNDY

The new town walls were also built in reply to the invasion of Brussels by the Count of Flanders. However, in 1369 Philip, Duke of Burgundy, married the daughter of the Count of Flanders, and when the count died in 1384 the Low Countries and eastern France came under the couple's Burgundian rule.

In the 1430s Brussels became the capital of Burgundy, a situation that was to change the city forever. Brussels

Richly detailed Brussels tapestries such as this *Allegory of Hope* (1525) were prized commodities

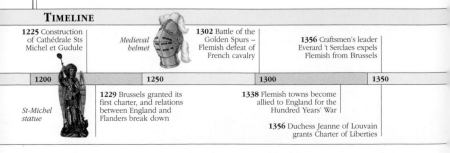

## TIMELINE

| 1200 | 1250 | 1300 | 1350 |
|------|------|------|------|

**1225** Construction of Cathédrale Sts Michel et Gudule

*Medieval helmet*

**1302** Battle of the Golden Spurs – Flemish defeat of French cavalry

**1356** Craftsmen's leader Everard 't Serclaes expels Flemish from Brussels

*St-Michel statue*

**1229** Brussels granted its first charter, and relations between England and Flanders break down

**1338** Flemish towns become allied to England for the Hundred Years' War

**1356** Duchess Jeanne of Louvain grants Charter of Liberties

**Painting of the family of the Hapsburg King of Austria, Maximillian I and Mary of Burgundy**

was now an administrative and cultural centre, famous for its grand architecture, in the form of mansions and churches, and its luxury crafts trade.

### THE HAPSBURG DYNASTY

In 1477 Mary of Burgundy, the last heir to the duchy, married Maximillian of Austria. Mary died in 1482, leaving Maximillian and the Hapsburg dynasty rulers of the city at a time when Brussels was experiencing serious economic depression. In 1488 Brussels and the rest of Flanders rebelled against this new power which had reinstated relations with France. The Austrians held on to power largely because of the plague of 1490 which halved Brussels' population. Maximillian passed his rule of the Low Countries to his son, Philip the Handsome in 1494 the year after he became Holy Roman Emperor. When

**Portrait of Charles V, Holy Roman Emperor**

Maximillian died, his daughter, Regent Empress Margaret of Austria, moved the capital of Burgundy from Brussels to Mechelen, where she educated her nephew, the future emperor Charles V.

### SPANISH RULE

In 1515, at the age of 15, Charles became Sovereign of Burgundy. The following year he inherited the Spanish throne and, in 1519, became the Holy Roman Emperor. As he was born in Ghent, and considered Flanders his real home, he restored Brussels as the capital of Burgundy. Dutch officials arrived to run the three government councils that were now based here.

For the first time the city had a court. Both aristocratic families and immigrants, eager to cash in on the city's expansion, were drawn to the heady mix of tolerance, intellectual sophistication and business. Brussels quickly emerged as the most powerful city in Flanders, overtaking its long-standing rivals Bruges and Antwerp.

However, the Reformation, begun in Germany by Martin Luther, was to usher in a period of religious conflict. When Charles V abdicated in 1555, he fractured the empire's unity by leaving the Holy Roman Empire to his brother Ferdinand and all other dominions to his devoutly Catholic son, Philip II of Spain. His persecution of the Protestant movement finally sparked the Revolt of the Netherlands led by the House of Orange. Brussels' Protestant rulers surrendered to Philip in 1585. His power ended when the English defeated the Spanish Armada in 1588, by which time 8,000 Protestants had been put to death.

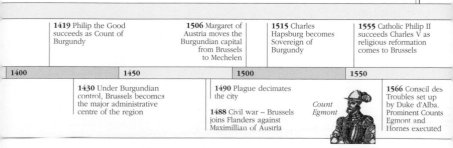

**1419** Philip the Good succeeds as Count of Burgundy

**1430** Under Burgundian control, Brussels becomes the major administrative centre of the region

**1506** Margaret of Austria moves the Burgundian capital from Brussels to Mechelen

**1490** Plague decimates the city

**1488** Civil war – Brussels joins Flanders against Maximillian of Austria

*Count Egmont*

**1515** Charles Hapsburg becomes Sovereign of Burgundy

**1555** Catholic Philip II succeeds Charles V as religious reformation comes to Brussels

**1566** Conseil des Troubles set up by Duke d'Alba. Prominent Counts Egmont and Hornes executed

1400　　　　1450　　　　1500　　　　1550

The armies of Louis XIV, the Sun King, bombard Brussels' city walls

## THE COUNTER-REFORMATION

From 1598 Archduchess Isabella and Archduke Albert were the Catholic rulers of the Spanish Netherlands, installing a Hapsburg governor in Brussels. They continued to persecute Protestants: all non-Catholics were barred from working. Thousands of skilled workers moved to the Netherlands. But such new trades as lace-making, diamond-cutting and silk-weaving flourished. Isabella and Albert were great patrons of the arts, and supported Rubens in Antwerp (see pp96–7).

Protestant prisoners paraded in Brussels during the Counter-Reformation under Albert and Isabella

## INVASION OF THE SUN KING

The 17th century was a time of of religious and political struggle all over Europe. The Thirty Years War (1618–48) divided western Europe along Catholic and Protestant lines. After 1648, France's Sun King, Louis XIV, was determined to add Flanders to his territory.

By 1633 both Albert and Isabella were dead and Philip IV of Spain, passed control of the Spanish Netherlands to his weak brother, the Cardinal-Infant Ferdinand. Keen to pursue his ambitions, Louis XIV besieged Maastricht in the 1670s and took Luxembourg. Having failed to win the nearby enclave of Namur, the piqued Sun King moved his army to Brussels, whose defences were weaker.

On August 13, 1695, the French bombarded Brussels from a hill outside the city walls, destroying the Grand Place (see pp42–3) and much of its environs. The French withdrew, but their desire to rule the region was to cause conflict over subsequent decades.

## A PHOENIX FROM THE ASHES

Despite the destruction incurred by the bombardment, Brussels was quick to recover. The guilds ensured that the Grand Place was rebuilt in a matter of years, with new guildhouses as a testament to the on-going success of the city's economic life and craftsmanship.

The building of the Willebroek canal during the 17th century gave Brussels access to the Rupel and Scheldt rivers, and thus to Antwerp and the North Sea. Large industries began to replace local market trading. Factories and mills grew up around the city's harbour, and Brussels became an export centre.

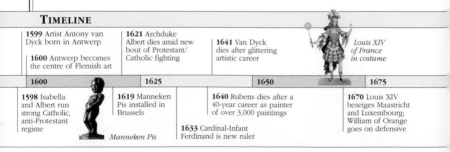

## TIMELINE

| | | | | |
|---|---|---|---|---|
| **1599** Artist Antony van Dyck born in Antwerp | **1621** Archduke Albert dies amid new bout of Protestant/ Catholic fighting | **1641** Van Dyck dies after glittering artistic career | | *Louis XIV of France in costume* |
| **1600** Antwerp becomes the centre of Flemish art | | | | |
| **1600** | **1625** | **1650** | | **1675** |
| **1598** Isabella and Albert run strong Catholic, anti-Protestant regime | **1619** Manneken Pis installed in Brussels | **1640** Rubens dies after a 40-year career as painter of over 3,000 paintings | | **1670** Louis XIV beseiges Maastricht and Luxembourg; William of Orange goes on defensive |
| | *Manneken Pis* | **1633** Cardinal-Infant Ferdinand is new ruler | | |

## AUSTRIAN SUCCESSION

Subsequent decades were dogged by war as Austria and England sought to stave off French ambitions. When Philip of Anjou succeeded to the Spanish throne, it looked as if the combined threat of Spain and France would overwhelm the rest of Europe. Emperor Leopold I of Austria, together with England and many German states, declared war on France. The resulting 14-year War of the Spanish Succession ended with the Treaty of Utrecht in 1713, which ceded the Netherlands, including Brussels, to Austria.

**Governor of Brussels,
Duke Charles of Lorraine**

The treaty did not end the conflict. Emperor Charles VI of Austria ruled after Leopold, but failed to produce a male heir. His death in 1731 sparked another 17 years of war – The War of the Austrian Succession over whether his daughter Maria Theresa should be allowed to inherit the crown. It was not until 1748, with the signing of the Treaty of Aix-la-Chapelle, that Maria Theresa gained control.

## THE BOOM PERIOD

The endless fighting took its toll, and Brussels, along with the rest of Belgium, was impoverished. Despite the sophistication of the aristocratic elite, the majority of the population were still ruled by feudal laws: they could not change jobs or move home without permission; and only three per cent of the population was literate.

In the 1750s Empress Maria Theresa of Austria installed her brother, Charles of Lorraine, in Brussels. Under the influence of the Enlightenment, his court attracted European artists and intellectuals, and Brussels became the most glamorous city in Europe. Industry also boomed with the construction of new roads and waterways. Brussels was transformed as the Place Royale and Parc de Bruxelles were laid out.

## THE WORKERS' REVOLT

While the aristocracy and new middle classes flourished, Brussels' workers were suffering. As the city's population grew there were more workers than jobs: wages plummeted and factory conditions were harsh.

When Joseph II succeeded Maria Theresa in 1780, he enforced a series of reforms including freedom of religion. However, he also cancelled the 500-year-old Charter of Liberties.

Influenced by the ideas of the French Revolution of 1789, the Belgians now demanded reform. Their rebellion was to result in an independent state.

**French prince Philip of Anjou became Philip V of Spain, sparking the War of the Spanish Succession**

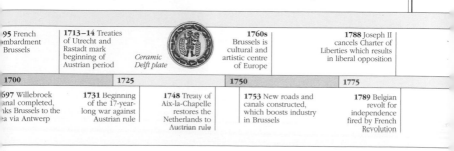

**95 French bombardment Brussels**

**1713–14 Treaties of Utrecht and Rastadt mark beginning of Austrian period**

*Ceramic Delft plate*

**1760s Brussels is cultural and artistic centre of Europe**

**1788 Joseph II cancels Charter of Liberties which results in liberal opposition**

**1700** | **1725** | **1750** | **1775**

**697 Willebroek canal completed, links Brussels to the sea via Antwerp**

**1731 Beginning of the 17-year-long war against Austrian rule**

**1748 Treaty of Aix-la-Chapelle restores the Netherlands to Austrian rule**

**1753 New roads and canals constructed, which boosts industry in Brussels**

**1789 Belgian revolt for independence fired by French Revolution**

# The Fight for Independence

**B**ELGIUM WAS AGAIN occupied by foreign powers between 1794 and 1830. First, by the French Republican armies, then, after Napoleon's defeat at Waterloo in 1815, by the Dutch. French radical reforms included the abolition of the guild system and fairer taxation laws. Although French rule was unpopular, their liberal ideas were to influence the Belgian drive for independence. William I of Orange was appointed King of the Netherlands (which included Belgium) after 1815. His autocratic style, together with a series of anti-Catholic measures, bred discontent, especially in Brussels and among the French-speaking Walloons in the south. The south was also angered when William refused to introduce tariffs to protect their trade – it was the last straw. The uprising of 1830 began in Brussels and Léopold I became king of the newly independent nation.

**King William I of Orange**
*William's rule as King of the Netherlands after 1815 was unpopular.*

**A Cultural Revolution in Brussels**
*French ideas not only influenced the revolution, but also Belgian culture. Under Napoleon the city walls were demolished and replaced by tree-lined boulevards.*

**Liberals joined** workers already protesting in the square outside.

**The Battle of Waterloo**
*Napoleon's influence came to an end after the battle of Waterloo on 18 June, 1815. A Prussian army came to Wellington's aid, and by 5:30pm Napoleon faced his final defeat. This led to Dutch rule over Belgium.*

**Agricultural workers**
*Harsh weather in the winter of 1829 caused hardship for both farmers and agricultural labourers, who also joined the protest.*

THE HISTORY OF BRUSSELS

**The Revolution in Industry**
*Unemployment, low wages and factory closures during the early decades of the 19th century sparked unrest in 1830.*

**La Théâtre de la Monnaie**
*A patriotic song,* L'Amour Sacré de la Patrie *led the audience in the theatre on the night of 25 August, 1830, to join demonstrators outside.*

L'INDÉPENDANCE DE LA BELGIQUE

Le Théâtre de la Monnaie le 25 août 1830 d'après le dessin de Hendricks.

## BELGIAN REVOLUTION

High unemployment, poor wages and a bad winter in 1829 provoked protests about living and working conditions. The revolution was ignited by a patriotic and radical opera at the Brussels' opera house, and the largely liberal audience rushed out into the street, raising the Brabant flag. Ten thousand troops were sent by William to quash the rebels, but the Belgian soldiers deserted and the Dutch were finally driven out of Belgium.

**The initial list of** demands asked for administrative independence from the Dutch, and for freedom of press.

**This symbolic** illustration of the revolution shows both liberals and workers ready to die for their country.

**King of Belgium, Léopold I**
*The crowning of German prince, Léopold of Saxe-Coburg, in Brussels in 1831 finally established Belgium's independence.*

## TIMELINE

| 1790 Republic of United Belgian States formed. Temporary end of Austrian rule | 1799 Emperor Napoleon rules France *Wellington* | | 1815 Battle of Waterloo. Napoleon defeated by army led by the Duke of Wellington | 1830 Rebellion begins at the Théâtre de la Monnaie in Brussels |
|---|---|---|---|---|
| **1790** | **1800** | **1810** | **1820** | **1830** |
| | 1794 Brussels loses its importance to The Hague | 1815 Belgium, allied with Holland under the United Kingdom of the Netherlands, is ruled by William I of Orange. Brussels becomes second capital | 1831 State of Belgium formed on 21 July. Treaty of London grants independence | |
| | 1790 War between France and Austria | | 1835 Continental railway built from Brussels to Mechelen | |

## THE FLEMISH AND THE WALLOONS: THE BELGIAN COMPROMISE

Linguistically and culturally, Belgium is divided. In the north, the Flemish have their roots in the Netherlands and Germany. In the south are the Walloons, the French-speaking Belgians, culturally connected to France. The "Linguistic Divide" of 1962 officially sanctioned this situation, dividing Belgium into Flemish- and French-speaking zones. The exception is Brussels, an officially bilingual city since the formation of Bruxelles-Capitale in 1963, and a national region by 1989 when it came to comprise 19 outlying districts. Conflicts still erupt over the issue, but the majority of Belgians seem to be in favour of a united country.

**Bilingual road signs**

### CONSOLIDATING THE NEW STATE

During its early days as an independent nation, Brussels was a haven for free-thinkers, including the libertarian poet Baudelaire, and a refuge for exiles, such as Karl Marx and Victor Hugo. Belgium's industries also continued to expand throughout the 19th century.

By 1870 there were no less than four main railway stations in Brussels able to export goods all over Europe. However, the population of Brussels had almost doubled, resulting in poor-quality housing and working conditions. Towards the end of the reign of Belgium's second monarch, Léopold II (r.1865–1909), industrial unrest led to new legislation which improved conditions, and all men over 25 gained the right to vote in 1893. But the king's principal concern was his colonialist policy in the Congo in Central Africa.

### THE GERMAN OCCUPATIONS

Albert I succeeded Léopold II as Belgium's new king. He encouraged the nation's artists and architects, and was a keen supporter of Art Nouveau *(see pp16–17)*. All of this ended as the country entered its bleakest period.

Despite its neutral status, Belgium was invaded by the German army in the summer of 1914. All of the country, except for the northern De Panne region, was occupied by the Germans. Some of the bloodiest battles of World War I were staged on Belgian soil. Flanders was the scene of brutal trench warfare, including the introduction of poison gas at Ypres *(see p107)*. Today, Belgium contains several vast graveyards, which include the resting places of the tens of thousands of soldiers who died on the Western Front.

The Belgians conducted resistance from their stronghold in De Panne, cutting telephone wires and destroying train tracks. The Germans responded by confiscating property, deporting Belgians to German labour camps

**King Léopold III visits a goldmine in the Congo in Africa**

## TIMELINE

| | 1847 Opening of Europe's first shopping mall, the Galéries St Hubert | 1871 Under Léopold II, the River Senne is reclaimed, and new districts built to cope with the growing city | 1898 Flemish language given equal status to French in law | 1914–18 World War I. Germany occupies Belgium |
|---|---|---|---|---|
| **1840** | | **1870** | **1900** | **1925** |
| | *The Belgian Congo* | 1884 Léopold II is granted sovereignty over the Congo | 1910 World Fair in Brussels promotes Belgium's industrial boom. Art Nouveau flourishes | 1929–31 Great Depression and reduction in foreign trade |
| 1839 Treaty of London grants neutrality to Belgium | | | | |

German troops raising the German flag at the Royal Castle at Laeken, near Brussels

## INTERNATIONAL STATUS

Belgium's history in the latter half of the 20th century has been dominated by the ongoing language debate between the Flemish and the French-speaking Walloons. From 1970 to 1994 the constitution was redrawn, creating a federal state with three separate regions; the Flemish north, the Walloon south and bilingual Brussels. While this smoothed over conflicts, cultural divisions run deep. Today, all parliamentary speeches have to be delivered in both French and Flemish.

Like most of Europe, Belgium went from economic boom in the 1960s to recession and retrenchment in the 1970s and 1980s. Throughout these decades Brussels' stature at the heart of Europe was consolidated. In 1958, the city became the headquarters for the European Economic Community (EEC), later the European Union. In 1967 NATO also moved to Brussels.

## THE EUROPEAN CAPITAL

Modern Brussels is a multilingual and cosmopolitan city at the forefront of Europe. This historically industrial city now prospers as a base for many large corporations such as ICI and Mitsubishi.

and murdering random hostages. Belgium remained under German occupation until the last day of the war, 11 November, 1918.

The 1919 Treaty of Versailles granted Belgium control of Eupen-Malmédy, the German-speaking area in the southeast. But by 1940 the country was again invaded by the Germans under Hitler. In May of that year, King Léopold III surrendered.

Despite national resistance to the Occupation, the King was interned at Laeken until 1944, after which he was moved to Germany until the end of the war. Rumours that Léopold had collaborated with the Nazis led to his abdication in 1951, in favour of his 20-year-old son, Baudouin.

The European Parliament, Brussels

Despite its flourishing status, the city has had its fair share of disasters, including the deaths of 38 Italian football supporters at the Heysel stadium in 1985. Also, two tragic paedophile murder cases in the 1990s led many Belgians to protest against the apparent failures of the police system. However, Brussels' future as a city of world importance seems certain as it lies at the political centre of the European Union.

| 1939–45 World War II. Germany again occupies Belgium | 1951 Abdication of Léopold III; Baudouin I succeeds | 1962 The Belgian Congo is granted independence | | 1993 King Baudouin I dies; Albert II succeeds | 2002 The euro becomes legal tender |
|---|---|---|---|---|---|
| | *Baudouin I* | *European flag* | | | |
| | 1950 | 1975 | | 2000 | |
| | 1944 Benelux Unions with Holland and Luxembourg formed | 1967 Brussels is new NATO HQ | 1985 Heysel Stadium disaster | 1989 Brussels is officially a bilingual city with 19 outlying districts | 2001 Crown Prince Philippe and Princess Mathilde have a daughter, Elisabeth |
| 1934 Albert I is killed in a climbing accident | | | | | |

# BRUSSELS
# AREA BY AREA

# THE LOWER TOWN

**M**OST VISITS TO Brussels begin with a stroll around the Lower Town, the ancient heart of the city and home to its most famous area, the Grand Place. The original settlement of the city was here; most of the streets surrounding this huge market square date from as far back as the Middle Ages up to the 18th century. The architecture is an eclectic blend of Gothic, Baroque and Flemish Renaissance.

Maison du Cygne, Grand Place

In and around the Place de Brouckère and the busy Boulevard Anspach are the more recent additions to the city's history. These appeared in the 19th century when the slums around the River Senne were cleared to make way for ornate constructions such as the financial centre, La Bourse, and Europe's first shopping arcade, Galéries St-Hubert. With its many restaurants and cafés, the Lower Town is also popular at night.

## SIGHTS AT A GLANCE

**Historic Buildings and Monuments**
Hôtel de Ville see pp44–45 **2**
Manneken Pis **3**
La Bourse **7**

**Museums and Galleries**
Musée du Costume et de la Dentelle **1**
Bruxella 1238 **8**
Centre Belge de la Bande Dessinée see pp50–51 **14**
Maison de la Bellone **21**

**Churches**
Notre-Dame de la Chapelle **4**
Eglise St-Nicolas **9**
Eglise St-Jean-Baptiste **19**
Eglise Ste-Catherine **22**

**Shopping**
Galeries St-Hubert **10**
Rue Neuve **16**

**Streets and Squares**
Rue des Bouchers **11**
Place de Brouckère **18**

**Theatres**
Théâtre Marionnettes de Toone **12**
Théâtre Royal de la Monnaie **13**
Théâtre Flamand **20**

**Cultural Centres**
Le Botanique **15**

**Historic Districts**
Quartier Marolles **5**
Halles St-Géry **6**

**Hotels**
Hôtel Métropole **17**

### KEY

🚊 Tram stop
Ⓜ Metro station
🚌 Bus terminus
ℹ Tourist information
🅿 Parking

### GETTING AROUND
The area is well served by trams which encircle the old town. However, the tiny streets are often pedestrianized, and usually the quickest and most enjoyable means of transport for short distances is on foot. Otherwise metro stations are well placed.

0 metres      500
0 yards       500

◁ Detail of the façade of the Hôtel de Ville in the Grand Place – centre of the Lower Town

# The Grand Place

THE GEOGRAPHICAL, HISTORICAL and commercial heart of
the city, the Grand Place is the first port of call for
most visitors to Brussels. This bustling cobblestone square
remains the civic centre, centuries after its creation,
and offers the finest surviving example in one area of
Belgium's ornate 17th-century architecture. Open-air
markets took place on or near this site as early as the
11th century, but by the end of the 14th century Brussels'
town hall, the Hôtel de Ville, was built, and city traders
added individual guildhouses in a medley of styles. In
1695, however, two days of cannon fire by the French
destroyed all but the town hall and two guild façades.
Trade guilds were urged to rebuild their halls to styles
approved by the Town Council, producing the harmonious unity of Flemish Renaissance buildings here today.

**The morning flower market in
bloom in the Grand Place**

**The Maison du Roi** was first
built in 1536 but redesigned in
1873. Once the residence of
ruling Spanish
monarchs, it is
now home to
the Musée de
la Ville, which
includes 16th-
century paint-
ings, tapestries,
and the 400
tiny outfits of
Manneken Pis.

① **NORTHEAST CORNER**      ② **MAISON DU ROI**

**The Hôtel de Ville** occupies the
entire southwest side of the
square. Still a functioning civic
building, Brussels' town hall is
the architectural masterpiece of
the Grand Place (see pp44–5).

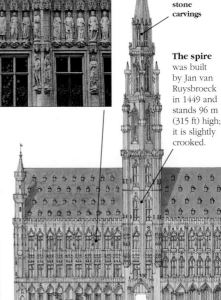

Ornate
stone
carvings

**The spire**
was built
by Jan van
Ruysbroeck
in 1449 and
stands 96 m
(315 ft) high;
it is slightly
crooked.

**Everard 't Serclaes** was murdered
defending Brussels in the 14th
century; touching the bronze
arm of his statue is said
to bring luck.

⑤ **EVERARD 'T SERCLAES**      ⑥ **HÔTEL DE VILLE**

**Le Pigeon** was home to Victor Hugo, the exiled French novelist who chose the house as his Belgian residence in 1852. Some of the most complimentary comments about Brussels emerged later from his pen.

**LOCATOR MAP**
See Brussels street finder, map 2

**La Maison des Ducs de Brabant** is a group of six guildhouses. Designed by the Controller of Public Works, Guillaume de Bruyn, the group is Neo-Classical with Flemish additions.

**Stone busts** of the ducal line along the façade gave this group of houses their name.

③ LE PIGEON

① LA MAISON DES DUCS DE BRABANT

**Le Renard** was built in the 1690s as the guildhouse of the haberdashers by the Flemish architects Marc de Vos and van Nerum. Façade details show St Nicolas, patron saint of merchants, and cherubs playing with haberdashery ribbons.

**Le Cornet** displays Italianate Flemish style. This Boatmen's Guildhouse (1697) is most notable for its gable, which is constructed in the form of a 17th-century frigate's bow.

**La Maison des Boulangers**, also known as "Le Roi d'Espagne", was a showpiece built by the wealthy and powerful guild of bakers. The 1676 octagonal copper dome is topped by a dancing golden figure.

**Le Roi d'Espagne** now houses the Grand Place's finest bar with a view of the bustling square and its splendours above ground level. (see p154). The gilt bust over the front entrance represents Saint Aubert, patron saint of bakers. A vast bust of Charles II of Spain sits in stone drapery on the third floor.

⑦ LE RENARD, LE CORNET AND LE ROI D'ESPAGNE

## Musée du Costume et de la Dentelle ❶

Rue de Violette 6, 1000 BRU.
**Map** 2 D3. **☎** (02) 213 4450.
**Ⓜ** Gare Centrale, de Brouckère.
**⏰** 10am–12:30pm, 1:30–5pm
Mon–Fri; 2–5pm Sat, Sun.
**📷** **♿** **📹** on request.

**A wedding dress at the Musée du Costume et de la Dentelle**

FOUND WITHIN two 18th-century gabled houses is the museum dedicated to one of Brussels' most successful exports, Belgian lace *(see pp20–21)*. The intricate skill employed by Belgian lace-makers has contributed a vital economic role in the city since the 12th century, and the collection explains and displays the history of this delicate craft. On the ground floor costumes from the 18th to the 20th centuries are displayed on mannequins, demonstrating how lace has adorned fashions of every era. The second floor houses a collection of antique lace, carefully stored in drawers and demonstrating the various schools of lacemaking in France, Flanders and Italy.

## Manneken Pis ❸

Rues de l'Etuve & du Chêne, 1000 BRU. **Map** 1 C3. **🚌** 34, 48, 95, 96. **🚊** 23, 52, 55, 56, 81. **Ⓜ** Bourse, Gare Centrale.

AN UNLIKELY ATTRACTION, this tiny statue of a young boy barely 30 cm (1 ft) high relieving himself into a small pool is as much a part of Brussels as

## Hôtel de Ville ❷

**Stone gargoyle**

THE IDEA OF having a town hall to reflect Brussels' growth as a major European trading centre had been under consideration since the end of the 13th century. It was not until 1401 that the first foundation stone was laid and the building was finally completed in 1459, emerging as the finest civic building in the country, a stature it still enjoys.

**A detail of the delicately carved façade with stone statues**

Jacques van Thienen was commissioned to design the left wing and belfry of the building, where he used ornate columns, sculptures, turrets and arcades. The tower and spire begun in 1449 by Jan van Ruysbroeck helped seal its reputation. In 1995, the 1455 statue of the city's patron saint, Michael, was restored and returned to its famous position on top of the tower in 1997, where it is used as a weather vane. Tours are available of the interior, which contains 15th-century tapestries and works of art.

**137 statues** adorn walls and many mullioned windows.

**★ Aldermen's Room**
*Still in use today for the meetings of the aldermen and mayor of Brussels, this council chamber contains a series of 18th-century tapestries depicting the history of 6th-century King Clovis.*

**STAR SIGHTS**

★ **Conference Room Council Chamber**

★ **Aldermen's Room**

the Trevi Fountain is part of Rome or Trafalgar Square's reclining lions are of London.

The original bronze statue by Jérôme Duquesnoy the Elder, was first placed on the site in 1619, the tongue-in-cheek design reflecting a genuine need for fresh drinking water in the area. Its popularity led, in 1770, to the addition of an ornate stone niche, giving more prominence to the small figure. Several attempts to steal the statue were made during the 18th century, notably by the French and then British armies in 1745, but it was the theft in

1817 by a former convict, Antoine Licas, which caused the most alarm – the robber smashed the bronze figure shortly after procuring it. A replica of the statue was cast the following year and returned to its revered site, and it is this copy that is seen today. In 1698 governor Maximilian-Emmanuel donated a suit of clothing with which to dress the statue. It was to be the beginning of a tradition that continues to this day. Visiting heads of state to Brussels donate miniature versions of their national costume for the boy, and now 400 outfits, including an Elvis suit, are housed in the Musée de la Ville (see p42).

(see p42)

## THE LEGENDS OF MANNEKEN PIS

The inspiration for this famous statue remains unknown, but the mystery only lends itself to rumour and fable and increases the little boy's charm. One theory claims that in the 12th century the son of a duke was caught urinating against a tree in the midst of a battle and was thus commemorated in bronze as a symbol of the country's military courage.

**The belfry** was built by architect Jan van Ruysbroeck. A statue of St Michael tops the 96 m (315 ft) spire

**Aldermen's Room**

**The gabled roof**, like much of the town hall, was fully restored in 1837, and cleaned in the 1990s.

## VISITORS' CHECKLIST

Grand Place, 1000 BRU. **Map** 2 D3. (02) 279 4365. 29, 34, 47, 48, 60, 63, 65, 66, 71, 95, 96. 23, 52, 55, 56, 81. M *Bourse, Gare Centrale.* **Museum** 10am–5pm Tue–Sun (to 1pm Sat & Sun). pub hols, election days. 11:30am & 3:15pm Tue, 12:15pm Sun (call for details).

**Cabinets des Echevins**

★ **Conference Room Council Chamber**
*The most splendid of all the public rooms, ancient tapestries and gilt mirrors line the walls above an inlaid floor.*

**Ornamental stone balcony staircase**

**Wedding Room**
*A Neo-Gothic style dominates this civil marriage office, with its many ornate carved timbers, including ancient ebony and mahogany.*

## Notre-Dame de la Chapelle ❹

Place de la Chapelle 1, 1000 BRU. **Map** 1 C4. *(02) 513 5348.* *27, 34, 95, 96.* *91, 92, 93, 94.* *Porte de Namur.* *5:30pm Mon–Sat; Mass 6:30pm daily.*

In 1134 king Godefroid I decided to build a chapel outside the city walls. It quickly became a market church, serving the many craftsmen living nearby. In 1210 its popularity was such that it was made a parish church, but it became really famous in 1250, when a royal donation of five pieces of the True Cross turned the church into a pilgrimage site.

Originally built in Romanesque style, the majority of the church was destroyed by fire in 1405. Rebuilding began in 1421 in a Gothic style typical of 15th-century Brabant architecture, including gables decorated with finials and interior capitals decorated with cabbage leaves at the base. The Bishop of Cambrai consecrated the new church in 1434.

One of the most striking features of the exterior are the monstrously lifelike gargoyles which peer down on the community – a representation of evil outside the sacred interior. The Baroque belltower was added after the 1695 bombardment by the French *(see p32)*. Another moving feature is the carved stone memorial to the 16th-century Belgian artist Pieter Brueghel the Elder *(see p14)*, who is buried here.

**The cool, elegant interior of Notre-Dame de la Chapelle**

**Rue Haute in the Quartier Marolles, with old-style shops and cafés**

## Quartier Marolles ❺

**Map** 1 C5. *20, 27, 48.* *91.* *Louise, Porte de Hal.*

Known colloquially as "Les Marolles", this quarter of Brussels is traditionally working class. Situated between the two city walls, the area was home to weavers and craftsmen. Street names of the district, such as Rue des Brodeurs (Embroiderers' St) and Rue des Charpentiers (Carpenters' St), reflect its artisanal history.

Today the area is best known for its fine daily flea market, held in the **Place du Jeu de Balle**. The flea market has been held on this site since 1640. Between 7am and 2pm, with the biggest and best markets on Thursday and Sunday, almost anything from junk to pre-war collector's items can be found among the stalls.

Shopping of a different kind is on offer on nearby Rue Haute, an ancient Roman road. A shopping district since the 19th century, it is still popular with arty types with its specialist stores, interior and antique shops. The street has a long artistic history, too – the elegant red-brick house at No. 132 was home to Pieter Brueghel the Elder and the sculptor Auguste Rodin had a studio at No. 224. No. 132 now houses the small **Maison de Brueghel**, dedicated to the 16th-century painter.

At the southern end of Rue Haute is **Porte de Hal**, the stone gateway of the now-demolished outer city walls. Looming over the Marolles is the imposing Palais de Justice *(see p69)*, which has hilltop views of the area west of the city, including the 1958 Atomium *(see p83)* and the Basilique Sacré-Coeur *(see p81)*.

**Maison de Brueghel**
Rue Haute 132, 1000 BRU.
*May–Sep: Wed & Sun pm (groups with written permission only).*
*Oct–Apr.*

**Busy restaurants and cafés outside Halles St-Géry**

## Halles St-Géry ❻

Place St-Géry, 1000 BRU. **Map** 1 C2. *47.* *23, 52, 55, 56, 81.* *de Brouckère.*

In many ways, St-Géry can be considered the birthplace of the city. A chapel to Saint Géry was built in the 6th century, then in AD 977 a fortress took over the site. A 16th-century church followed and occupied the location until the 18th century. In 1881 a covered meat market was erected in Neo-Renaissance style. The glass and intricate ironwork was renovated in 1985, and the hall now serves as a cultural centre with an exhibition on local history.

## La Bourse ❼

Palais de la Bourse, 1000 BRU. **Map** 1 C2. ▐ *(02) 509 1211.* ▆ *47.* ▛ *3, 52, 55, 56, 81.* Ⓜ *Bourse.* ◯ *10am daily, by appointment.* ◉ *Sat & Sun, public hols.* ▟ *of the exchange market.*

**B**RUSSELS' Stock Exchange, La Bourse, is one of the city's most impressive buildings, dominating the square of the same name. Designed in Palladian style by architect Léon Suys, it was constructed from 1867 to 1873. Among the building's most notable features are the façade's ornate carvings. The great French sculptor, Auguste Rodin, is thought to have crafted the groups representing Africa and Asia, as well as four caryatids inside. Beneath the colonnade, two beautifully detailed winged figures representing Good and Evil were carved by sculptor Jacques de Haen. Some areas of the building are open to the public, but a screen divides visitors from the frantic bidding and trading that takes place on weekdays on the trading floor.

## Bruxella 1238 ❽

Rue de la Bourse, 1000 BRU. **Map** 1 C3. ▐ *(02) 279 4350.* ▆ *34, 48, 95, 96.* ▛ *3, 52, 55, 56, 81.* Ⓜ *Bourse, de Brouckère.* ◯ *10:15am (English), 11:15am, 1:45pm, 2:30pm, 3:15pm, Wed.* ▟ ▟ *obligatory, starts from Maison du Roi, Grand Place.*

**O**NCE HOME to a church and 13th-century Franciscan convent, in the early 19th century this site became a Butter Market until the building of the Bourse commenced in 1867. In 1988 municipal roadworks began alongside the Place de la Bourse. Medieval history must have been far from the minds of the city authorities but, in the course of working on the foundations for the Bourse, important relics were found, including 13th-century bones, pottery and the 1294 grave of Duke John I of Brabant. Visitors can now see these and other pieces of Burgundian history in a small museum built on the site.

## Eglise St-Nicolas ❾

Rue au Beurre 1, 1000 BRU. **Map** 1 C2. ▐ *(02) 513 8022.* ▆ *34, 48, 95, 96.* ▛ *3, 52, 55, 56, 81.* Ⓜ *Bourse, de Brouckère.* ◯ *9am–6:30pm daily, except during services.*

**A**T THE END of the 12th century a market church was constructed on this site, but, like much of the Lower Town, it was damaged in the 1695 French Bombardment. A cannon ball lodged itself directly into an interior pillar and the belltower finally collapsed in 1714. Many restoration projects were planned but none came to fruition until as late as 1956, when the west side of the building was given a new, Gothic-style façade. Named after St Nicolas, the patron saint of merchants, the church contains choir stalls dating from 1381 which display detailed medallions telling St Nicolas's story. Another interesting feature is the chapel, constructed at an angle, reputedly to avoid the flow of an old stream. Inside the church, works of art by Bernard van Orley and Peter Paul Rubens are well worth seeing.

**Detail of a Rodin statue, La Bourse**

**The 19th-century domed glass roof of Galéries St-Hubert**

## Galeries St-Hubert ❿

Rue des Bouchers, 1000 BRU. **Map** 2 D2. ▆ *29, 38, 60, 63, 65, 66, 71.* Ⓜ *Gare Centrale.* ▟

**S**IXTEEN YEARS after ascending the throne as the first king of Belgium, Léopold I inaugurated the opening of these grand arcades in 1847.

St-Hubert has the distinction of being the first shopping arcade in Europe, and one of the most elegant. Designed in Neo-Renaissance style by Jean-Pierre Cluysenaar, the vaulted glass roof covers its three sections, Galerie du Roi, Galerie de la Reine and Galerie des Princes, which house a range of luxury shops and cafés. The ornate interior and expensive goods on sale soon turned the galleries into a fashionable meeting place for 19th-century society, including resident literati – Victor Hugo and Alexandre Dumas attended lectures here. The arcades remain a popular venue, with shops, a cinema, theatre, cafés and restaurants.

**Gothic-style façade of Eglise St Nicolas**

Pavement displays of restaurants along Rue des Bouchers

## Rue des Bouchers ⓫

**Map** 2 D2. 🚋 *29, 60, 63, 65, 66, 71.* 🚃 *3, 52, 55, 56, 81, 90.* Ⓜ *de Brouckère, Gare Centrale, Bourse.*

L IKE MANY streets in this area of the city, Rue des Bouchers retains its medieval name, reminiscent of the time when this meandering, cobble-stoned street was home to the butchers' trade. Aware of its historic importance and heeding the concerns of the public, the city council declared this area the Ilot Sacré (sacred islet) in 1960, forbidding any of the architectural façades to be altered or destroyed, and commanding those surviving to be restored. Hence Rue des Bouchers abounds with 17th-century stepped gables and decorated doorways.

Today, this pedestrianized thoroughfare is best known as the "belly of Brussels", a reference to its plethora of cafés and restaurants. Many cuisines are on offer here, including Chinese, Greek, Italian and Indian. But the most impressive sights during an evening stroll along the street are the lavish pavement displays of seafood, piled high on mounds of ice, all romantically lit by an amber glow from the streetlamps.

At the end of the street, at the Impasse de la Fidélité, is a recent acknowledgement of sexual equality. Erected in 1987, Jeanneke Pis is a coy, cheeky female version of her "brother", the more famous Manneken Pis *(see p45)*.

## Théâtre Marionettes de Toone ⓬

Impasse Schuddeveld 6, off the Petite Rue des Bouchers, 1000 BRU. **Map** 2 D2. 🛈 *(02) 511 7137.* 🚋 *29, 34, 48, 60, 63, 65, 66, 71, 95, 96.* 🚃 *3, 52, 55, 56, 81.* Ⓜ *Bourse, Gare Centrale.* ☐ *bar: noon–midnight daily; theatre: performance times (8:30pm Tue–Sat).* ⬤ *Sun, pub hols.* 🖼 🎫 *on request, for tour reservations* 🛈 *(02) 217 2753.* **Museum** ☐ *intervals.*

A POPULAR pub by day, at night the top floor of this tavern is home to a puppet theatre. During the time of the Spanish Netherlands *(see p32)*, all theatres were closed because of the satirical performances by actors aimed at their Latin rulers.

**Harlequin puppet** This began a fashion for puppet shows, the vicious dialogue more easily forgiveable from inanimate dolls. In 1830, Antoine Toone opened his own theatre and it has been run by the Toone family ever since; the owner is the seventh generation, Toone VII. The classics are enacted by these wooden marionettes in the local Bruxellois dialect, and occasionally in French, English, German or Dutch.

## Théâtre Royal de la Monnaie ⓭

Place de la Monnaie, 1000 BRU. **Map** 2 D2. 🛈 *(07) 023 3939.* 🚋 *29, 60, 65, 66.* 🚃 *3, 52, 55, 56, 81.* Ⓜ *de Brouckère, Bourse.* ☐ *performance times, Mon–Sat; box office: 11am–6pm Tue–Sat.* ⬤ *Sun, public hols.* 🖼 🎫 *noon Sat only.*

T HIS THEATRE was first built in 1817 on the site of a 15th-century mint (Hôtel des Monnaies) but, following a fire in 1855, only the front and pediment of the original Neo-Classical building remain. After the fire, the theatre was redesigned by the architect, Joseph Poelaert, also responsible for the imposing Palais de Justice *(see p69)*.

The original theatre was to make its historical mark before its destruction, however, when on 25 August, 1830, a performance of *La Muette de Portici* (*The Mute Girl*) began a national rebellion. As the tenor began to sing the nationalist *Amour Sacré de la Patrie* (*Sacred love of the homeland*), his words incited an already discontented city, fired by the libertarianism of the revolutions taking place in France, into revolt. Members of the audience ran out into the street in a rampage that developed into the

The original Neo-Classical façade of Théâtre Royal de la Monnaie

The 19th-century glasshouse of Le Botanique in summer

September Uprising *(see p34–5)*. The theatre today remains the centre of Belgian performing arts; major renovations took place during the 1980s. The auditorium was raised 4 m (13 ft) to accommodate the elaborate stage designs, but the luxurious Louis XIV-style decor was carefully retained and blended with the new additions. The central dome is decorated with an allegory of Belgian arts.

## Centre Belge de la Bande Dessinée ⓮

*See pp50–51.*

## Le Botanique ⓯

Rue Royale 236, 1210 BRU. **Map** 2 E1. 🕿 *(02) 226 1211.* 🚌 *38, 58, 61.* 🚊 *92, 93, 94.* Ⓜ *Botanique.* 🕐 *10am–6pm daily.* ♿

I N 1797, THE CITY of Brussels created a botanical garden in the grounds of the Palais de Lorraine as a source of reference for botany students. The garden closed in 1826, and new gardens were relocated in Meise, 13 km (9 miles) from Brussels.

A grand glass-and-iron rotunda was designed at the centre of the gardens by the French architect Gineste. This

iron glasshouse still stands, as does much of the 19th-century statuary by Constantin Meunier *(see p15)*, including depictions of the Four Seasons. The glasshouse is now home to the French Community Cultural Centre and offers plays, concerts and exhibitions.

## Rue Neuve ⓰

**Map** 2 D2. 🚌 *29, 60, 63, 65, 66, 71.* 🚊 *3, 52, 55, 56, 81, 90.* Ⓜ *Bourse, de Brouckère, Rogier.*

B RUSSELS shoppers have been flocking to the busy Rue Neuve since the 19th century for its reasonably priced goods and well-located stores.

Rue Neuve, the longest pedestrian shopping street in the city

Similar to London's Oxford Street, but now pedestrianized, this is the heart of commercial shopping. It houses well-known international chainstores and shopping malls, such as **City 2**, which has shops, cafés and the media store Fnac all under one roof. Inno department store was designed by Horta *(see p78)*, but after a fire in 1967 was entirely rebuilt.

To the east of Rue Neuve is Place des Martyrs, a peaceful square where a monument pays tribute to the 450 citizens killed during the 1830 uprising.

### 🏠 City 2
Rue Neuve 123, 1000 BRU. 🕿 *(02) 211 4060.* 🕐 *10am–7pm Mon–Thu & Sat, 10am– 8pm Fri.* 🔴 *Sun, public hols.*

## Hôtel Métropole ⓱

Place de Brouckère 31, 1000 BRU. **Map** 2 D2. 🕿 *(02) 217 2300.* 🚌 *29, 60, 65, 66.* 🚊 *23, 52, 55, 56, 81.* Ⓜ *de Brouckère.*

T HE AREA lying between Place Rogier and Place de Brouckère is known as the hotel district of Brussels, and one of the oldest and grandest hotels in the area is the Métropole.

In 1891 the Wielemans Brewery bought the building and commissioned the architect Alban Chambon to redesign the interior, with money no object. The result was a fine Art Nouveau hotel which opened for business in 1895 and has since accommodated numerous acclaimed visitors to the city, including actress Sarah Bernhardt. In 1911 the hotel was the location of the science conference Conseil Physique Solvay, attended by the great scientists Marie Curie and Albert Einstein.

The Hôtel Métropole continues to welcome guests from all walks of life, at surprisingly reasonable cost given its beauty, history and location. It is particularly popular for drinks in its café and heated pavement terrace, which are both open to non-residents to enjoy cocktails and cappuccinos in elegant surroundings.

# Centre Belge de la Bande Dessinée ⓮

**A**FFECTIONATELY KNOWN as *cébébédé*, the Museum of Comic Strip Art pays tribute to the Belgian passion for comic strips or *bandes dessinées* and to many world-famous comic strip artists from Belgium and abroad.

Arranged over three levels, the collection is housed in a Horta-designed Art Nouveau building. One of the most popular perma-nent exhibitions is a tour of the great comic strip heroes, from *Tintin* to *The Smurfs*, both of whose creators were Belgian. Other displays detail the stages of putting together a comic strip, from examples of initial ideas and pencil sketches

**The famous Tintin rocket**

**Three Comic Figures**
*Tintin, Professor Calculus and Captain Haddock greet visitors on the 1st floor.*

through to final publication. The museum regularly holds major exhibitions featuring the work of fam-ous cartoonists and studios, and also houses some 6,000 original plates, displayed in rotation, as well as a valuable archive of photographs and artifacts.

**The Smurfs**
*These tiny blue characters first appeared in the* Spirou *journal in 1958. By the 1980s they had their own TV show and hit records.*

**A Suivre**
*Founded in 1978,* A Suivre *expanded the comic strip genre, and led to the new form of graphic novels: adult stories in cartoon form.*

★ **Life-size Cartoon Sets**
*A series of authentic comic scenes encourages children to enter the world of their favourite comic strip characters.*

---

**STAR SIGHTS**

★ **Entrance Hall**

★ **Life-size Cartoon sets**

## VISITORS' CHECKLIST

20 rue des Sables, 1000 BRU.
**Map** 2 E2. 🎧 *(02) 219 1980.* 🚌
*38, 58, 61.* 🚊 *56, 81, 90.* Ⓜ
*Botanique, Rogier, Centrale.* ⭕
*10am–6pm Tue–Sun.* ⬤ *Mon,
1 Jan, 25 Dec.* 🖼 ⛊ 🛇 ⬛

### ★ Entrance Hall
*This airy space designed by
Victor Horta features stained
glass and wrought-ironwork.*

**Comic Library**
*The museum library
doubles as a study
centre for both art
students and enthu-
siasts of all ages. This
unique collection
includes a catalogue
of hundreds of old
comic strips, artists'
equipment, biogra-
phies, comic novels
and photographs.*

## A HORTA-DESIGNED BUILDING

This beautiful building was constructed
between 1903 and 1906 to the design
of the Belgian Art-Nouveau architect
Victor Horta. Originally built as a fabric
warehouse, and known as the Waucquez
Building, it was one in a series of department stores and warehouses in the city
designed by him. Saved from demolition by
the French Cultural Commission of Brussels,
in 1989 the building re-opened as a museum
dedicated to the comic strip, Belgium's so-
called Ninth Art *(see pp18–19)*. Carefully
restored, the building has many classic
features of Art Nouveau design, including
the use of curves on structural iron pillars.
In the impressive entrance hall is a display of Horta's architectural drawings

**Cast-iron
pillar**

for the building, and on the right the
Brasserie Horta serves traditional Belgian dishes in a
charming glass and marble Art Nouveau setting.

### THE CHANGING FACE OF HERGÉ'S TINTIN
Perhaps the best-known Belgian
comic character, *Tintin* made his
debut in a children's paper in 1929.
He began life as a simple black line
drawing, featuring the famous quiff,
but no mouth. By 1930 Hergé began
to produce *Tintin* in book-form and
gave him both a mouth and a more
complex character suggested by a
greater range of facial expressions.
By the 1940s *Tintin* was appearing
in colour, alongside such new
characters as Captain Haddock, the
Thompsons and Professor Calculus.

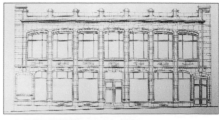

**Horta's drawing of the CBBD building**

**Nineteenth-century building in Place de Brouckère**

## Place de Brouckère 🔞

**Map** 2 D2. 🚌 29, 60, 63, 65, 66, 71. 🚊 3, 52, 55, 56, 81, 90. Ⓜ de Brouckère, Bourse.

In 1872 a design competition was held to encourage the construction of buildings of architectural interest in de Brouckère. Twenty winning applicants were selected and commissioned to give prominence to this Brussels junction. The Parisian contractor Jean-Baptiste Mosnier was responsible for taking the original plans through to completion.

The French influence of Mosnier and his workers is still evident on the square. Many of the buildings were erected in stone, common in France at the end of the 19th century, whereas brickwork was more usual in Brussels. Several original façades survive today, including the 1874 Hôtel Continental by Eugene Carpentier.

One of the great hotels of Brussels, the Hôtel Métropole (see p49) is situated on the south side of the square. The 1900–10 interior is splendidly gilded and can be seen either through the doorway or by pretending to be a guest. Café Métropole next door is, however, open to the public; here the lavishly ornate surroundings date from around 1890.

In the 20th century, architectural style was still at a premium in the district. In 1933 a Neo-Classical cinema was erected with an impressive Art Deco interior. During the 1960s, two imposing glass buildings blended the contemporary with the classical. Today, the varied historic architecture of Place de Brouckère enhances one of the city's busiest squares, despite recent additions of advertising hoardings.

## Eglise St-Jean-Baptiste-au-Béguinage 🔞

Place du Béguinage, 1000 BRU. **Map** 1 C1. 📞 (02) 217 8742. 🚌 47. Ⓜ Ste-Catherine. ⏰ 9am–5pm Tue–Sat, 10am–8pm Sun. ⏺ Mon. ♿

This stone-clad church was consecrated in 1676 around the long-standing and largest béguine community in the country, established in 1250. Fields and orchards around the site contained cottages and houses for up to 1,200 béguine women, members of a lay religious order who took up charitable work and enclosed living after widowhood or failed marriages. In medieval times the béguines ran a laundry, hospital and windmill for the people of the city. Still a popular place of worship, the church is also notable for its Flemish Baroque details from the 17th century, especially the onion-shaped turrets and ornamental walls. The nave is also Baroque, decorated with ornate winged cherubs, angels and scrolls. The confessionals are carved with allegorical figures and saints. A more unusual feature are the aisles, which have been widened to allow more light in. In the apse is a statue of St John the Baptist. The 1757 pulpit is a fine example of Baroque woodcarving, showing St Dominic and a heretic.

## Théâtre Flamand 🔞

Rue de Laeken 146, 1000 BRU. **Map** 1 C1. 🚌 47. 🚊 18. Ⓜ Yser. 🌐 www.kvs.be

The former quay area of Brussels, on the banks of the old River Senne, still survives as a reminder that the city was once a thriving port. In 1882, architect Jean Baes was commissioned to enlarge one of the former waterfront warehouses and then turn it into a theatre but was instructed to retain the original 1780 façade. Baes solved this problem ingeniously by placing the façade directly behind the frontage of the new building. In

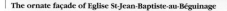

**The ornate façade of Eglise St-Jean-Baptiste-au-Béguinage**

addition to this, the Théâtre Flamand has other interesting design features peculiar to the late 19th century. The four exterior metal terraces and a staircase leading to the ground were built for audience evacuation in the event of fire. The theatre has recently undergone a major restoration programme, which has not only restored the fabric of the original building but has also improved the facilities.

**The 19th-century interior staircase of Théâtre Flamand**

## Maison de la Bellone ㉑

Rue de Flandre 46, 1000 BRU. **Map** 1 C2. [ (02) 513 3333. 🚌 63. 🚊 18. [M] Ste-Catherine. [ 10am–6pm Tue–Fri (exhibition centre open noon–6pm). 🌑 Sat–Mon, Jul.

THIS 17TH-CENTURY aristocratic residence, now shielded under a glass roof and no longer visible from the street, was once the headquarters of the Ommegang procession (see p25). The original façade is notable for its decoration. There is a statue of Bellona (goddess of war), after whom the house is named, above the central arch, and the window ledges have medallions of Roman emperors.

**Stonework on the Maison de la Bellone**

Today the house, its exhibition centre and once-private theatre are open for dance and cinema shows, and temporary exhibitions of art and furniture.

## THE BÉGUINE MOVEMENT

The béguine lifestyle swept across Western Europe from the 12th century, and Brussels once had a community of over 1,200 béguine women. The religious order is believed to have begun among widows of the Crusaders, who resorted to a pious life of sisterhood on the death of their husbands. The women were lay nuns, who opted for a secluded existence devoted to charitable deeds, but not bound by strict religious vows. Most béguine convents disappeared during the Protestant Reformation in much of Europe during the 16th century, but begijnhofs (béguinages) continued to thrive in Flanders. The grounds generally consisted of a church, a courtyard, communal rooms, homes for the women and extra rooms for work. The movement dissolved as female emancipation spread during the early 1800s, although 20 convents remain, including those in Bruges (see p117) and Ghent.

**Béguine lay nun at prayer in a Brussels béguinage**

## Eglise Ste-Catherine ㉒

Place Ste-Catherine 50, 1000 BRU. **Map** 1 C2. [ (02) 513 3481. 🚌 47. 🚊 3, 52, 55, 56, 81, 90. [M] Ste-Catherine, De Brouckère. [ 8:30am–5:30pm daily. 🔔 on request.

SADLY, THE ONLY remnant of the first church here, built in the 15th century, is its Baroque tower, added in 1629. Inspired by the Eglise St-Eustache in Paris, the present church was redesigned in 1854–59 by Joseph Poelaert in a variety of styles. Notable features of the interior include a 14th-century statue of the Black Madonna and a portrait of St Catherine herself. A typically Flemish pulpit was installed at some stage; it may have come from the parish of Mechelen. Two impressive tombs were carved by Gilles-Lambert Godecharle. To the east of the church is the Tour Noire (Black Tower), a surviving remnant of the 12th-century stone city walls.

Although this area has been dedicated to the saint since the 13th century, the square of Place Ste-Catherine was only laid in front of this large church after the basin once here was filled in. Paved in 1870, the square contrasts the peacefulness of the religious building with today's vigorous trade in good fish restaurants.

The central square was once the city's main fish market, and this is still the best place to indulge in a dish or two of Brussels' famous seafood, but prices are generally high. Flanking the square, Quai aux Briques and Quai au Bois à Brûler (Brick Quay and Timber Quay, named after their industrial past), contain lively parades of fish restaurants.

**Eglise Ste-Catherine showing the spacious Victorian interior**

# THE UPPER TOWN

**B**RUSSELS' UPPER TOWN is separated from the lower part of the city by an escarpment that runs roughly north-south from the far end of Rue Royale to the Palais de Justice. Modern developments are now scattered across the whole city, and the difference between the two areas is less distinct than in the past; traditionally the Lower Town was mainly Flemish-speaking and a bustling centre

**Peter Pan statue in Palais d'Egmont**

for trade, while the Upper Town was home to French-speaking aristocrats and royalty. Today the Upper Town is known for its beautiful Gothic churches, modern architecture and fine museums. The late 18th-century elegance of the Parc de Bruxelles and Place Royale is complemented by Emperor Leopold II's sweeping 19th-century boulevards that connect the Parc du Cinquantenaire to the city centre.

## SIGHTS AT A GLANCE

**Historic Streets and Buildings**
Hôtel Ravenstein **6**
Palais de Charles
 de Lorraine **8**
Palais d'Egmont **14**
Palais de Justice **15**
Palais Royal pp58–9 **2**
Parliament Quarter **22**
Place du Grand Sablon **11**
Place du Petit Sablon **13**
Place Royale **4**
Square Ambiorix **19**

**Parks and Gardens**
Parc du Cinquantenaire
 pp74–5 **25**
Parc Léopold **24**

**Museums and Galleries**
Institut Royal des Sciences
 Naturelles **23**
Musée Charlier **9**
Musée de la Dynastie **1**
Musée Instrumental **7**
Musée Wiertz **21**
Musées Royaux des Beaux-
 Arts pp62–7 **10**

**Churches and Cathedrals**
Cathédrale Sts Michel et Gudule
 pp70–71 **17**

Chapelle de la Madeleine **18**
Eglise St-Jacques-sur-
 Coudenberg **3**
Notre-Dame du Sablon **12**

**Theatres and Concert Halls**
Palais des Beaux-Arts **5**

**Modern Architecture**
Quartier Européen **20**

**Shopping**
Galérie Bortier **16**

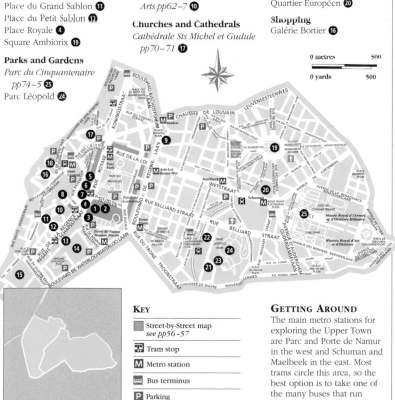

0 metres 500

0 yards 500

## KEY

| | |
|---|---|
| ▨ | Street-by-Street map see pp56–57 |
| 🚋 | Tram stop |
| M | Metro station |
| 🚌 | Bus terminus |
| P | Parking |

## GETTING AROUND

The main metro stations for exploring the Upper Town are Parc and Porte de Namur in the west and Schuman and Maelbeek in the east. Most trams circle this area, so the best option is to take one of the many buses that run through the Upper Town

◁ **Detail of a façade in a terrace of Art Nouveau houses in Square Ambiorix**

# Street-by-Street: Quartier Royal

**Fountain in park**

THE QUARTIER ROYAL has traditionally been home to Brussels' nobility and rulers. Chosen because the air was purer on the hill than it was in the Lower Town, the area once known as Coudenberg Hill was occupied by the 15th-century Coudenberg Palace, home to the Dukes of Brabant and Renaissance rulers. In 1731, the palace was destroyed in just six hours by a fire. Slowly rebuilt during the 18th and 19th centuries, four new palaces and much of the park were designed in Neo-Classical style chosen by Charles de Lorraine (*see p33*). Today the Royal Quarter presents a peaceful elegance, with some of Europe's finest 18th-century buildings framing the tree-lined paths and fountains of Parc de Bruxelles.

**Rue Royale** runs for 2 km (1 mile) from the Quartier Royal to Jardin Botanique. In contrast to the 18th-century Neo-Classicism of its beginnings, along its route many fine examples of Victorian and Art Nouveau architecture stand out.

### Eglise St-Jacques-sur-Coudenberg

*One of Brussels' prettiest churches, St-Jacques' 18th-century façade was modelled exactly on a classical temple. The barrel-vaulted nave and half-domed apse are sprinkled with floral plasterwork and contain several fine Neo-Classical paintings* ③

### ★ Place Royale

*In the centre of this attractive, symmetrical square is a statue of Godefroi of Bouillon, a Brabant soldier who fought the first Catholic Crusades and died in Palestine* ④

RUE ROYALE

PLACE ROYALE

## KEY

– – – Suggested route

## STAR SIGHTS

★ **Palais Royal**

★ **Parc de Bruxelles**

★ **Place Royale**

**Place des Palais** divides Palais Royal and the park. In French, "Palais" refers to any large stately building, and does not have royal connotations.

| 0 metres | 100 |
| 0 yards | 100 |

★ **Parc de Bruxelles**
*On the site of medieval hunting grounds once used by the dukes of Brabant, the park was redesigned in the 1770s with fountains, statues and tree-lined walks.*

**LOCATOR MAP**
*See Streetfinder Map 2*

RUE DE LA LOI

RUE DUCALE

ACE DES PALAIS

**Palais de la Nation**
*Designed by French architect Barnabé Guimard, the Palais de la Nation was built in 1783 and restored in 1883 after a fire. Since 1831, it has been the home of both chambers of the Belgian Parliament.*

★ **Palais Royal**
*The largest of the palaces, the low-rise Palais Royal is the official home of the Belgian monarch and family. A flag flies to indicate when the king is in the country* ❷

**Palais des Académies**
*Built in 1823 as the residence of the Crown Prince, this has been the private premises of the Académie Royale de Belgique since 1876.*

## Musée de la Dynastie ❶

Place des Palais 7, 1000 BRU.
**Map** 2 E4. ☎ (02) 545 0800.
🚌 20, 27, 34, 38, 54, 60, 71, 95, 96.
🚊 92, 93, 94. Ⓜ Trone, Parc.
◯ 10am–5pm Tue–Sun. ● Mon,
1 Jan, 21 Jul, 25 Dec.

T HE MUSÉE de la Dynastie
contains a broad collection
of paintings, documents and
other royal memorabilia chart-
ing the history of the Belgian
monarchy from independence
in 1830 to the present day.
Since 1992 it has been housed
in the former Hôtel Bellevue,
an 18th-century Neo-Classical
building lying adjacent to the
Palais Royal, which was
annexed to the palace in 1902.
A permanent exhibition in
honour of the late, immensely
popular, King Baudouin
(r.1951–1993) was added in

**The Neo-Classical façade of the
Musée de la Dynastie**

1998. As well as official
portraits, informal photographs
are on display which give a
fascinating insight into the
private lives of the Belgian
royal family. The collection
is displayed in chronological
order in a series of rooms
with a bust of the sovereign
to which it is devoted at the
entrance to each one.

## Eglise St-Jacques-sur-Coudenberg ❸

Place Royale, 1000 BRU. **Map** 2 E4. ☎
(02) 511 7836. 🚌 20, 27, 34, 38, 54,
60, 71, 95, 96. 🚊 92, 93, 94. Ⓜ
Trone, Parc. ◯ 3–5pm Mon,
10am–6pm Tue–Sat, 9am–noon Sun.

T HE PRETTIEST building in the
Place Royale, St-Jacques-
sur-Coudenberg is the latest
in a series of churches to
have occupied this site. There
has been a chapel here since
the 12th century, when one
was built to serve the dukes
of Brabant. On construction
of the Coudenberg Palace in
the 13th century, it became
the ducal chapel. The chapel
suffered over the years: it was
ransacked in 1579 during
conflict between Catholics
and Protestants, and was so
badly damaged in the fire
of 1731 that destroyed the

## Palais Royal ❷

T HE PALAIS ROYAL is the most important of the palaces
around the Parc de Bruxelles. An official residence of
the Belgian monarchy, construction of the modern palace
began in the 1820s on the site of the old Coudenberg
Palace. Work continued under Léopold II (r.1865–1909),
when much of the exterior was completed. Throughout
the 20th century the palace underwent interior improvements and restoration of its older sections. It is open
only from July to September, but this is a
fine opportunity to tour Belgium's
lavish state reception rooms.

**The Field Marshal's
Room** contains a portrait
of the first Belgian king,
Léopold I, after Winter-
halter's 1843 original.

STAR SIGHTS

★ Throne Room

★ Small White Room

**★ Throne Room**
*One of Brussels' original state-
rooms, the huge throne room is
decorated in grand style, with
huge pilastered columns, 11
large candelabras and 28
wall-mounted chandeliers.*

**The 19th-century cupola of Eglise St-Jacques-sur-Coudenberg**

Coudenberg Palace that it was demolished soon after. The present church was built in the Neo-Classical style of the rest of the area and was consecrated in 1787, although it served several years as a Temple of Reason and Law during the French Revolution,

returning to the Catholic Church in 1802. The cupola was completed in 1849. The interior is simple and elegant, with two large paintings by Jan Portaels on either side of the transept, and a royal pew.

## Place Royale ④

**Map** 2 E4. 🚌 *20, 27, 34, 38, 54, 60, 71, 95, 96.* 🚋 *92, 93, 94.* Ⓜ *Trone, Parc.*

THE INFLUENCE of Charles de Lorraine is still keenly felt in the Place Royale. As Governor of Brussels from 1749 to 1780 he redeveloped the site once occupied by the Coudenberg Palace along Neo-Classical lines reminiscent of Vienna, a city he greatly admired.

When the area was being worked on, the ruins of the burnt-down palace were demolished and the entire site

was rebuilt as two squares. However, in 1995, excavation work uncovered ruins of the 15th-century Aula Magna, the Great Hall of the former palace. This was part of the extension of the palace started under the dukes of Brabant in the early 13th century and then developed under the rule of the dukes of Burgundy, in particular Philip the Good. It was in this room that the Hapsburg emperor Charles V abdicated in favour of his son, Philip II. The ruins can now be seen in a corner of the Place Royale.

Although criss-crossed by tramlines and traffic, the Place Royale maintains a feeling of dignity with its tall, elegant, cream buildings symmetrically set around a cobbled square. Visitors can tour the area on foot, admiring the exceptional Neo-Classical buildings.

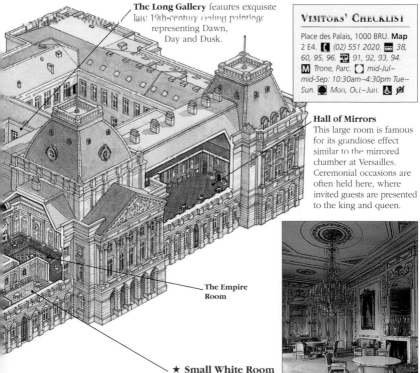

**The Long Gallery** features exquisite late 19th-century ceiling paintings representing Dawn, Day and Dusk.

**Hall of Mirrors**
This large room is famous for its grandiose effect similar to the mirrored chamber at Versailles. Ceremonial occasions are often held here, where invited guests are presented to the king and queen.

**The Empire Room**

**★ Small White Room**
*Rows of 19th-century royal portraits dominate this gilt chamber with its large candle-lit chandeliers and late 18th-century rococo furnishings.*

The Victor Horta-designed façade of the Palais des Beaux-Arts

## Palais des Beaux-Arts ❺

Rue Ravenstein 23, 1000 BRU.
**Map** 2 E3. 📞 *(02) 507 8200,
511 3433.* 🚌 *20, 71, 60, 95, 96.*
🚊 *92, 93, 94.* Ⓜ *Centrale.*
🕐 *11am–7pm daily.* ⬤ *public hols.*
📠 *(02) 507 8468.* ▢ ▯

THE PALAIS des Beaux-Arts
owes its existence to Henri
Le Boeuf, a music-loving finan-
cier who gave his name to the
main auditorium. In 1922 he
commissioned the architect
Victor Horta (*see p78*) to
design a cultural centre which
would house concert halls
and exhibition areas open
to all visitors and embracing
the artistic fields of music,
theatre, cinema and art. The
construction took seven years
as the building was on a
slope but could not be so tall
as to block the view of the
town from the Palais Royal:
Horta had to revise his plans
six times. The centre was the
first of its kind in Europe.

The complex has a fine
reputation and has played a
key role in the cultural life of
Brussels for over 70 years. It
is the focus for the city's music
and dance, and is home to
the Belgian National Orchestra.

The complex also houses the
**Musée du Cinema**, set up in
1962, with its fine archive and
exhibition of old cameras and
lenses. Its main activity is the
daily screening of classic films.

🏛 **Musée du Cinema**
Rue Baron Horta 9, 1000 BRU.
📞 *(02) 507 8370.* 🕐 *5:30–10:30pm
daily.* 📠

## Hôtel Ravenstein ❻

Rue Ravenstein 3, 1000 BRU.
**Map** 2 E3. 🚌 *20, 60, 71, 95, 96.*
🚊 *92, 93, 94.* Ⓜ *Centrale, Parc.*
🕐 *restaurant only.*

OVER THE centuries the
Hôtel Ravenstein has
been the home of patrician
families, soldiers and court
officials, and, for the past 100
years, the Royal Society of
Engineers. The building
was designed at the
end of the 15th
century for Adolphe
and Philip Cleves-
Ravenstein; in
1515 it became the
birthplace of Anne
of Cleves.
Consisting of two
parts, joined by
gardens and
stables, it is the last
remaining example of a
Burgundian-style manor
house. The Hôtel Ravenstein
was acquired by the town in
1896 and used to store

The pretty open courtyard of the
Hôtel Ravenstein

artworks. Sadly, it fell into dis-
repair and renovation took
place in 1934. One half is now
a Belgian restaurant, the other
the Royal Society of Engineers'
private HQ. However, the
pretty, original inner courtyard can still be seen.

## Musée Instrumental ❼

Rue Montagne de la Cour 2, 1000
BRU. **Map** 2 E4. 📞 *(02) 545 0130.*
🕐 *9:30am–5pm Tue–Fri (to 8pm
Thu), 10am–5pm Sat & Sun.* 🚌 *20,
38, 60, 71, 95, 96.* 🚊 *92, 93, 94.*
Ⓜ *Gare Centrale, Parc.* 📠 📷 ▯
🍴 ♿

ONCE A department store, the
building known as Old
England is a striking showpiece
of Art Nouveau architecture
located by the Place Royale.

Architect Paul Saintenoy
gave full rein to his imagina-
tion when he designed these
shop premises for the Old
England company in 1899.
The façade is made
entirely of glass and
elaborate wrought
iron. There is a
domed gazebo on
the roof, and a
turret to one side.
Surprisingly, it was
only in the 1990s
that a listed
buildings policy
was adopted in
Brussels, which
has secured treasures such as
this. Much preservation work
is now taking place. Old
England is one of the buildings that has undergone
extensive renovation work,
having been used until
recently as a temporary exhibition space. The building is
now home to the Musée
Instrumental, moved from the
Sablon. Meanwhile, the Old
England company is still
flourishing, with its premises
now at No. 419 in the
fashionable Avenue Louise.

The collection of the Musée
Instrumental began in the 19th
century when the state bought
80 ancient and exotic instru-
ents. It was doubled in 1876
when King Léopold II don-
ated a gift of 97 Indian musical
instruments presented to him

Old England, home to
the Musée Instrumental

by a maharajah. A museum displaying all of these artifacts opened in 1877, and by 1924 the museum boasted 3,300 pieces and was recognized as a leader in its field. Today the collection contains more than 6,000 items and includes many fine examples of wind, string and keyboard instruments from medieval times to the present. Chief attractions include prototype instruments by Adolphe Sax, the Belgian inventor of the saxophone, mini violins favoured by street musicians and a violin maker's studio. In June 2000 the museum moved to its specially designed home in the newly renovated Old England building, where there is much more room in which to display this world-class collection.

**Antique violin**

## Palais de Charles de Lorraine ❽

Place du Musée 1, 1000 BRU. **Map 2** D4. ☎ (02) 519 5371. 🚌 27, 34, 60, 65, 66, 71, 95, 96. 🚋 92, 93, 94. Ⓜ Centrale, Parc. ◯ 1–5pm Tue, Thu–Fri. ◐ pub hols, last two weeks in Aug, 25 Dec–1 Jan. 🎫 for details ☎ (02) 519 5786.

**H**IDDEN BEHIND this Neo-Classical façade are the few rooms that remain of the

**The state room with marble floor at the Palais de Charles de Lorraine**

palace of Charles de Lorraine, Governor of Brussels during the mid-18th century. He was a keen patron of the arts, and the young Mozart is believed to have performed here. Few original features remain, as the palace was ransacked by marauding French troops in 1794. Extensive renovations were recently completed. The bas-reliefs at the top of the stairway, representing air, earth, fire and water, reflect Charles de Lorraine's keen interest in alchemy. Most spectacular of all the original features is the 28-point star set in the floor of the circular drawing room. Each of the points is made of a different Belgian marble, a much sought-after material which was used in the construction of St Peter's Basilica in Rome.

## Musée Charlier ❾

Avenue des Arts 16, 1210 BRU. **Map** 2 F2. ☎ (02) 218 5382, 220 2690. 🚌 23, 63, 65, 66. Ⓜ Madou, Arts-Loi. ◯ noon–5pm Tue–Sat. 🎫 🎫

**T**HIS QUIET MUSEUM was once the home of Henri van Cutsem, a wealthy collector and patron of the arts. In 1890 he asked the young architect Victor Horta to re-design his house as an exhibition space for his extensive collections. Van Cutsem died, and his friend, the sculptor Charlier, installed his own art collection in the house. Charlier commissioned Horta to build another museum, at Tournai in southern Belgium, to house van Cutsem's collection. On Charlier's death in 1925 the house and contents were left to the city as a museum.

The Musée Charlier opened in 1928. It contains paintings by a number of different artists, including portraits by Antoine Wiertz *(see p72)* and early landscapes by James Ensor. The collection also includes sculptures by Charlier, and the ground floor contains collections of glassware, porcelain, chinoiserie and silverware. Of special note are the tapestries, some from the Paris studios of Aubusson, on the staircases and the first floor, and the displays of Louis XV- and Louis XVI-style furniture on the first and second floors.

**Musée Charlier, home to one of Belgium's finest individual collections of art and furnishings**

# Musées Royaux des Beaux-Arts: Musée d'art ancien ❿

Hercules Sculpture

J OINTLY KNOWN AS the Musées Royaux des Beaux-Arts, The Musée d'art ancien and Musée d'art moderne are Brussels' premier art museums. The museums' buildings, adjacent to the Place Royale, are home to exhibits from two eras, *ancien* (15th–18th century) and *moderne* (19th century– present day). Housed in a Neo-Classical building designed by Alphonse Balat between 1874 and 1880, the Musée d'art ancien is the larger of the two sections. The art collection dates back to the 18th century when it consisted of the few valuable works left behind by the French Republican army, which had stolen many of Brussels' treasures and taken them back to Paris. This small collection was initially exhibited in the Palais de Charles de Lorraine (*see p61*), but donations, patronage and the recovery of some pieces from the French, enlarged the collection. The present gallery opened in 1887. The Musée d'art ancien is best known for the finest collection of Flemish art in the world, and many Old Masters, including van Dyck and Rubens, are also well represented.

**Façade of museum**
*Corinthian columns and busts of Flemish painters adorn the entrance.*

★ **The Assumption of the Virgin** (*c.1610*)
*Pieter Paul Rubens (1577–1640) was the leading exponent of Baroque art in Europe, com-bining Flemish precision with Italian flair. Here, Rubens suppresses background colours to emphasize the Virgin's blue robes.*

Ground level

**Interior of the Main Hall**
*Founded by Napoleon in 1801 to relieve the packed Louvre in Paris, these are the oldest muse-ums in Belgium. More than 2,500 works are exhibited in the museums' buildings.*

Entrance

Entrance to Musée d'art moderne

Lower level

## STAR EXHIBITS

- ★ **The Assumption of the Virgin by Rubens**

- ★ **The Annunciation by the Master of Flémalle**

Upper level

**VISITORS' CHECKLIST**

Rue de la Régence 3, 1000 BRU.
**Map** 2 D4. ☎ *(02) 508 3211.*
🚌 *25, 95, 96.* 🚋 *91, 92, 93, 94.* Ⓜ *Gare Centrale, Parc.* ◯ *10am–5pm Tue–Sun.* ● *Mon, public hols.* ♿ 🎁 📷 🛗 🍴
🅆 www.fine-arts-museum.be

**The Census at Bethlehem** *(1610)*
*Pieter Brueghel the Younger (c.1564–1638) produced a version of this subject some 40 years after the original by his father. Shown together, the two works illustrate the development of Flemish painting in its peak period.*

**Madonna with Saint Anne and a Franciscan donor** *(1470)*
*Hugo van der Goes (c.1440–82) was commissioned to paint this symbolic work for the monk shown on the right for his personal devotional use.*

**★ The Annunciation** *(c.1406–7)*
*The Master of Flémalle (c.1378–1444) sets the holy scene of the Archangel Gabriel announcing the impending birth of the Messiah in a homely, contemporary setting, with daily objects an apparent contrast to the momentous event.*

**KEY**

| | |
|---|---|
| 🟦 | 15th–16th century (blue route) |
| 🟫 | 17th–18th century (brown route) |
| ⬜ | Sculpture gallery |
| ⬜ | Temporary exhibitions |
| ⬜ | Non-exhibition space |

**GALLERY GUIDE**
*In the gallery different coloured signs are used to lead the visitor through different eras of art (see pp66–7). On the first floor, in rooms 10 to 34, the blue route covers the 15th and 16th centuries. The brown route is in rooms 50 to 62 and covers the 17th and 18th centuries. The sculpture gallery is housed on the lower ground floor.*

# Musées Royaux des Beaux-Arts: Musée d'art moderne

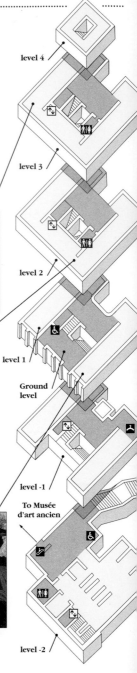

O PENED IN 1984, the Musée d'art moderne is situated in a unique setting: eight levels of the building are underground, but a lightwell allows many of the works to be seen by natural daylight filtering in from the Place du Musée. The top three levels above ground are temporary exhibition space. As is the case for the Musee d'art ancien, the collection of works is wide and varied, displayed in chronological order. Many well-known 20th-century artists from 1900 to the present day are included, but the most popular paintings are those of the Belgian Surrealists.

level 4

level 3

**Skeletons Fighting over a Pickled Herring** (1891)
*Moving from a naturalistic style, James Ensor became the leading light of the Belgian Surrealist artists. His uneasy preoccupation with death and the macabre is shown in this witty, disturbing oil.*

level 2

**View of London** (1917)
*Heavily influenced by Monet's work, Emile Claus developed a variant of Impressionism with fellow artists called "Luminism". The Belgian Claus was a refugee to London, and his Luminist interest in light effects is shown through the damp fog of this London twilight. The painting shows a clarity of definition that is almost realist in technique.*

level 1

Ground level

level -1

To Musée d'art ancien

**The Orange Market at Blidah** (1898)
*Henri Evenepoel is known for his use of raw colour and tone; here, the market bustle is secondary to the arrangement of the shades in the traders' bright robes.*

level -2

## STAR EXHIBITS

★ **Woman in a Blue Dress by Rik Wouters**

★ **The Domain of Arnheim by René Magritte**

## GALLERY GUIDE

*The yellow route, in rooms 69–91, is dedicated to the 19th century. Level -4 covers work from the first quarter of the 20th century and its various art movements, such as Fauvism and Cubism. Level -5 contains the Surrealist collection. Level -6 includes the Magritte exhibition, the Jeune Peinture Belge and COBRA schools. Levels -7 and -8 exhibit works from the 1960s to the present day. Levels 2, 3 and 4 contain temporary exhibitions that are changed regularly.*

**Composition** *(1921)
(detail shown)*
*Two stylized human
figures form the centre
of this work by Belgian
painter Pierre-Louis
Flouquet, combining
Futurism and Cubism
in a "plastic" style.*

★ **Woman in a Blue
Dress in front of a
Mirror** *(1914)
Rik Wouters was a
Fauvist painter
whose fascination
with colour led him
to innovative spatula
painting techniques,
as seen here.*

**Draped Woman on
Steps** *(1957–8)
The prolific British
artist Henry Moore
is the world's most
exhibited sculptor.
This piece reveals
his characteristic
fluidity of line,
together with
tension in
the waiting
figure.*

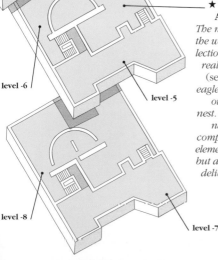

level -4

level -3

★ **The Domain of
Arnheim** *(1962)
The museum contains
the world's largest col-
lection of work by sur-
realist René Magritte
(see p15). Here, an
eagle-mountain rears
over a small bird's
nest. The inexplicable
nature of the eerie
composition draws its
elements into question,
but answers are made
deliberately difficult.*

level -6

level -5

level -8

level -7

### KEY

☐ 19th century (yellow route)

☐ 20th century (green route)

☐ Non-exhibition space

# Exploring the Musées Royaux des Beaux-Arts

S IX CENTURIES OF ART, both Belgian and international, are displayed in the two museums that make up the Musées Royaux des Beaux-Arts. The combination of the two museums contains works from many artistic styles, from the religious paintings of the 15th-century Flemish Primitives to the graphic art of the 1960s and 1970s. The Musée d'art moderne also stages regular temporary exhibitions. The museums are very well set out, guiding the visitor easily through the full collection or, if time is short, directly to the art era of special interest. Each section is highly accessible, as both museums are divided into different coloured routes which relate to the art of each century, taking the visitor through galleries representing the varied schools of art by period.

Flemish still life, *Vase of Flowers* (1704) by Rachel Ruysch

## THE BLUE ROUTE

T HIS ROUTE leads visitors through a large display of works dating mostly from the 15th and 16th centuries. In the first few rooms are works by the renowned Flemish Primitive School (*see p14*). As is the case with much painting of the Middle Ages, the pictures are chiefly religious in nature and depict a variety of biblical scenes and details from the lives of saints. A work of particular note is *The Annunciation* by the Master of Flémalle, which shows the Archangel Gabriel appearing to the Virgin Mary as she sits at her fireside in a typically Flemish parlour. Also on display are a number of pictures by Rogier van der Weyden, the most famous of all the Flemish Primitive artists and city painter to Brussels during the mid-15th century; of note is his version of the

*Lamentation*. The work of Bruges artist Hans Memling is mostly shown in his native city, but his *The Martyrdom of Saint Sebastian* is found here.

The most important works in this collection are the paintings by the Brueghels, father and son. Both were renowned for their scenes of peasant life, and on display are *The Bird Trap* (1565) by Pieter Brueghel the Elder, and *The Village Wedding* (1607) by his son, Pieter.

Also on view are beautiful tapestries and the Delporte Collection, which groups sculpture, paintings and *objets d'art* from around the world.

## THE BROWN ROUTE

T HE SECOND route wends its way through the works of the 17th and 18th centuries. The rooms are wider and taller here in order to house the larger canvases of that time.

A highlight of the route is the world-famous collection of works by Pieter Paul Rubens (1557–1640), which affords a fine overview of the artist's work. As well as key examples of his religious works, there are some excellent portraits, such as *Hélène Fourment*, a portrait of his young wife. Of special interest are the sketches and paintings made in preparation for Rubens' larger works, such as *Four Negro Heads*, a work made in preparation of the 1620 *Adoration of the Magi*.

Other works of note in this section are the paintings by Old Masters such as van Dyck's *Portrait of a Genoese Lady with her Daughter* of the 1620s and Frans Hals' *Three Children with Goatcart*, as well as several paintings by representatives of later Flemish schools, including Jacob Jordaens and his depiction of myths, such as *Pan and Syrinx* (c.1645) and *Satyr and Peasant*. Baroque and Flemish art are all well represented on the tour, a journey through the best painting of the time.

Also on display are some small sculptures which were studies of larger works by Laurent Delvaux, a leading sculptor of the 18th century, particularly *Hercules and Erymanthian Boar*, a study for the sculpture by the staircase in the Palais de Charles de Lorraine (*see p61*). Works of the Italian, Spanish and French schools of this era are also represented, notably a depiction by Claude Le Lorrain in 1672 of the classical poetic scene *Aeneas hunting the Stag on the Coast of Libya*.

*Lamentation* (c. 1420–50) by Rogier van der Weyden

## THE YELLOW ROUTE

This section covers the 19th century and is closer to the contemporary collection both in position and period. It is an informed introduction to the cutting-edge displays nearby.

The works along the yellow route vary greatly in style and subject matter, from Romanticism, exemplified by David, and Neo-Classicism, to Realism and Symbolism. There are, as in the other sections, examples of work by artists from outside Belgium, including Pierre Bonnard's *Nude against the Light* (1907), Edouard Vuillard's *Two Schoolchildren* (1894) and Monet's *Sunset at Etretat* (1885), but once again most emphasis is on Belgian artists.

Social realist artist Constantin Meunier (1831–1905) is represented by many of his sculptures, including *Firedamp* (1888). Much of the work of James Ensor (1890–1949) remains in his native city Ostend, but many of his macabre works are displayed here, such as *Scandalized Masks* (1883) and *Two Skeletons Fighting over a Pickled Herring* (1891). This section also offers the chance to see pictures by artists who are less well known outside Belgium, such as Henri Evenepoel (1872–99) whose lively Arab scene *Orange Market at Blidah* (1898) provides a contrast to the stark works of painters such as Ensor. The work of Impressionist Emile Claus is of value to followers of the movement. Of local interest is the landscape of Brussels by van Moer, painted in 1868,

*Le Joueur Secret* (1927) by Magritte

which clearly shows the River Senne before it was covered over for hygiene reasons. Moving from the passion of Romanticism to grim industrial realism and gentle Impressionism, this survey is definitive.

The underground Sculpture Gallery, with carvings and bronzes

## THE ORANGE ROUTE

Anyone with an interest in sculpture should follow this route down to the lower ground level in the Musée d'art ancien. Here, 18th- and 19th-century stone, marble and bronze Belgian sculpture is displayed alongside an exhibition explaining various methods behind many of the works on show, from carving to casting and burnishing in the materials of past centuries. There is also access to a sculpture terrace from outside the entrance of the Musée d'art ancien.

*Death of Marat* (1793) by David, a leading work on the yellow route

## THE GREEN ROUTE

The collection of modern art is wide and varied and includes works by well-known 20th-century painters from Belgium and around the world. There is no clearly defined route to follow within this section, nor are the exhibits strictly grouped by period or movement, so it is best to wander through the collection, stopping at areas of interest.

There are a number of works by the leading Belgian artists of the 20th century, such as Fauvist painter Rik Wouters' (1882–1916) *The Flautist* (1914). International artists include Matisse, Paul Klee and Chagall. But the real draw for most people is the collection of pictures by the Belgian Surrealists, in particular René Magritte (1898–1967). His best-known paintings, including *The Domain of Arnheim* (1962), are on display here. Another noted Surrealist, Paul Delvaux, is also well represented with works such as *Evening Train* (1957) and *Pygmalion* (1939).

Belgian art of the 20th century tends to be severe and stark, but the postwar *Jeune Peinture Belge* school reintroduced colour in an abstract way and is represented in works such as Marc Mendelson's 1950s *Toccata et fugue*. Sculpture highlights in this section include Ossip Zadkine's totem pole-like *Diana* (1937) and Henry Moore's *Draped Woman on Steps* (1957–8).

**Busy café scene at Place du Grand Sablon**

## Place du Grand Sablon ⓫

**Map** 2 D4. 🚌 27, 34, 48, 95, 96. 🚊 92, 93, 94. Ⓜ Gare Centrale, Louise, Parc.

Sⁱᵗᵁᴬᵀᴱᴰ ᴏɴ the slope of the escarpment that divides Brussels in two, the Place du Grand Sablon is like a stepping stone between the upper and lower halves of the city. The name "sablon" derives from the French "sable" (sand) and the square is so-called because this old route down to the city centre once passed through an area of sandy marshes.

Today the picture is very different. The square, more of a triangle in shape, stretches from a 1751 fountain by Jacques Berge at its base uphill to the Gothic church of Notre-Dame du Sablon. The fountain was a gift of the Englishman Lord Bruce, out of gratitude for the hospitality shown to him in Brussels. The square is surrounded by elegant town houses, some with Art Nouveau façades. This is a chic, wealthy and busy part of Brussels, an area of up-market antiques dealers, fashionable restaurants and trendy bars, which really come into their own in warm weather when people stay drinking outside until the early hours of the morning: a good place in which to soak up the

atmosphere. Wittamer, at No. 12, is a justifiably well-known *patisserie* and chocolate shop, which also has its own tea room on the first floor.

Every weekend the area near the church plays host to a lively and thriving, if rather expensive, antiques market.

## Notre-Dame au Sablon ⓬

Rue Bodenbroeck 6, 1000 BRU. **Map** 2 D4. ☎ (02) 511 5741. 🚊 92, 93, 94. Ⓜ Gare Centrale, Louise. ◗ 8am–6pm Mon–Fri, 10am–7pm Sat & Sun. ♿ 📷 on request.

Aʟᴏɴɢ ᴡɪᴛʜ ᴛʜᴇ Cathédrale Sts Michel et Gudule (see p70–71), this lovely church is one of the finest remaining examples of Brabant Gothic architecture in Belgium.

A church was first erected here when the guild of crossbowmen was granted permission to build a chapel to Our Lady on this sandy hill. Legend has it that a young girl in Antwerp had a vision of the Virgin Mary who instructed her to take her statue to Brussels. The girl carried the statue of the Virgin to Brussels down the Senne river by boat and gave it to the crossbowmen's chapel, which rapidly became a place of pilgrimage. Work to enlarge the church began around 1400 but, due to lack of funds, was not completed until 1550. All that remains today of the

**Notre-Dame du Sablon window**

incident are two carvings depicting the young girl in a boat, since the statue was destroyed in 1565.

The interior of the church is simple but beautifully proportioned, with inter-connecting side chapels and an impressive pulpit dating from 1697. Of particular interest, however, are the 11 magnificent stained-glass windows, 14 m (45 ft) high, which dominate the inside of the church. As the church is lit from the inside, they shine out at night like welcoming beacons. Also worth a visit is the chapel of the Tour et Taxis family, whose mansion once stood near the Place du Petit Sablon. In 1517 the family had tapestries commissioned to commemorate the legend that led to the chapel becoming a place of pilgrimage. Some now hang in the Musées Royaux d'art et d'histoire in Parc du Cinquantenaire (see p75), but others were stolen by the French Revolutionary army in the 1790s.

**The magnificent interior of the church of Notre-Dame du Sablon**

## Place du Petit Sablon ⓭

**Map** 2 D4. 🚌 20, 27, 34, 48, 95, 96. 🚊 92, 93, 94. Ⓜ Gare Centrale, Louise, Parc.

Tʜᴇꜱᴇ ᴘʀᴇᴛᴛʏ, formal gardens were laid out in 1890 and are a charming spot to stop for a rest. On top of the railings that enclose the gardens are 48 bronze statuettes by Art Nouveau artist Paul Hankar, each one representing a differ-

One of the lavish fountains in the gardens of Petit Sablon

ent medieval guild of the city. At the back of the gardens is a fountain built to commemorate Counts Egmont and Hornes, the martyrs who led a Dutch uprising against the tyrannical rule of the Spanish under Philip II, and were beheaded in the Grand Place in 1568 (*see p31*). On either side of the fountain are 12 further statues of 15th- and 16th-century figures, including Bernard van Orley, whose stained-glass windows grace the city's cathedral, and the Flemish mapmaker Gerhard Mercator, whose 16th-century projection of the world forms the basis of most modern maps.

**Statue of Peter Pan in Palais d'Egmont gardens**

has twice been rebuilt, in 1750 and again in 1891, following a fire. Today it belongs to the Belgian Foreign Ministry. It was here that Great Britain, Denmark and Ireland signed as members of the EEC in 1972.

Though the palace itself is closed to the public, the gardens, whose entrances are on the Rue du Grand Cerf and the Boulevard de Waterloo, are open. There is a statue of Peter Pan, a copy of one found in Kensington Gardens, in London. Many of the gardens' buildings are now run down, and plans have started to restore the ancient orangery and the disused ice house.

## Palais d'Egmont ⓮

Rue aux Laines, 1000 BRU. **Map** 2 E4. 🚌 *27, 34, 95, 96.* 🚊 *91, 92, 93, 94.* Ⓜ *Louise, Parc.* ♿

THE PALAIS d'Egmont (also known as the Palais d'Arenberg) was originally built in the mid-16th century for Françoise of Luxembourg, mother of the 16th-century leader of the city's rebels, Count Egmont. This palace

## Palais de Justice ⓯

Place Poelaert 1, 1000 BRU. **Map** 1 C5. 🇨 *(02) 508 6111.* 🚌 *34.* 🚊 *91, 92, 93, 94.* Ⓜ *Louise.* ◯ *8am–5pm Mon–Fri.* ● *Sat & Sun, Jul, public hols.* ♿ 📷 *on request.*

THE PALAIS DE JUSTICE rules the Brussels skyline and can be seen from almost any vantage point in the city. Of all the ambitious projects of King Léopold II, this was perhaps the grandest. It occupies an area larger than St Peter's Basilica in Rome, and was one of the world's most impressive 19th-century buildings. It was built between 1866 and 1883 by architect Joseph Poelaert who looked for inspiration in classical temples, but sadly died mid-construction in 1879. The Palais de Justice is still home to the city's law courts.

Detail of a cornice at the Palais de Justice

## Galerie Bortier ⑯

Rue de la Madeleine 55, 1000 BRU.
**Map** 2 D3. 🚌 20, 38. 🚋 92, 93, 94. Ⓜ Gare Centrale. 🕐 9am–6pm Mon–Sat. ⬤ Sun, public hols. ♿

GALERIE BORTIER is the only shopping arcade in the city dedicated solely to book and map shops, and it has become the haunt of students, enthusiasts and researchers looking for secondhand French books and antiquarian finds.

The land on which the gallery stands was originally owned by a Monsieur Bortier, whose idea it was to have a covered arcade lined with shops on either side. He put

160,000 francs of his own money into the project, quite a considerable sum in the 1840s. The 65-m (210-ft) long Galérie Bortier was built in 1848 and was designed by Jean-Pierre Cluysenaar, the architect of the Galéries St-Hubert nearby (see p47). The Galérie Bortier opened along with the then-adjacent Marché de la Madeleine, but the latter was unfortunately destroyed by developers in 1958.

A complete restoration of Galérie Bortier was ordered by the Ville de Bruxelles in 1974. The new architects kept strictly to Cluysenaar's plans and installed a replacement glass and wrought-iron roof made

to the original 19th-century Parisian style. The Rue de la Madeleine itself also offers plenty of browsing material for bibliophiles and art lovers.

**Crammed interior of a bookshop at the Galérie Bortier**

## Cathédrale Sts Michel et Gudule ⑰

THE CATHEDRALE Sts Michel et Gudule is the national church of Belgium, although it was only granted cathedral status in 1962. It is the finest surviving example of Brabant Gothic architecture. There has been a church on the site of the cathedral since at least the 11th century. Work began on the Gothic cathedral in 1225 under Henry I, Duke of Brabant, and continued over a period of 300 years. It was finally completed with the construction of two front towers at the beginning of the 16th century under Charles V. The cathedral is made of a sandy limestone, brought from local quarries. The interior is very bare; this is due to Protestant iconoclast ransacking in 1579–80 and thefts by French revolutionists in 1783. It was fully restored and cleaned in the 1990s and now reveals its splendour.

**The twin towers** rise above the city. Unusually, they were designed as a pair in the 1400s; Brabant architecture typically has only one.

★ **Last Judgement window**
*At the front of the cathedral, facing the altar, is a magnificent stained-glass window of 1528 depicting Christ awaiting saved souls. Its vivid reds, blues and yellows place it in the 16th-century style. The Renaissance panes are surrounded by later Baroque garlands of flowers.*

### STAR SIGHTS

★ **Last Judgement window**

★ **Baroque pulpit**

**Romanesque remains** of the first church here, dating from 1047, were discovered during renovation work. They can be seen and toured in the crypt.

# Chapelle de la Madeleine ⑱

Rue de la Madeleine, 1000 BRU.
**Map** 2 D3. 🕿 *(02) 511 2845.*
🚌 *20, 38.* 🚊 *92, 93, 94.* Ⓜ *Gare Centrale.* ⭘ *7am–7pm Mon– Sat; 7am–noon, 5pm–8pm Sun.* ♿

THIS LITTLE church once stood on the site now occupied by the Gare Centrale, but it was moved, stone by stone, further down the hill to make way for the construction of the Art Deco-style station and its car park during the early 1950s.

The 17th-century façade of the church has been restored. The original 15th-century interior has been replaced by

**A view of the Chapelle de la Madeleine with restored brickwork**

a plain, modest decor, with simple stone pillars and modern stained-glass windows. Off the regular tourist track, the

chapel is used by people as a quiet place for worship. The Baroque chapel which was once attached has now gone.

**The transept** windows represent the rulers of Belgium in 1538. Jan Haeck made the designs after Bernard van Orley's sketches.

**Sainte Gudule**
*This 7th-century saint is very dear to the people of Brussels. Her relics were scattered to the winds by ransacking Protestants in 1579, but this only served to reinforce her cult.*

**VISITORS' CHECKLIST**

Parvis Ste-Gudule, 1000 BRU.
**Map** 2 E2. 🕿 *(02) 217 8345, 219 1170.* 🚌 *65, 66.* 🚊 *92, 93, 94.* Ⓜ *Gare Centrale* ⭘ *8am–6pm daily.* 🎫 *to crypt.* ✝ *regular services throughout the day.* ♿ *on request.*

**The Statue of St Michael** is the cathedral's symbol of its links with the city. While the gilded plaster statue is not itself historically exceptional, its long heritage is; the patron saint of Brussels, the Archangel St Michael is shown killing the dragon, symbolic of his protection of the city.

**The Lectern**

★ **Baroque pulpit**
*The flamboyantly carved pulpit in the central aisle is the work of an Antwerp-born sculptor, Henri-François Verbruggen. Designed in 1699, it was finally installed in 1776.*

**The Art Nouveau façade of No. 11 Square Ambiorix**

## Square Ambiorix ⑲

**Map** 3 B2. 🚌 54, 63. Ⓜ Schuman.

CLOSE TO THE EU district, but totally different in style and spirit, lies the beautiful Square Ambiorix. Together with the Avenue Palmerston and the Square Marie-Louise below that, this marshland was transformed in the 1870s into one of the loveliest residential parts of Brussels, with a large central area of gardens, ponds and fountains.

The elegant houses, some Art Nouveau, some older, have made this one of the truly sought-after suburbs in the city. The most spectacular Art Nouveau example is at No. 11. Known as the Maison St Cyr after the painter

whose home it once was, this wonderfully ornate house, with its curved wrought-iron balustrades and balconies, is a fine architectural feat considering that the man who designed it, Gustave Strauven, was only 22 years old when it was built at the turn of the 20th century.

## Quartier Européen ⑳

**Map** 3 B3. 🚌 20, 21, 22, 27, 34, 38, 54, 68, 80, 95, 96. Ⓜ Maelbeek, Schuman.

THE AREA at the top of the Rue de la Loi and around the Schuman roundabout is where the main buildings of the European Union's administration are found.

The most recognizable of all the EU seats is the star-shaped Berlaymont building, now nearing completion following the removal of large quantities of asbestos discovered in its structure. The Berlaymont, formerly the headquarters of the European Commission, will continue to be refurbished until further notice. The commission workers (the civil servants of the EU) are at present dotted around the area. The Council of Ministers, which comprises representatives of member-states' governments, now meets in the sprawling pink granite block across the road from the Berlaymont, known as Justus Lipsius, after a Flemish philosopher. Further down the road from the Justus Lipsius building is the Résidence Palace, a luxury 1920s housing complex that boasts a theatre, a pool and a roof garden as well as

several floors of private flats. It now houses the International Press Centre. Only the theatre is open to the public, but EU officials are allowed into the Art Deco swimming pool.

This area is naturally full of life and bustle during the day, but much quieter in the evenings and can feel almost deserted at weekends. What is pleasant at any time, though, is the proximity of the city's green spaces including Parc du Cinquantenaire (*see pp74–5*), Parc Léopold and the verdant Square Ambiorix.

**Paintings and sculpture on show in the Musée Wiertz gallery**

## Musée Wiertz ㉑

Rue Vautier 62, 1000 BRU. **Map** 3 A4. 📞 (02) 648 1718. 🚌 21, 22, 27, 34, 38, 54, 59, 60, 80, 95, 96. Ⓜ Maelbeek, Schuman, Trone. 🕐 10am– noon, 1–5pm Tue –Fri; every 2nd weekend. ⬤ Mon, weekends Jul–Aug, public hols. 🖼

MUSEE WIERTZ houses some 160 works, including oil paintings, drawings and sculptures, that form the main body of Antoine Wiertz's (1806–65) artistic output. The collection fills the studio built for Wiertz by the Belgian state, where he lived and worked from 1850 until his death in 1865, when the studio became a museum.

The huge main room contains Wiertz's largest paintings, many depicting biblical and Homeric scenes, some in the style of Rubens. Also on display are sculptures and his death mask. The last of the six rooms contains his more gruesome efforts, one entitled *Madness, Hunger and Crime*.

**The Justus Lipsius, the pink granite EU Council building**

A tall European parliament building rising up behind the trees of Parc Léopold in the Parliament Quarter

## Parliament Quarter ㉒

Map 3 A4. 🚌 21, 22, 27, 34, 38, 64, 60, 00, 95, 96. Ⓜ Maalbuuk, Schuman.

THE VAST, MODERN, steel-and-glass complex, situated just behind Quartier Léopold train station, is one of three homes of the European Parliament, the elected body of the EU. Its permanent seat is in Strasbourg, France, where the plenary sessions are held once a month. The administrative centre is in Luxembourg and the committee meetings are held in Brussels.

This gleaming state-of-the-art building has many admirers, not least the parliamentary workers and MEPs themselves. But it also has its critics: the huge domed structure housing the hemicycle that seats the 600-plus MEPs has been dubbed the "*caprices des dieux*" ("whims of the gods"), which refers both to the shape of the building which is similar to a French cheese of the same name, and to its lofty aspirations. Many people also regret that, to make room for the new complex, a large part of Quarticr Léopold has been lost. Though there are still plenty of restaurants and bars, a lot of the charm has gone. When the MEPs are absent, the building is often used for meetings of European Union committees.

## Institut Royal des Sciences Naturelles ㉓

Rue Vautier 29, 1000 BRU. Map 3 A4. ☎ (02) 627 4238. 🚌 20, 21, 22, 34, 38, 54, 59, 60, 80, 95, 96. Ⓜ Maelbeek, Schuman. 🕒 9:30am–4:45pm Tue–Fri, 10am–6pm Sat & Sun. ⬛ Mon, 1 Jan, 1 May, 25 Dec.

THE INSTITUT Royal des Sciences Naturelles is best known for its fine collection of iguanadon skeletons dating back 250 million years. The museum also contains interactive and educational displays covering all aspects and evolutionary eras of natural history.

## Parc Léopold ㉔

Rue Belliard. Map 3 B4. 🚌 20, 27, 59, 80. Ⓜ Maelbeek, Schuman.

PARC LÉOPOLD occupies part of the grounds of an old estate and a walk around its lake follows the old path of the Maelbeek river which was covered over in the 19th-century for reasons of hygiene.

At the end of the 19th century, scientist and industrialist Ernest Solvay put forward the idea of a science park development. Solvay was given the Parc Léopold, the site of a zoo since 1847, and set up five university centres here. Leading figures including Marie Curie and Albert Einstein met here to discuss new scientific issues. The park is still home to many scientific institutes, as well as a haven of peace in the heart of this busy political area.

Whale skeleton inside the Institut Royal des Sciences Naturelles

# Parc du Cinquantenaire 25

Musée de l'Armée gun

THE FINEST OF LEOPOLD II's grand projects, the Parc and Palais du Cinquantenaire were built for the Golden Jubilee celebrations of Belgian independence in 1880. The park was laid out on unused town marshes. The palace, at its entrance, was to comprise a triumphal arch and two large exhibition areas, but by the time of the 1880 Art and Industry Expo, only the two side exhibition areas had been completed. Further funds were eventually found, and work continued for 50 years. Before being converted into museums, the large halls on either side of the central archway were used to hold trade fairs, the last of which was in 1935. They have also been used for horse races and to store homing pigeons. During World War II, the grounds of the park were used to grow vegetables to feed the Brussels people.

★ **Musée de l'Armée**
*Opened in 1923, the museum covers all aspects of Belgium's military history, and exhibits over 200 years of militaria. Historic aircraft are on display in the hall next door.*

**View of Park with Arch**
*Based on the Arc de Triomphe in Paris, the arch was not completed in time for the 50th Anniversary celebrations but was finished in 1905.*

**The Grand Mosque** was built in Arabic style as a folly in 1880. It became a mosque in 1978.

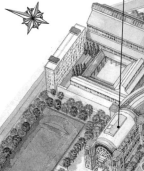

**Pavillon Horta**

**Tree-lined Avenue**
*In part formal garden, part forested walks, many of the plantations of elms and plane trees date from 1880.*

---

**STAR SIGHTS**

★ **Musées Royaux d'Art et d'Histoire**

★ **Musée de l'Armée**

---

**Underpass**

0 metres        100

0 yards         100

## The Central Archway

*Conceived as a gateway into the city, the arch is crowned by the symbolic bronze sculpture* Brabant Raising the National Flag.

### Autoworld

*Housed in the south wing of the Cinquantenaire Palace, Autoworld is one of the best collections of automobiles in the world. There are some 300 cars, including an 1886 motor, and a 1924 Model-T Ford that still runs.*

**The park** is popular with Brussels' Eurocrats and families at lunchtimes and weekends.

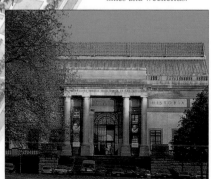

### ★ Musées Royaux d'Art et d'Histoire

*Belgian architect Bordiau's plans for the two exhibition halls, later permanent showcases, were partly modelled on London's Victorian museums. The use of iron and glass in their construction was inspired by the Crystal Palace.*

### Musées Royaux d'Art et d'Histoire

*Parc du Cinquantenaire 10.* 📞 *(02) 741 7211.* ⏰ *9:30am–5pm Tue–Sun (from 10am Sun and pub hols).* ● *1 Jan, 1 May, 1 & 11 Nov, 25 Dec.* 🏠

Also known as the Musée du Cinquantenaire, this excellent museum has occupied its present site since the early 1900s, but the history of the collections goes back as far as the 15th century, and the quantity of exhibits is vast. Sections on ancient civilizations include Egypt and Greece, and also Persia and the Near East. Other displays feature Byzantium and Islam, China and the Indian Subcontinent, and the Pre-Columbian civilizations of the Americas. There are decorative arts from all ages, with glassware, silverware and porcelain as well as a fine collection of lace and tapestries. Religious sculptures and stained glass are displayed around a courtyard in the style of church cloisters.

The aircraft display at the Musée Royal de l'Armée

### Musée Royal de l'Armée et d'Histoire Militaire

*Parc du Cinquantenaire 3.* 📞 *(02) 737 7811.* ⏰ *9am–noon, 1–4:30pm Tue–Sun.* ● *Mon, 1 Jan, 1 May, 1 Nov, 25 Dec.*

Together with the section on aviation, displays cover the Belgian Army and its history from the late 1700s to today, including weapons, uniforms, decorations and paintings. There is a section covering the 1830 struggle for independence *(see p34–5).* Two new sections show both World Wars, including the activities of the Resistance.

# GREATER BRUSSELS

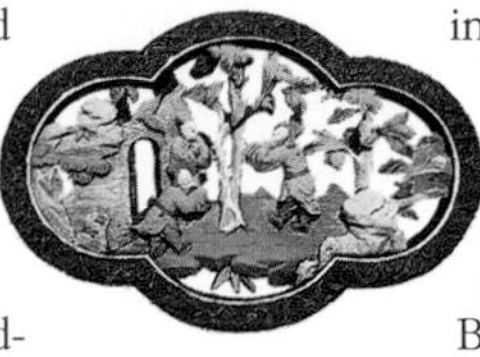

PAST THE heart-shaped ring-road of Brussels city centre lie 19 suburbs (*communes*) which form the Bruxelles-Capitale region. While many are residential, a handful are definitely worth the short ride to sample outlying treasures of Brussels' fascinating history. For fans of early 20th-century architecture, the suburb of St-Gilles offers numerous original examples of striking Art Nouveau buildings including Musée Horta. In Koekelberg and visible from the Upper Town is the huge Sacré-Coeur basilica, started

**Detail from annexe of Chinese Pavilion, Laeken**

in 1904. To the north, Heysel offers attractions whose modernity contrasts with the historical city centre. The 1958 Atomium, now restored, stands next to the Bruparck theme park. To the east, the Central Africa Museum reflects Belgium's colonial past in the Congo, and the tram museum takes a journey through Brussels' urban past. Peace and tranquillity can be found close to the metropolis, in the orderly landscape of Royal Laeken and the lush green spaces of the Bois de la Cambre and the Fôret de Soignes.

## SIGHTS AT A GLANCE

**Churches and Cathedrals**
Basilique Nationale du
 Sacré-Coeur **8**

**Historic Monuments,
Buildings and Districts**
Anderlecht **7**
Avenue Louise **2**
Ixelles **4**
St-Gilles **3**
Uccle **6**

**Parks and Gardens**
Bruparck **13**
Domaine de Laeken
 see pp82–3 **11**
Fôret de Soignes **5**

**Museums and
Exhibition Areas**
The Atomium **12**
Musée Horta see p78 **1**
Musée du Tram **9**

Musée Royal de
 l'Afrique Centrale **10**

**KEY**

| | |
|---|---|
| ■ | Central Brussels |
| □ | Greater Brussels |
| ✈ | Airport |
| ▬ | Major Road |
| ▬ | Minor Road |

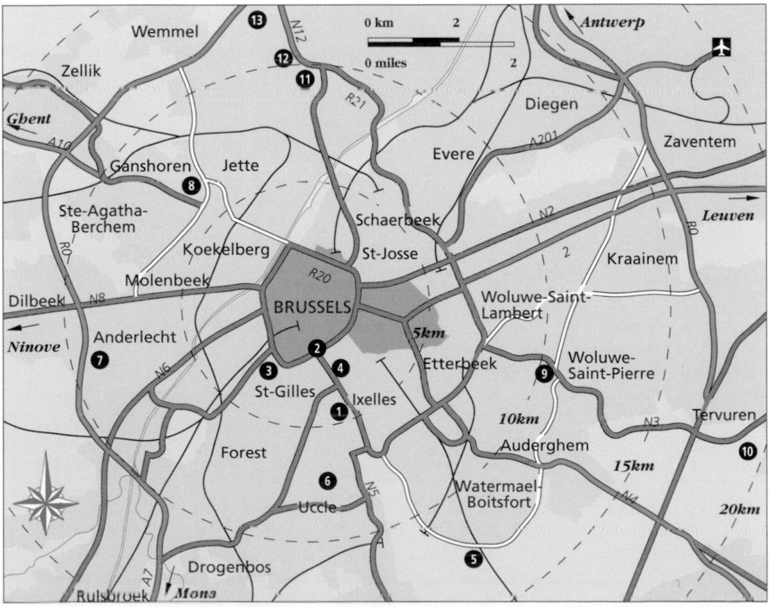

◁ **The Atomium towering over Mini-Europe in the Bruparck**

# Musée Horta ❶

ARCHITECT VICTOR HORTA (1861–1947) is considered by many to be the father of Art Nouveau, and his impact on Brussels architecture is unrivalled by any other designer of his time. A museum dedicated to his unique style is today housed in his restored family home, which he designed from 1898 to 1901. His skill lay not only in his grand, overall vision but in his equal talent as an interior designer, blending themes and materials into each detail. The airy interior of the building displays trademarks of the architect's style – iron, glass and curves – in every detail, while retaining a functional approach.

**Art Nouveau candelabra**

**VISITORS' CHECKLIST**

Rue Américaine 23–25, 1060 BRU. ☎ (02) 543 0490. 🚌 54. 🚊 81, 82, 91, 92. Ⓜ Albert, Louise. ◯ 2–5:30pm Tue–Sun. ⬤ Mon, public hols.

**★ Central Staircase**
*Decorated with curved wrought iron, the stairs are enhanced further by mirrors and glass, bringing natural light into the house.*

**The bedroom** features Art Nouveau furniture, including a wardrobe inlaid with pale and dark wood.

**★ Dining Room**
*White enamel tiles line the walls, rising to an ornate ceiling, decorated with the scrolled metalwork used in other rooms.*

**Madame Horta's sitting-room** features blue-and-cream wool rugs woven to Horta's design, and a marble fireplace.

**Front Entrance**

**STAR FEATURES**

★ Central Staircase

★ Dining Room

**Living Room**
*The detail of Horta's work can be best seen here, from sculpted bannister ends to finely wrought door handles that echo larger forms.*

Exclusive boutique in the chic Avenue Louise

## Avenue Louise ❷

**Map** 2 D5. 🚋 *34, 54.* 🚌 *81, 82,
93, 94.* Ⓜ *Louise.*

MOST VISITORS to Brussels
travelling by car will
come across this busy thoroughfare, its various under-
passes constructed in the
1950s and 1960s to link up
the city centre with its suburbs.
In fact, the avenue was constructed in 1864 to join the
centre with the suburb of
Ixelles. However, the north
end of the avenue retains a
chic atmosphere; by the Porte
de Namur, fans of designer
labels can indulge themselves
in Gucci and Versace, as well
as investigating the less expensive but no less chic boutiques.
   The avenue also has its architectural treasures. The **Hôtel
Solvay** at No. 224 was built by
Victor Horta in 1894 for the
industrialist Solvay family. Its
ornate doorway, columns and
balconies are a fine example
of Art Nouveau style *(see
p16–17)*. The house is still
a private home. At No. 346,
**Hôtel Max Hallet** is one of
Horta's masterpieces, built in
1903. Continuing south leads
to the peaceful atmosphere
of Ixelles and its parkland.

## St-Gilles ❸

🚋 *20, 48.* 🚌 *23, 55, 81, 82, 90.*
Ⓜ *Porte de Hal, Parvis St-Gilles.*

NAMED AFTER THE patron
saint of this district's
main church, St-Gilles is
traditionally one of Brussels'
poorer areas. However, amid

the low-quality functional
housing are architectural
survivors which make the
suburb well worth a visit.
Art Nouveau and *sgraffiti*
gems *(see p17)* can be found
in streets such as Avenue
Jean Volders and Rue
Vanderschrick. The **Hôtel
Hannon** (1902), now a
photography gallery, remains
one of the city's most
spectacular Art Nouveau
structures. Restored in 1985,
it has a stained-glass window
and ornate statuary that take
this architectural style to its
peak *(see p16)*.
Art Nouveau
details can be seen
in the nearby
streets, particu-
larly in Rue Felix
Delhasse and in
the nearby Rue
Africaine.
   One of the
most striking features of St-
Gilles is the **Porte de Hal**.
Brussels' second set of town
walls, built in the 14th
century, originally included
seven gateways, of which
Porte de Hal is the only
survivor *(see p12)*. Used as a
prison from the 16th to 18th
centuries, it was restored in
1870. Today it houses a small
small museum of folk art, including a collection of
19th-century toys.

Art Nouveau detail on
façade in Rue Africaine

### 🏛 Hôtel Hannon
Ave de la Jonction 1, BRU 1060.
📞 *(02) 538 4220.* Ⓜ *Albert.*
### 🏛 Porte de Hal
Blvds de Midi & de Waterloo, BRU
1000. 📞 *(02) 534 1518.* 🚋 *20, 48.*
🚌 *3, 55, 90.* Ⓜ *Porte de Hal.* ⏰
*10am–4:45pm Tue–Sun.* ♿ ♿

## Ixelles ❹

🚋 *54, 71, 95, 96.* 🚌 *23, 81, 82, 90,
93, 94.* Ⓜ *Porte de Namur.*

ALTHOUGH ONE of Brussels'
largest suburbs and a busy
transport junction, the heart
of Ixelles remains a peaceful
oasis of lakes and woodland.
   The idyllic **Abbaye de la
Cambre** was founded in 1201,
achieving fame and a degree
of fortune in 1242, when Saint
Boniface chose the site for his
retirement. The abbey then
endured a troubled history in
the wars of religion during the
16th and 17th centuries. It
finally closed as an operational
abbey in 1796 and now houses
a school of architecture. The
abbey's pretty Gothic church
can be toured and its grassy
grounds and courtyards offer
a peaceful walk.
   South of the abbey, the
Bois de la Cambre remains
one of the city's most popular
public parks. Created in 1860,
it achieved popularity almost
immediately when royalty
promenaded its main route.
Lakes, bridges and lush grass
make it a favoured picnic site.
   The **Musée Com-
munal d'Ixelles**
nearby has a fine
collection of
posters by 19th-
and 20th-century
greats, such as
Toulouse Lautrec
and Magritte, as
well as sculptures
by Rodin. The former home of
one of Belgium's finest sculp-
tors is now **Musée Constantin
Meunier**, with 170 sculptures
and 120 paintings by the artist,
and his studio preserved in its
turn-of-the-century style.

### 🏛 Abbaye de la Cambre
Ave de Général de Gaulle, BRU 1050.
📞 *(02) 648 1121.* ⏰ *9am–noon,
3–6:30pm daily.* ● *public hols.*
### 🏛 Musée Communal
d'Ixelles
Rue J Van Volsem 71, BRU 1050.
📞 *(02) 515 6421.* ⏰ *1–6:30pm
Tue–Fri, 10am–5pm Sat–Sun.*
● *Mon, public hols.*
### 🏛 Musée Constantin
Meunier
Rue de l'Abbaye 59, BRU 1050.
📞 *(02) 648 4449.* ⏰ *10am noon,
1–5pm Tue–Sun.* ● *Mon, public hols.*

The Forêt de Soignes, once a royal hunting ground and now a park

## Forêt de Soignes ❺

🚃 71, 72. 🚊 23, 90. Ⓜ Demey, Hermann Debroux. 🐾 Thu, Sun. 📞 (02) 215 1740.

THE LARGE FORESTED area to the southeast of Brussels' city centre has a long history: thought to have had prehistoric beginnings, it was also here that the Gallic citizens suffered their defeat by the Romans (see p29). However, the forest really gained renown in the 12th century when wild boar roamed the landscape, and local dukes enjoyed hunting trips in the woodland.

The density of the landscape has provided tranquillity over the ages. In the 14th and 15th centuries it became a favoured location for monasteries and abbeys. Few have survived, but Abbaye de Rouge-Cloître is a rare example from this era.

In a former 18th-century priory is the **Groenendaal Arboretum**, in which more than 400 forest plants are housed, many of which are extinct elsewhere. The most common sight, however, is the locals enjoying a stroll.

🌸 **Groenendaal Arboretum**
Duboislaan 14, 1560 BRU.
📞 (02) 657 0386.
⏰ 8:30am–5pm, Mon–Fri.

## Uccle ❻

🚃 49, 50, 60. 🚊 18, 23, 52, 90.

UCCLE IS A smart residential district, nestling in its tree-lined avenues. Not immediately a tourist destination, it is worthwhile taking a trip to the

**Musée David et Alice van Buuren**. The 1920s residence of this Dutch couple is now a small museum, displaying their eclectic acquisitions. Amid the Dutch Delftware and French Lalique lamps are great finds, such as original sketches by Van Gogh. Visitors will also enjoy the modern landscaped gardens at the rear.

🏛 **Musée David et Alice van Buuren**
Ave Léo Errera 41, 1180 BRU. 📞 (02) 343 4851. ⏰ 1–6pm Sun, 2–6pm Mon. Group visits by appointment. ● 24–31 Dec. 📷

## Anderlecht ❼

🚃 46, 49, 63, 89. 🚊 56, 82. Ⓜ Bizet, Clemenceau, St-Guidon.

CONSIDERED to be Brussels' first genuine suburb (archaeological digs have uncovered remnants of Roman housing), Anderlecht is now best known

Mirò-style drawings, Anderlecht

as an industrial area, for its meat market, and its successful football club of the same name. Despite this, the Modernist Spanish painter Joan Mirò added a unique artistic contribution inspiring bright cartoon-like murals on Rue Porcelaine.

Although only a few pockets of the suburb are now residential, during the 15th century this was a popular place of abode and some houses remain from that era. **Maison Erasme**, built in 1468, is now named after the great scholar and religious reformer, Erasmus (1466–1536), who lived here for five months in 1521. The house was restored in the 1930s. Now a museum dedicated to the most respected thinker of his generation, it displays a collection of 16th-century furniture and portraits of the great humanist by Holbein and van der Weyden.

Nearby is the huge edifice of **Eglise Sts-Pierre-et-Guidon**. This 14th-century Gothic church, completed with the addition of a tower in 1517, is notable for its sheer size and exterior gables, typical of Brabant architecture. The life of St Guidon, patron saint of peasants, is depicted on interior wall murals.

Illustrating a more recent history, the **Musée Gueuze** is an operational family brewery that has opened its doors to the public to witness the production of classic Belgian beers such as lambic, gueuze and kriek (see pp142–3).

Maison Erasme in Anderlecht, with its courtyard and fountain

The Basilique Nationale du Sacré-Coeur rising over the city

🏛 **Maison Erasme**
Rue du Chapitre 31, 1070 BRU.
📞 *(02) 521 1383.* 🕐 *10am–5pm Tue–Sun* 🚫 *Mon, 1 Jan, 25 Dec.*
♿

⛪ **Eglise Sts-Pierre-et-Guidon**
Place de la Vaillance, 1070 BRU.
🕐 *2–5pm Mon–Fri.* 🚫 *Sat & Sun.*

🏛 **Musée Gueuze**
Rue Gheude 56, 1070 BRU.
📞 *(02) 521 4928.* 🕐 *9am–5pm Mon–Fri, 10am–5pm Sat.*
🚫 *Sun, public hols* 💶 *including 1 free beer.*

## Basilique Nationale du Sacré-Coeur ❽

Parvis de la Basilique 1, Koekelberg,
1083 BRU. 📞 *(02) 425 8822.*
Ⓜ *Simonis.* 🚌 *49, 87.* 🚊 *19.*
🕐 *9am–4pm (8am–6pm summer), daily.* 📷 *by appointment.*

ALTHOUGH A small and popular suburb among Brussels' residents, there is little for the visitor to see in Koekelberg other than the striking Basilique Nationale du Sacré-Coeur, but this does make the journey worthwhile for those interested in the best of Art Deco.

King Léopold II was keen to build a church in the city which could accommodate vast congregations to reflect the burgeoning population of early 20th-century Brussels.

He commissioned the church in 1904, although the building was not finished until 1970. Originally designed by Pierre Langerock, the final construction, which uses sandstone and terracotta, was the less expensive adaptation by Albert van Huffel. Very much a 20th-century church, in contrast to the many medieval religious buildings in the city centre, it is dedicated to those who died for Belgium, in particular the thousands of Belgian soldiers who were never to return from the two world wars, killed in battles fought on their own terrain.

The most dominating feature of the church is the vast green copper dome, rising 90 m (295 ft) above ground. For those who do not manage to visit the church itself, it is this central dome that is visible from many points in the city, including the Palais de Justice.

## Musée du Tram ❾

Ave de Tervuren 364b, BRU 1150. 📞
*(02) 515 3108.* 🚊 *39, 44.* 🕐 *Apr–Sep: 1:30pm–7pm Sat & Sun, pub hols. Group tours possible. Every Sun and pub hol, the museum organizes a tour to Heysel (9:45am).* 🚫 *Oct–Mar.* ♿

THIS MUSEUM traces the history of public transport in Belgium, with marvellous displays of heritage machinery. Horse-drawn trams are available to transport visitors round the site, which features fully-working early versions of the electric tram, buses and plenty of interactive exhibits.

## Musée Royal de l'Afrique Centrale ❿

Leuvensesteenweg 13, Tervuren 3080.
📞 *(02) 769 5211.* 🚊 *44.*
🕐 *10am–5pm Tue–Fri, 10am–6pm Sat & Sun,* 📷 *Mon, public hols.* ♿

IN THE 19th century, the colony of the Belgian Congo was Belgium's only territorial possession. It was handed back to self-government in 1960 and eventually renamed Zaire (now the Democratic Republic of Congo). This museum, opened in 1899, is a collection gleaned from over 100 years of colonial rule. Galleries show ceremonial African dress and masks, and displays on colonial life.

Dugout canoes, pagan idols, weapons and stuffed wildlife, feature heavily. There is a horrifying collection of conserved giant African insects, much beloved by children. The museum has been adding constantly to its collection and is now a memento to a past way of life in the Congo.

The Musée Royal de l'Afrique Centrale façade in Tervuren

# Domaine de Laeken ⓫

IN THE 11TH CENTURY Laeken became popular among pilgrims after reported sightings of the Virgin Mary. Since the 19th century, however, it has been firmly etched in the minds of all Belgians as the residence of the nation's monarchy. A walk around the sedate and peaceful area reveals impressive buildings constructed in honour of the royal location, not least the sovereign's official residence and its beautifully landscaped parkland. More surprising is the sudden Oriental influence. The great builder, King Léopold II, wanted to create an architectural world tour; the Chinese and Japanese towers are the only two buildings that came to fruition, but show the scope of one monarch's vision.

**★ Pavillon Chinois**
*Architect Alexandre Marcel designed this elaborate building in 1909; inside are examples of Oriental porcelain.*

**Tour Japonais**

**Parc Royal**

**Villa Belvedere**
was once the residence of the Royal Family, and is now home to the heir to the throne.

**Monument Léopold**
stands as the focus of the park complex and layout. It honours Léopold I, first king of the Belgians. Built in Neo-Gothic style, it has a filigree cast-iron canopy and tracery around the base.

**Place de la Dynastie**
is part of the attractive park that was once the Royal Family's private hunting ground.

**★ Serres Royales**
*These late 19th-century glasshouses are home to exotic trees, palms and camellias. Open to the public annually in April, they are the King's private property.*

**Château Royal**
*The Belgian royal residence, in the heart of the 160-ha (395-acre) estate, was heavily restored in 1890, with a façade by architect Poelaert covering the 18th-century original.*

**Domaine Royale de
Laeken** is the royal estate,
adjacent to the Parc de
Laeken in the city district
of Laeken; the woodland
features old magnolias
and blooming hawthorns.

The Atomium rising 100 m (325 ft) over the Bruparck at dusk

## The Atomium ⑫

Boulevard du Centenaire, 1020 BRU.
📞 (02) 475 4777. 🚌 84, 89. 🚊
23, 81. Ⓜ Heysel. ⚫ until 2005 for
restoration work. 🎦

BUILT FOR THE 1958 World
Fair (see p37), the Atomium
is probably the most identifi-
able symbol of Brussels. As
the world moved into a new
age of science and space
travel at the end of the 1950s,
so the design by André
Waterkeyn reflected this with
a structure of an iron atom,
magnified 165 billion times.
Each of the nine spheres that
make up the "atom" are 18
m (60 ft) in diameter, and
linked by escalators.
They include exhibition
rooms and a smart
restaurant at the top of
the structure.

## Bruparck ⑬

Boulevard du Centenaire, 1020 BRU.
📞 (02) 474 8377. 🚌 84, 89. 🚊
23, 81. Ⓜ Heysel. **Mini-Europe
& Océade** 📞 (02) 478 4944 (Mini-
Europe); (02) 478 4220 (Océade).
◯ Apr–Sep: 9:30am–6pm daily
(Jul–Aug: to midnight); Oct–mid-Jan:
10am–5pm daily. ⚫ end Jan–Mar.
🎦 **Kinepolis** 📞 (02) 474 2600. ◯
perfomances. 🎦 for film screenings.

ALTHOUGH NOWHERE near as
large or as grand as many
of the world's theme parks,
Bruparck's sights and range of
fast-food restaurants are always
a popular family destination.
The first and favourite port
of call for most visitors is Mini-

Europe, where more than 300
miniature reconstructions take
you around the landscapes of
the European Union. Built at
a scale of 1:25, the collection
displays buildings of social or
cultural importance, such as
the Acropolis in Athens, the
Brandenburg Gate of Berlin
and the Houses of Parliament
from London. Even at this
scale the detail is such that it
can be second only to visiting
the sights themselves.
For film fans, Kinepolis
cannot be beaten. Large
auditoriums show a range of
popular films from different
countries on 29 screens. The
IMAX cinema features surround
sound and a semi-circular 600
sq m (6,456 sq ft) widescreen.
If warmth and relaxation
are what you are looking for,
Océade is a tropically heated
water park, complete with
giant slides, wave machines,
bars, cafés and even realistic
re-created sandy beaches.

London's Houses of Parliament in
small scale at Mini-Europe

# BEYOND BRUSSELS

# BEYOND BRUSSELS

**B**RUSSELS IS AT THE HEART *not only of Belgium, but also of Europe. The city marks the divide between the Flemish north and the French-speaking Walloon south. Its central position makes Brussels an ideal base for visitors: within easy reach are the ancient Flemish towns of Antwerp, Ghent and Bruges, each with their exquisite medieval architecture, superb museums and excellent restaurants.*

Although Belgium is a small country, it has one of the highest population densities in Europe. An incredibly efficient road and rail network also means that large numbers of people move around the country every day, with around half the population employed in industry, particularly in textiles, metallurgy and chemicals. Despite this, parts of Belgium are still farmed. Stretching south from the defences of the North Sea is the plain of Flanders, a low-lying area which, like the Netherlands, has reclaimed land or *polders*, whose fertile soil is intensively cultivated with wheat and sugar beet. Bordering the Netherlands is the Kempenland, a sparsely populated area of peat moors, which in the 19th century was mined for coal.

There are small farms here today which cultivate mainly oats, rye and potatoes. Northeast Belgium also contains the large port of Antwerp, a major centre of European industry, with its ship-building yards, oil-refineries and car factories. The towns of Leuven, Lier and Mechelen are noted for their medieval town centres, while Oudenaarde produces exceptionally fine tapestries in a trade dating back to the 13th century.

Brussels itself is surrounded by both Flemish and Walloon Brabant, a fertile region famous for its wheat and beet farms and pasture for cows. Just a few kilometres south of the capital is Waterloo, the most visited battlefield in the world, where Napoleon was defeated by Wellington in 1815.

Visitors sail under the Blinde Ezelstraat Bridge on a tour of Bruges

◁ The Brabo Fountain in Antwerp's Grote Markt

# Exploring Beyond Brussels

B ELGIUM OCCUPIES one of the most densely populated parts of Europe, with a concentration of towns and villages across the flat landscapes of the Flemish plain. Along the North Sea coast there are fewer settlements, set among fertile farmland. To the north and west of Brussels are the three easy-to-reach towns of Antwerp, Ghent and Bruges which, with their ancient buildings and vibrant cultural life, are attractive destinations. East of Brussels is the charming university town of Leuven, and further on is the open-air museum of Bokrijk, whose restored buildings focus on the the history of the Flemish people.

**Bronze statue of Silvius Brabo in Antwerp's Grote Markt**

## KEY

| | |
|---|---|
| ▬ | Motorway |
| ▬ | Major road |
| ▬ | Minor road |
| ▬ | River |

0 km      20

0 miles      20

**View over Bruges from the Belfort**

## SIGHTS AT A GLANCE

| | |
|---|---|
| Antwerp ❶ | Leuven ❾ |
| Ath ⓯ | Liège ⓫ |
| Bokrijk Museum ❿ | Lier ❷ |
| Bruges ⓴ | Mechelen ❸ |
| Charleroi ⓭ | Mons ⓮ |
| Dendermonde ❹ | Namur ⓬ |
| Ghent ⓳ | Nivelles ❽ |
| Halle ❻ | Pajottenland ❺ |
| Ieper ⓱ | Ronse ⓰ |
| Oudenaarde ⓲ | Waterloo ❼ |

## GETTING AROUND

In Belgium distances are short, with a wide choice
of routes – even the tiniest village is easily reached.
Brussels sits at the hub of several major highways
such as the E19 and the E40 (which link the capital
to the country's principal towns). The fully integ-
rated public transport system has frequent train
services and a comprehensive bus network.

**Namur's Citadel from the River Meuse**

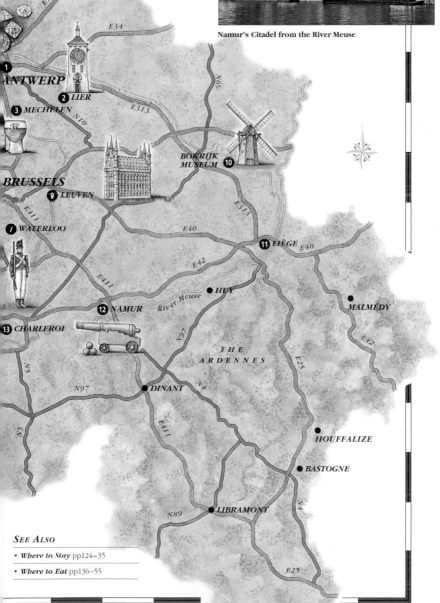

# Street-by-Street: Antwerp ❶

**F**ANNING OUT FROM the east bank of the River Scheldt, Antwerp is Belgium's second-largest city. It is also the centre of the international diamond trade, which is run from the unassuming buildings that line the streets near Centraal Station. Today, the city's industries lie away from its medieval core whose narrow streets and fine buildings cluster around the cathedral and the Grote Markt. Most sites of interest are within easy walking distance of the Grote Markt whose surrounding streets house museums, shops and exuberant cafés and bars.

**Gilt statue on guildhouse**

**Nationaal Scheepvaart-museum**
*This model of an 18th-century armed merchant ship is in Antwerp's Maritime Museum.*

**To Koninklijk Museum voor Schone Kunsten**

**The Vleeshuis**
*Occupied by the Butcher's Guild for three centuries, this beautiful 1504 building has striking layers of brick and stone that look like alternating strips of fat and lean meat.*

**The Ethnografisch Museum** has artifacts from around the world.

**Stadhuis**

**KEY**

- - - Suggested route

**STAR SIGHTS**

★ **Grote Markt**

★ **Kathedraal**

**The Brabo Fountain**
*This statue, in the centre of the Grote Markt, depicts the fearless soldier, Silvius Brabo. Said to be the nephew of Julius Caesar, Brabo is shown throwing the hand of the mythical giant, Antigonius, into the River Scheldt.*

### Sint Pauluskerk

*This imposing
church was built
in 1517, but has
a magnificent
Baroque gate and
spire dating from
the late 17th century.
Inside, there is a noted
collection of paintings,
including one especially
fine work by Rubens.*

### ★ Grote Markt

*Antwerp's golden
age of trade in the
16th century is
reflected in the
square's cosmopo-
litan 1564 town
hall, built by
architects from
all over Europe.*

To
Centraal
Station

### ★ Onze Lieve Vrouwe Kathedraal

*The largest Gothic cathedral in
Belgium, this building occupies a
1-ha (2.5-acre) site in Antwerp's
centre. Work began on this elegant
church, noted for its spire, in 1352
and took two centuries to complete.*

To Rubenshuis

### Groenplaats

*The Groenplaats or Green
Square is a pleasant open
space with trees and flower
beds. Lined with cafés, bars
and restaurants, the square
is a popular spot with both
locals and visitors for a
peaceful stroll or meal.*

0 metres   50

0 yards   50

# Exploring Antwerp

THERE HAS BEEN a settlement here, on the banks of the River Scheldt, since the 2nd century. The city of Antwerp grew up and became part of the Duchy of Brabant in 1106. Within 200 years it was a thriving hub of the European cloth industry and Brabant's main port. Today, Antwerp is the principal city of Flemish-speaking Belgium. It is a large metropolis whose port and older residential areas surround a compact centre packed with evidence of its rich history. There are exquisite guild-houses, where the medieval merchants once traded, and imposing churches and several museums, where collections of paintings by the city's most famous son, Pieter Paul Rubens (1577–1640), are also to be found. Antwerp also has many contemporary attractions, such as excellent restaurants, busy nightclubs and bars. Thanks to the Antwerp Six, a group of adventurous designers, the city also has a reputation for cutting-edge fashion.

**Carvings above the cathedral door depict the Last Judgement**

**Visitors tour Antwerp on an historic horse-drawn bus**

## Getting Around

The best way to get around Antwerp is by using the public transport system. The excellent bus and tram network is focused on Centraal Station, where most visitors arrive. Fast and frequent trams and buses travel from here to the centre. Most of the city's main sights are within walking distance of the Grote Markt.

### 🏛 Grote Markt

Grote Markt. 【 *(03) 232 0103.* 🛔

Antwerp's central square, or Grote Markt, is flanked by the ornately gabled Stadhuis (town hall), which was built in 1564 by the architect and sculptor Cornelis Floris. Its interior was restored in the 19th century and houses a series of paintings which celebrate the city's history. The north side of the square has a series of guild-houses, each of which is decorated with gilded figures. The tallest of these is the House of the Crossbowmen at number seven, on top of which is a statue of St George and the dragon. The Brabo fountain in the middle of the square is one of Antwerp's noted landmarks.

### 🔒 Onze Lieve Vrouwe Kathedraal

Groenplaats 21 or Handschoenmarkt. 【 *(03) 213 9940.* ◯ *10am–5pm Mon–Fri, 10am–3pm Sat, 1–4pm Sun.* 🗝 🛔

The building of Antwerp's Onze Lieve Vrouwe Kathedraal (Cathedral of Our Lady) took almost two centuries, from 1352 to 1521. This magnificent structure has a graceful tiered spire that rises 123 m (404 ft) above the winding streets of the medieval city centre. Inside, the impression of light and space owes much to its seven-aisled nave and vaulted ceiling. The collection of paintings and sculpture includes three works by Rubens, of which two are triptychs – the *Raising of the Cross* (1610) and the *Descent from the Cross* (1612).

### 🔒 Sint Pauluskerk

St-Paulusstraat 22 or Veemarkt 14. 【 *(03) 231 3321.* ◯ *Easter Sat–Sep: 2–5pm daily.* 🗝 *3pm Sun & pub hols.*

Completed in the early 17th century, this splendid church is distinguished by its combination of both Gothic and Baroque features. The exterior dates from about 1517, and has an added elaborate Baroque gateway. The interior is noted for its intricately carved wooden choir stalls. St Paulus also possesses an outstanding series of paintings illustrating the Fifteen Mysteries of the Rosary, one of which, *The Scourging of the Pillar*, is an exquisite canvas by Rubens. There are also paintings by van Dyck and Jordaens.

**Fresco paintings of the dukes of Brabant adorn the Stadhuis walls**

### ♛ Vleeshuis

Vleeshouwersstraat 38–40. ☎ (03) 233 6404. ⏰ 10am–4:45pm Tue–Sun, Easter Mon. ● 1 & 2 Jan, 1 May, Ascension, 1 & 2 Nov, 25 & 26 Dec. ♿

The Vleeshuis (Meat Hall) was completed in 1504 to a design by Herman de Waghemakere. The structure features slender towers with five hexagonal turrets and rising gables, all built in alternate strips of stone and brick – giving it a streaky bacon-like appearance.

Inside, there is an impressive collection of medieval wood carvings and old musical instruments. In the 17th century, Antwerp was renowned for its manufacture of instruments, including the eccentrically shaped harpsichords and clavichords on display here. There are also paintings, but the highlight is the retable (altarpiece), depicting Christ's Entombment, Crucifixion and Ascent to Heaven, which was carved in wood by Jacob van Cothem in 1514.

### 🏛 Nationaal Scheepvaartmuseum

Steenplein 1. ☎ (03) 201 9340. ⏰ 10am–5pm Tue–Sun. ● Mon. ♿

The Maritime Museum is located in the gatehouse of Antwerp's original fortress, or

**View of the Vleeshuis' striking façade**

**Statue of an ogre outside the Maritime Museum**

Steen, the oldest building in the city. Built from the 10th to 16th centuries, it was used in medieval times as a prison. Today, this restored building has 12 rooms devoted to the history of all things nautical, from fearsome Viking ships' heads to the small but elegant gondola built for the visit of Napoleon to the city in 1808. Outside, moored along the riverside, is a selection of old canal tugs and barges.

### ♛ Rubenshuis

See pp96–7.

### ⛪ Sint Jacobskerk

Lange Nieuwstraat 73–75, Eikenstraat. ☎ (03) 225 0414. ⏰ Apr–Oct: 2–5pm Mon–Sat; Nov–Mar: 9am–noon, Mon–Sat; Sun services only. ♿

Noted as Rubens' burial place, this sandstone chuch, built over three centuries from 1491 to 1656, occupies the site of a chapel which lay along the pilgrimage route of St James of Compostella. The rich interior contains the tombs of several other notable Antwerp families, as well as much 17th-century art, including sculptures by Hendrik Verbruggen, and paintings by van Dyck, Otto Venius (Rubens' first master) and Jacob Jordaens. When Rubens died, in 1640, he was buried in his family chapel, located directly behind the high altar. The chapel altar is where one of Rubens' last paintings, *Our Lady Surrounded by Saints* (1634), is displayed.

### 🏛 Koninklijk Museum voor Schone Kunsten

See pp94–5.

### 🏛 Modenatie

Nationalestraat 28. ☎ (03) 226 1447. ⏰ 10am–6pm Tue–Sun, 2–6pm Mon.

The Fashion Museum houses the Flanders Fashion Institute, the Fashion Department of Antwerp's Royal

Academy, as well as a museum of fashion (MOMU).

### 🏛 Provincial Diamond Museum

Koningin Astridplein 19–24. ☎ (03) 202 4890. ⏰ 10am–5pm (6pm in summer) daily. ♿

This museum is dedicated to the world of diamonds.

**Late 16th-century printing press in the Museum Plantin-Moretus**

### 🏛 Museum Plantin-Moretus

Vrijdagmarkt 22–23. ☎ (03) 221 1450. ⏰ 10am–5pm Tue–Sun, Easter Mon. ● Mon, 1 & 2 Jan, 1 May, Ascension, 1 & 2 Nov, 25 & 26 Dec. ♿

This fascinating museum occupies a large 16th-century house that belonged to the printer Christopher Plantin, who moved here in 1576. The house is built around a courtyard, and its ancient rooms and narrow corridors resemble the types of interiors painted by Flemish and Dutch masters. The museum is devoted to the early years of printing, when Plantin and others began to produce books that bore no resemblance to earlier, illuminated medieval manuscripts.

Antwerp was a centre for printing in the 15th and 16th centuries, and Plantin was its most successful printer. Today, his workshop displays several historic printing presses, as well as woodcuts and copper plates. Plantin's library is also on show and includes an array of beautifully made volumes. One of the gems here is an edition of the Gutenberg Bible – the first book to be printed using moveable type, a new technique invented by Johannes Gutenberg in 1455.

# Koninklijk Museum voor Schone Kunsten

ANTWERP'S LARGEST and most impressive fine art
collection is exhibited in the Museum voor Schone
Kunsten, which occupies a massive late 19th-century Neo-
Classical building almost 2 km (1 mile) to the south of the
Grote Markt. The permanent collection contains both
ancient and modern works. The earlier collection on the
upper floor begins with medieval Flemish painting and
continues through the 19th century, with the 'Antwerp
Trio' of Rubens, van Dyck and Jordaens well represented.
At ground level, modern exhibits include the work of
Belgian artists René Magritte, James Ensor and Paul
Delvaux, as well as a major collection of work by Rik
Wouters, an Impressionist influenced by Cézanne. Tissot
and van Gogh are among the foreign artists on show.

First Floor

**Façade of Gallery**
*Building began on
this imposing struc-
ture in 1884. The
Neo-Classical façade
with its vast pillars
has carved women
charioteers atop
each side. It was
opened in 1890.*

★ **Saint Barbara** *(1437)*
*Jan van Eyck's painting of
Saint Barbara in several
tones of grey shows the
saint sitting in front
of a huge Gothic
cathedral tower
still under
construction,
while a prayer
book lies open
on her lap.*

Main
Entrance

---

## STAR PAINTINGS

★ **Saint Barbara
by Jan van Eyck**

★ **Adoration of
the Magi by Pieter
Paul Rubens**

★ **Woman Ironing
by Rik Wouters**

★ **Woman Ironing** *(1912)*
*This peaceful domestic scene by
Rik Wouters employs the muted
colours of Impressionism. This was
a productive period for Wouters
who painted 60 canvases in 1912.*

## GALLERY
## GUIDE

*The gallery is divided
into two floors. Flemish
Old Masters and 19th-
century painters are
housed on the first floor,
while the ground floor
focuses on James Ensor
and the 20th century.
Each room is lettered and
visitors may view exhibits
chronologically, starting
in the entrance hall.*

## ★ Adoration of the Magi (1624)

*One of Rubens' master-pieces, this painting displays a remarkable freedom of composition.*

### VISITORS' CHECKLIST

Leopold de Waelplaats 1–9. 🚋
(03) 238 7809. 🚌 1, 23, 290. 🚋
4, 8. 🕙 10am–5pm Tue–Sun.
🔴 1 & 2 Jan, 1 May, Ascension,
25 Dec. ♿ 🔲 📷 📹 🔄

## As the Old Sang, the Young Play Pipes (1638)

*Jacob Jordaens' (1593–1678) joyous celebration of life in this painting of a family enjoying a musical evening contrasts with his religious paintings.*

## Pink Bows (1936)

*Paul Delvaux's dream-like style clearly shows the influence of Sigmund Freud's psycho-analytic theories on Surrealist painting.*

## Madame Récamier (1967)

*René Magritte's macabre version of the original painting by David is a classic Surrealist work.*

### KEY

- 🟦 15th-century paintings
- 🟦 16th-century paintings
- 🟦 17th-century paintings
- 🟦 17th century in Holland
- 🟦 19th-century paintings
- 🟦 19th-century salon
- 🟦 20th-century paintings
- 🟦 Temporary exhibitions
- 🟦 Non-exhibition space

**Ground Floor**

# Rubenshuis

**Statue of Neptune**

RUBENSHUIS, ON Wapper Square, was Pieter Paul Rubens' home and studio for the last thirty years of his life, from 1610 to 1640. The city bought the premises just before World War II, but by then the house was little more than a ruin, and what can be seen today is the result of careful restoration. It is divided into two sections. To the left of the entrance are the narrow rooms of the artist's living quarters, equipped with period furniture. Behind this part of the house is the kunstkamer, or art gallery, where Rubens exhibited both his own and other artists' work, and entertained his friends and wealthy patrons, such as the Archduke Albert and the Infanta Isabella. To the right of the entrance lies the main studio, a spacious salon where Rubens worked on – and showed – his works. A signposted route guides visitors through the house.

**Façade of Rubenshuis**
*The older Flemish part of the house sits next to the later house, whose elegant early Baroque façade was designed by Rubens.*

**Formal Gardens**
*The small garden is laid out formally and its charming pavilion dates from Rubens' time. He was influenced by such architects of the Italian Renaissance as Vitruvius when he built the Italian Baroque addition to his house in the 1620s.*

**★ Rubens' Studio**
*It is estimated that Rubens produced some 2,500 paintings in this large, high-ceilinged room. In the Renaissance manner, Rubens designed the work which was usually completed by a team of other artists employed in his studio.*

| STAR SIGHTS |
| --- |
| ★ Kunstkamer |
| ★ Rubens' Studio |

### Bedroom
*The Rubens family lived in the Flemish section of the house, with its small rooms and narrow passages. The portrait by the bed is said to be of Rubens' second wife, Helena Fourment.*

**The Familia Kamer**, or family sitting room, is cosy and has a pretty tiled floor. It overlooks Wapper Square.

**VISITORS' CHECKLIST**

Wapper 9–11. ☎ (03) 201 1555.
🚌 1, 9, 19. 🚊 2, 15. ⬤ 10am–
5pm Tue–Sun, Easter Mon. ⬤ 1 &
2 Jan, 1 & 2 Nov, 25 & 26 Dec. 🖼

### Dining Room
*Intricately fashioned leather panels line the walls of this room, which also displays a noted work by Frans Snyders.*

### ★ Kunstkamer
*This art gallery contains a series of painted sketches by Rubens. At the far end is a semi-circular dome, modelled on Rome's Pantheon, displaying a number of marble busts.*

**Chequered mosaic tiled floor**

### Baroque Portico
*One of the few remaining original features, this portico was designed by Rubens, and links the older house with the Baroque section. It is adorned with a frieze showing scenes from Greek mythology.*

The Centenary Clock on Lier's
Zimmertoren or watchtower

## Lier ❷

🏃 30,000. 🚇 🚌 ❓ Grote Markt
57, (03) 800 0555. 🆆 www.lier.be

Lier is an attractive small
town, just 20 km (12 miles)
southeast of Antwerp. The
Grote Markt is a spacious
cobbled square framed by
handsome historic buildings.
The Stadhuis (town hall) was
built in 1740, and its elegant
dimensions contrast strongly
with the square, turreted 14th-
century Belfort (belfry) adjoining. Nearby is the **Stedelijk
Museum Wuyts**, with its
collection of paintings by
Flemish masters including Jan
Steen, Brueghel and Rubens.
East of here the church of St
Gummaruserk, with its soaring
stone pillars and vaulted roof,
evokes medieval times, and
the carved altarpiece is
notable for the intricate detail
of its biblical scenes. The
stained-glass windows are
among the finest in Belgium
and were a gift from Emperor
Maximillian I in 1516.

One of Lier's highlights is
the **Zimmertoren**, a 14th-
century watchtower that
now houses the clocks of
Lodewijk Zimmer (1888–
1970). This Lier merchant
wanted to share his
knowledge of timepieces.

🏛 **Stedelijk Museum
Wuyts**
Florent van Cauwen straat 14.
📞 (03) 491 1396. ⭕ Apr–Oct:
10am–midday 1–5pm Tue–Sun. 📷
🕍 **Zimmertoren**
Zimmerplein 18. 📞 (03) 491 1395.
⭕ daily. 📷

## Mechelen ❸

🏃 75,000. 🚇 🚌 ❓ Hallestraat 2,
Grote Markt, (015) 29 7655.

The seat of the Catholic
Archbishop of Belgium,
Mechelen was the administrative capital of the country
under the Burgundian prince,
Charles the Bold, in 1473.
Today, it is an appealing town
whose expansive main square
is flanked by pleasant cafés
and bars. To the west of the
square is the main attraction,
**St Romboutskathedraal**, a
huge cathedral that took some
300 years to complete. The
building might never have
been finished but for a deal
with the Vatican: the cathedral
was allowed to sell special
indulgences (which absolved
the purchaser of their sins) to
raise funds, on condition that
the pope received a percent-
age. Completed in 1546, the
cathedral's tower has Belgium's
finest carillon, a set of 49 bells,
whose peals ring out at
weekends and on pub-
lic holidays. The church
also contains *The
Crucifixion* by Antony
van Dyck (1599–1641).

Less well-known
in Mechelen are three
16th-century houses
by the River Dilje.
They are not open
to visitors, but their
exteriors are delight-
ful. The "House of
the Little Devils"
is adorned with
carved demons.

Mechelen is famous for its
local beers, and visitors should
try the Gouden Carolus, a
dark brew, which is said to
have been the favourite tipple
of the Emperor Charles V.

🏛 **St Romboutskathedraal**
St Romboutskerkhof. 📞 (015) 29
7655. 📷 obligatory. Easter–Sep:
2pm Sat, Sun & pub hols; Jun–mid-
Sep: 7pm Mon (Jul & Aug: also 2pm).
Tours depart from the Tourist Office.

Mechelen's main square, the
Grote Markt, on market day

## Dendermonde ❹

🏃 40,000. 🚇 🚌 ❓ Stadhuis,
Grote Markt, (052) 21 3956.

A quiet, industrial town,
Dendermonde is about
20 km (12 miles) southeast
of Ghent. Its strategic position, at the confluence of the
Scheldt and Dender rivers,
has attracted the attention
of a string
of invaders

Vleeshuis façade on the Grote Markt in Dendermonde

**Wood panelled walls and paintings adorn the hall at Gaasbeek Castle**

over the centuries, including the Germans who shelled Dendermonde in 1914. But the town is perhaps best-known as the site of the Steed Bayard, a carnival held every ten years at the end of August.

Today, the town's spacious main square is framed by the quaint turrets and towers of the the Vleeshuis or Meat Hall. The Town Hall is an elegant 14th-century building which was extensively restored in 1920. Dendermonde also possesses two exquisite early religious paintings by Anthony van Dyck which are on display in the Onze Lieve Vrouwekerk (Church of Our Lady).

## Pajottenland ❺

🏠 *111,700.* **ℹ** *Toerisme Pajottenland en Zennevalaaei, (02) 356 4259.* **w** *www.visitflanders.com*

T HE PAJOTTENLAND forms part of the Brabant province to the southwest of Brussels, and is bordered in the west by the Dender River. The gentle rolling hills of the landscape contain many farms, some of which date back to the 17th century. The village of Onze Lieve Vrouw Lombeek, just 12 km (7 miles) west of Brussels, is named after its church, an outstanding example of 14th-century Gothic architecture.

Just a few kilometres south of the village lies the area's main attraction, the castle and

grounds of **Gaasbeek**. The castle was remodelled in the 19th century, but actually dates from the 13th century, and boasts a moat and a thick curtain wall, strengthened by huge semi-circular towers. The castle's interior holds an excellent collection of fine and applied arts. Among the treasures are rich tapestries, 15th-century alabaster reliefs from England, silverware and a delightful ivory and copper hunting horn which belonged to the Protestant martyr Count Egmont in the 16th century.

The Pajottenland is also known for its beers, especially lambic and gueuze. Lambic is one of the most popular types of beer in Belgium *(see pp142–3)*.

### ♣ Gaasbeek
Kasteelstraat 40. **ℂ** *(02) 532 4372.* ☐ *Apr–Oct: 10am–5pm Tue–Sun.* ● *Nov–Mar.* 🅰

## Halle ❻

🏛 *30,000.* 🚉 🚌 **ℹ** *Stadhuis, Grote Markt, (02) 356 4259.* **w** *www.halle.be*

L OCATED ON THE outskirts of Brussels, in the province of Brabant, Halle is a peaceful little town. It has been a major religious centre since the 13th century because of the cult of the Black Virgin, an effigy in the Onze Lieve Vrouwebasiliek, the town's main church. The holy statue's blackness is due to its stained colour, which is said to have occurred through contact with gunpowder during the religious wars of the 17th century.

The virgin has long been one of Belgium's most venerated icons and each year, on Whit Sunday, the statue is paraded through the town.

### THE STEED BAYARD

Dendermonde's famous carnival of the Steed Bayard occurs every ten years at the end of August. The focus of the festival is a horse, the Steed Bayard itself, represented in the carnival by a giant model. It takes 34 bearers to carry the horse which weighs 700 kg (1,540 lb) and is 5.8 m (19 ft) high. A procession of locals dressed in medieval costume re-enact the Steed Bayard legend – a complex tale of chivalry and treachery, family loyalty and betrayal. The four Aymon brothers (who were said to be the nephews of Emperor Charlemagne) ride the horse, and it is their behaviour towards the animal which serves to demonstrate their moral worth.

# Waterloo 𝟕

**Death mask of Napoleon**

THE BATTLE OF WATERLOO was fought on 18 June, 1815. It pitted Napoleon and his French army against the Duke of Wellington, who was in command of troops mostly drawn from Britain, Germany and the Netherlands. The two armies met outside the insignificant hamlet of Waterloo, to the south of Brussels. The result was decisive. The battle began at 11:30am and just nine hours later the French were in full retreat. Napoleon abdicated and was subsequently exiled to the island of St Helena, where he died in mysterious circumstances six years later.

Despite its importance, the battlefield has not been conserved, and part of it has been dug up for a highway. However, enough remains to give a general sense of the battle. The best place to start a visit here is at the Musée Wellington, some 3 km (2 miles) from the battlefield.

predates the battle, after which it was extended, with the newer portions containing dozens of memorial plaques and flagstones dedicated to those British soldiers who died at Waterloo. Several of these plaques were paid for by voluntary contributions from ordinary soldiers in honour of their officers.

**The Butte de Lion viewed from the Waterloo battlefield**

## 🏛 Musée Wellington
Chaussée de Bruxelles 147. 📞 (02) 354 7806. ◯ daily. ● 1 Jan, 25 Dec. 📷 W www.museewellington.com
The Waterloo inn where Wellington spent the night before the battle has been turned into the Musée Wellington, its narrow rooms packed with curios alongside plans and models of the battle. One curiosity is the artificial leg of Lord Uxbridge, one of Wellington's commanders. His leg was blown off by a cannon ball during the

battle and buried in Waterloo. After his death, the leg was sent to join the rest of him in England and, as recompense, his relatives sent his artificial one back to Waterloo.

## 🔒 Eglise St-Joseph
Chaussée de Bruxelles.
📞 (02) 354 0011.
Across the road from the Musée Wellington is the tiny church of St-Joseph, which was built as a royal chapel at the end of the 17th century. Its dainty, elegant cupola

## ▦ Butte de Lion
149 Chaussée de Bruxelles, N5, 3km (2 miles) S of Waterloo.
📞 (02) 385 1912. ◯ daily. 📷
Dating from 1826, the Butte de Lion is a 45-m (148-ft) high earthen mound built on the

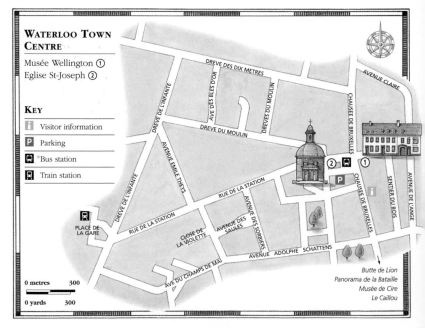

**WATERLOO TOWN CENTRE**

Musée Wellington ①
Eglise St-Joseph ②

**KEY**

| | |
|---|---|
| 🛈 | Visitor information |
| 🅿 | Parking |
| 🚌 | Bus station |
| 🚃 | Train station |

0 metres    300
0 yards     300

DREVE DES DIX METRES
DREVE DE L'INFANTE
AVE DES BLÉS D'OR
DREVES DU MOULIN
DREVE DU MOULIN
AVENUE ÉMILE THEYS
DREVE DE L'INFANTE
RUE DE LA STATION
PLACE DE LA GARE
RUE DE LA STATION
CLOSE DE LA VIOLETTE
AVÉ DU CHAMPS DE MAI
AVENUE DES SAULES
RUE DE LA STATION
AVENUE DES SORBIERS
AVENUE ADOLPHE SCHATTENS
AVENUE CLAIRE
CHAUSSÉE DE BRUXELLES
CHAUSSÉE DE BRUXELLES
CHAUSSÉE DE BRUXELLES
SENTIER DU BOIS
AVENUE DE L'ANGE

②🚌 ①
🅿

*Butte de Lion*
*Panorama de la Bataille*
*Musée de Cire*
*Le Caillou*

spot where one of Wellington's Dutch generals, the Prince of Orange, was wounded during the battle. Steps lead to the top, which is guarded by a huge cast-iron lion, and from here there is a great view over the battlefield. The French army approached from the south and fought up the slope across farmland that became increasingly marshy as the day went on, while their opponents had the drier ridge at the foot of the mound. A plan of the battle is displayed at the top.

### 🚩 Panorama de la Bataille
252–254 Route du Lion, Braine-L'Alleud. N5, 3 km (2 miles) S of Waterloo. ( (02) 385 1912. ○ daily. 🔖
This is perhaps the most fascinating of the several attractions located beneath the Butte de Lion. This circular painting of the battle by artist Louis Demoulin was erected in 1912. It is 110 m (360 ft) long and stretches right round a circular, purpose-built gallery. Panoramic, circular paintings came to be very popular in the late 19th century; this is one of the few works that remain intact.

### 🏛 Musée de Cire
315–317 Route du Lion, N5, 3 km (2 miles) S of Waterloo. ( (02) 384 6740. ○ Apr–Oct: daily; Nov–Mar: pub hols, Sat & Sun. 🔖
The Musée de Cire is a wax museum where pride of place goes to the models of soldiers dressed in the military regalia of 1815. It seems strange today that the various armies dressed their men in such vivid colours, which made them easy targets. Indeed, many commanders paid for the uniforms of their men themselves, competing with each other for the most flamboyant design.

### 🏛 Napoleon's Last Headquarters
66 Chaussée de Waterloo, Vieux-Genappe, N5, 7 km (4.5 miles) S of Waterloo. ( (02) 384 2424. ○ pm daily. ● 1 Jan, 25 Dec. 🔖
Napoleon spent the eve of the battle in a farmhouse, Le Caillou. This is now a museum containing some artifacts from Napoleon's army, a bronze death mask of the Emperor and his army-issue bed.

Southeast side of Nivelles' imposing church, Collégiale Ste-Gertrude

## Nivelles ❽
🏠 20,000. 🚆 🚌 ⓘ Waux-Hall, Place Albert I, (067) 88 2275.

T UCKED AWAY among the rolling hills of the province of Brabant, the little town of Nivelles was, for centuries, the site of one of the wealthiest and most powerful abbeys in the region. Earlier it was the cradle of the Carolingian dynasty, whose most celebrated ruler was the Emperor Charlemagne (747–814). The main sight today is the vast church, the Collégiale Ste-Gertrude, that dominates the town centre. Something of an architectural hotchpotch, the church dates back to the 10th century and is remarkable in that it has two imposing chancels – one each for the pope and the king.

## Leuven ❾
See pp102–103.

## Bokrijk Museum ❿
See pp104–105.

## Liège ⓫
🏠 400,000. 🚆 🚌 ⓘ En Féronstrée 92, (04) 221 9221.

B ELGIUM'S THIRD-biggest city, Liège is a major river port and industrial conurbation at the confluence of the rivers Meuse and Ourthe. The city

has an unusual history in that it was an independent principality from the 10th to the 18th century, ruled by Prince Bishops. However, the church became widely despised and when the French Republican army arrived in 1794, they were welcomed by the local citizens with open arms.

Today, Liège possesses some notable attractions and highlights include the **Musée de la Vie Wallonne** (Museum of Walloon Life), housed in an outstanding 17th-century friary. The museum focuses on Walloon folklore and culture, which is depicted in a series of reconstructed interiors and craft workshops from the city's history.

### 🏛 Musée de la Vie Wallonne
Cour des Mineurs. ( (04) 237 9040. ○ 10am–5pm Tue–Sat. 🔖

## Namur ⓬
🏠 100,000. 🚆 🚌 🚍 ⓘ Square Léopold, (081) 24 64 49.

F RENCH SPEAKING Namur is a friendly, attractive town whose narrow central streets boast several elegant mansions and fine old churches, as well as lots of lively bars and outstanding restaurants. Until the Belgian army left in 1978, Namur was also a military town. The soldiers were stationed within the Citadel, located on top of the steep hill on the south side of the centre, which remains the town's main attraction. An exploration of its bastions and subterranean galleries takes several hours.

Namur's ancient walls or Citadel seen from the River Meuse

# Leuven ❾

**W**ITHIN EASY STRIKING distance of Brussels, the historic Flemish town of Leuven traces its origins to a fortified camp constructed here by Julius Caesar. In medieval times, the town became an important centre of the cloth trade, but it was as a seat of learning that it achieved international prominence. In 1425, Pope Martin V and Count John of Brabant founded Leuven's university, and by the mid-1500s it was one of Europe's most prestigious academic institutions, the home of such famous scholars as Erasmus and Mercator.

**Font Sapienza**

Even today, the university exercises a dominant influence over the town, and its students give Leuven a vibrant atmosphere. The bars and cafés flanking the Oude Markt, a large square in the centre of town, are especially popular. Adjoining the square is the Grote Markt, a triangular open space which boasts two fine medieval buildings, the Stadhuis and St Pieterskerk.

Huge buttresses support the tower of the Church of Saint Peter

**Lively café society in the Oude Markt**

### 🏛 Oude Markt

This handsome, cobble-stoned square is flanked by a tasteful ensemble of high-gabled brick buildings. Some of these date from the 18th century; others are comparatively new. At ground level these buildings house the largest concentration of bars and cafés in town, and as such attract the town's university students in their droves.

### 🏛 Stadhuis

Grote Markt. ☎ (016) 21 1539. ○ daily. 🎫 🎥 obligatory. At 3pm daily (Apr–Sep: also at 11am Mon–Fri). Built between 1448 and 1463 from the profits of the cloth trade, Leuven's town hall, the Stadhuis, was designed to demonstrate the wealth of the city's merchants. This distinctive, tall building is renowned for its lavishly carved and decorated façade. A line of narrow windows rise up over three floors beneath a steeply pitched roof adorned with dormer windows and

pencil-thin turrets. It is, however, in the fine quality of its stonework that the building excels, with delicately carved tracery and detailed medieval figures beneath 300 niche bases. There are grotesques of every description as well as representations of folktales and biblical stories, all carved in exuberant late-Gothic style. Within the niche alcoves is a series of 19th-century statues depicting local dignitaries and politicians. Guided tours of the interior are available, and include three lavishly decorated reception rooms.

**Stone carvings of medieval figures decorate the Stadhuis façade**

### 🔒 St Pieterskerk and Museum voor Religieuze Kunst

Grote Markt. ☎ (016) 29 5133. ○ Mar–Oct: daily, Nov–Feb: Tue–Sun. 🎫 to museum. Across the square from the Stadhuis rises St Pieterskerk, a massive church built over a period of two hundred years from the 1420s. The nave and aisles were completed first, but when the twin towers of the western façade were finally added in 1507, the foundations proved inadequate and they soon began to sink. With money in short supply, it was decided to remove the top sections of the towers – hence the truncated versions of today.

Inside the church, the sweeping lines of the nave are intercepted by an impressive 1499 rood screen and a Baroque wooden pulpit, depicting the conversion of Saint Norbert. Norbert was a wealthy but irreligious German noble, who was hit by lightning while riding. He was unhurt but his horse died under him, and this led to his devoting himself to the church.

The church also houses the Religious Art Museum which has three exquisite paintings by Dieric Bouts (1415–75). Born in the Netherlands, Bouts spent most of his working life in Leuven, where he became the town's official artist. In his *Last Supper* (1468), displayed here, Bouts painted Judas's face in shadow, emphasizing the mystery of Holy Communion rather than the betrayal.

## 🦶 Fochplein

Adjacent to the Grote Markt is the Fochplein, a narrow triangular square containing some of Leuven's most popular shops, selling everything from fashion to food. In the middle is the Font Sapienza, a modern fountain that shows a student pouring water through his empty head – a pithy view of the town's student population.

## 🏛 Museum Vander Kelen-Mertens

Savoyestraat 6. 🕿 (016) 22 6906.
🕐 Tue–Sun. 🖼

The Museum Vander Kelen-Mertens has fair claim to be Leuven's most enjoyable museum, with its well-presented collection arranged over two floors. Once the home of the Vander Kelen-Mertens family, the rooms are furnished in a variety of historical styles, ranging from a Renaissance salon to a rococo dining room. Much of the art on display is by the early Flemish masters, including the work of Quentin Metsys (1466–1550), who was born in Leuven and is noted for introducing Italian style to north European art. The collection also includes a beautiful *Holy Trinity* by Rogier

van der Weyden (1400–1464). Fine art is located in the first-floor galleries where there is also an impressive display of 16th- and 17th-century embroidered vestments, stained glass and Oriental ceramics.

## ⛪ St Michielskerk

Naamsestraat.
🕐 Jun–Sep: Wed, Sat & Sun.

One of Leuven's most impressive churches, St Michielskerk was built for the Jesuits in the middle of the 17th century. The church was badly damaged during World War II, but has since been carefully restored. Its graceful façade with its flowing lines is an excellent illustration of the Baroque style. The interior is regularly open to visitors for three afternoons during the summer months. The stunning 1660 carved woodwork around the altar and choir are well worth seeing.

## ⛪ Groot Begijnhof

Schapenstraat. 🕐 daily, for street access only.

Founded around 1230, the Groot Begijnhof was once one of the largest béguinages in Belgium, home to several hundred béguines (see p53).

The complex of 72 charming red-brick cottages (dating mostly from the 17th century) is set around the grassy squares and cobbled streets near the River Dilje. Leuven university bought the complex in 1961 and converted the cottages into student accommodation.

**The red-brick houses of Leuven's Groot Begijnhof**

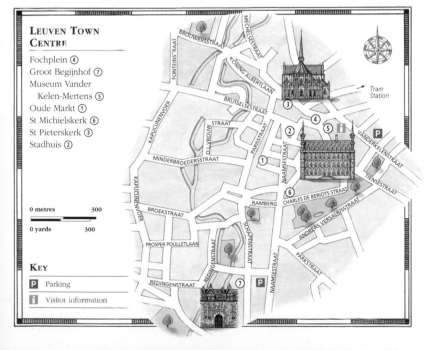

## LEUVEN TOWN CENTRE

0 metres 300
0 yards 300

### KEY

P Parking
🛈 Visitor information

# Bokrijk Openluchtmuseum ⑩

BOKRIJK VILLAGE CONTAINS an immensely popular open-air museum devoted to Flemish rural life before 1900. Set among the forest and rolling pasture of Limburg province, about 10 km (6 miles) northeast of the town of Hasselt, the open-air museum was established in 1953 by the provincial government. The land has been farmed since the Middle Ages, and in the early 20th century was used by the Belgian Farmer's Union for agricultural trials.

Bokrijk is made up several settlements which have been moved here and reconstructed, and has more than a hundred restored buildings. The collection is divided into three main sections, each representing a distinct geographical area. Manned by costumed guides, the farmhouses, barns and workshops offer various live demonstrations of an assortment of traditional crafts.

**Costumed character**
*Characters such as this man, dressed in typical peasant's clothing of the 19th century, enhance the Bokrijk's authentic atmosphere.*

**Visitor riding historic bike**
*The museum offers the chance to participate in a range of activities from cycling and rope-making to such traditional crafts as baking and wood-carving.*

**The Old Town**

**Pigeon Tower**
*The pigeon nests in this 1634 tower were located in the upper part of the building, which was accessible only by ladder, to prevent the theft of the young birds.*

**Fertile Uplands:
Limburg Haspengouw
and the Maasland**

★ **Interior features**
*Most of the buildings here have original interior features. This 18th-century fireplace has Delft tiles that depict biblical scenes such as the birth of Christ.*

**VISITORS' CHECKLIST**

Domain Bokrijk, 3600 Genk. ☎ (011) 26 5300. FAX (011) 26 5310. 🚉 Bokrijk. ⏰ Mar–Sep: 10am–6pm daily. ● Oct–Feb. ▨ 🚻
W www.limburg.be/bokrijk

The Fertile Lowlands: East and West Flanders

★ **Agricultural architecture**
*This 16th-century farmhouse was built in the style of houses seen in Brueghel's paintings. The windmill dates from 1788 and was used to grind grain. It still contains the original millstones.*

**The Poor Heathlands**, or the Kempen, is one of the principal geographical areas in the museum. It was an area of waste land where villagers eked out a living from their farms.

**Grain store**
*This elegant, timber-framed grain store, or* spijker, *dates from the 16th century. This building comes from Limburg province, where it probably formed part of a brewery.*

**Village priest**
*Many of the Bokrijk's costumed workers, such as this village priest, are on hand to explain what life was like in these pre-industrial rural areas.*

metres 50
yards 50

**STAR FEATURES**

★ **Agricultural architecture**

★ **Interior features**

# Charleroi ⑬

🏃 *200,000.* ✈ 🚇 🚌 🛈 *Square de la Gare du Sud, (071) 31 8218.*

WITH A POPULATION of more than 200,000, the industrial centre of Charleroi is one of the largest cities in French-speaking Belgium. Named after the Hapsburg king Charles II, who had the town fortified in 1666, it achieved prominence in the 1800s as the focus of a burgeoning coal-mining and steel area known as the Pays Noir (Black Country). Its busy centre fans out from the River Sambre, dividing into the Lower City, which is largely concerned with commerce and is of little interest to the casual visitor, and the Upper City, an older quarter around Place Charles II. The highlights are the **Museum of Fine Art** and the **Musée du Verre** (Glass Museum), with its collection of glass ranging from Assyrian necklaces to contemporary glasswork. From Charleroi, it is around 20 km (12 miles) west to the little town of Binche, the site of one of Belgium's most famous carnivals. Every year in March, parties lead up to a Shrove Tuesday festival.

**St Christophe's church in Charleroi's Upper City**

🏛 **Museum of Fine Art**
Place Charles II. 📞 *(071) 86 1132.* 🕐 *9am–12:30pm 1:15–5pm Tue–Sat.* 📷

🏛 **Musée du Verre**
Blvd Defontaine 10. 📞 *(071) 31 0838.* 🕐 *Tue–Sun.* ● *Mon.* 📷

# Mons ⑭

🏃 *90,000.* 🚇 🚌 🛈 *Grand Place 22, (065) 33 5580.*

PERHAPS BEST known for its association with both World Wars, Mons is actually an ancient town. The capital of the French-speaking province of Hainaut, Mons lies across the steep hill that first made

**The summer drawing room in the 18th-century Chateau d'Attre, near Ath**

it important. Natural strongpoints are rare in this part of the country and the Romans, observing the lay of the land, established a fortified camp here in the 1st century AD.

Today, Mons is a friendly town whose social life focuses around the Grand Place and its pavement cafés. Also overlooking the Grand Place is the 15th-century Hôtel de Ville, an imposing Gothic structure. A cast-iron monkey, known as the *Singe du Grand Garde*, sits on the outside wall near the main entrance, and is meant to bring good luck to those who stroke its head. South-west of the Grand Place are the town's well-preserved medieval streets and the Collégiale Ste-Waudru, a late-Gothic church.

Mons' other important sights are the **Musée du Guerre**, which focuses on the role of Mons in both World Wars, and the **Musée du Vieux Namy**, with its collection of ceramics and Delftware.

🏛 **Musée du Guerre**
Rue Houdain 13.
📞 *(065) 33 5213.*
🕐 *Tue–Sun.*

🏛 **Musée du Vieux Namy**
Rue Mouzain 31, Namy.
📞 *(065) 36 0825.*
🕐 *Apr–Sep: Sat–Sun.*

# Ath ⑮

🏃 *11,700.* 🚇 🚌 🛈 *Rue de Pintamont 54, (068) 26 9230, 26 5170.*

THIS QUIET TOWN grew up around the River Dendre. Ath is known for its festival – the Ducasse – which occurs every year on the fourth weekend in August. Held over two days, it features the "Parade of the Giants", a procession of gaily decorated giant figures representing characters from local folklore and the Bible, such as the Aymon brothers and the Steed Bayard (*see p99*), as well as David, Goliath and Samson.

The surrounding country of gently rolling hills is dotted with hamlets and farms, as well as historical sights. A few kilometres north-east of Ath is one of the most popular attractions

**The Gothic church Collégiale Ste-Waudru, Mons**

in the region, the **Château d'Attre**. This handsome 18th-century palace was built in 1752 by the Count of Gomegnies, chamberlain to the Hapsburg Emperor Joseph II, and was a favourite haunt of the Hapsburg aristocracy. Its interior is opulent, with ornate plasterwork, parquet floors and paintings. The River Dendre crosses the delightful grounds.

♣ **Château d'Attre**
Attre. ⟨ (068) 45 4460. ☐ to Attre. ☐ Jul–Aug: Thu–Tue; Apr–Jun & Sep–Oct: Sat & Sun. ● Nov–Mar.

**The southeast entrance of the chapel of St Hermes, Ronse**

## Ronse ⑯

⚐ 25,000. ☐ ☐ ⓘ Stadhuis, Grote Markt, Oudenaarde, (05) 531 7251.

SET AMONG the pretty hills of the Flemish Ardennes, Ronse is famous for its *Zotte Maandag*, or Crazy Monday festivities. Every year, on the second weekend in January, a boisterous procession of masked medieval characters parades through the town.

In medieval times, Ronse was where thousands of the mentally ill were taken to seek a cure. The object of the pilgrimage was a visit to the chapel of Hermes, a Roman saint thought to be an expert in exorcism. Today, the chapel retains three rusty iron rings that recall the days when the insane were chained up awaiting a miracle. A painting here depicts St Hermes on a horse, dragging a devil behind him.

## Ieper ⑰

⚐ 35,000. ☐ ☐ ⓘ 34 Market Square, (057) 23 9220.

IEPER IS THE Flemish name of the town familiar to hundreds of thousands of British soldiers as Ypres – its French appellation. During World War I, this ancient town, which was once a centre of the medieval wool trade, was used as a supply depot for the British army fighting in the trenches just to the east.

The Germans shelled Ieper to pieces, but after the war the town was rebuilt to its earlier design, complete with an exact replica of its imposing, 13th-century Lakenhalle (cloth hall). The original building was located by the River Ieperlee (which now runs underground), and boats could unload their wares on site. Today, part of the interior has been turned into the excellent "In Flander's Fields" Museum, a thoughtfully laid-out series of displays that attempt to conjure the full horrors of World War I. There is a simulated gas attack, personal artifacts and an array of photographs.

Another reminder of war is the huge Menin Gate memorial (just east of the Grote Markt) inscribed with the names of over 50,000 British and Commonwealth troops who died in and around Ieper but have no known resting place. The last post is sounded here every evening at 8pm.

**Weaving a tapestry at the Huis de Lalaing workshop, Oudenaarde**

## Oudenaarde ⑱

⚐ 30,000. ☐ ☐ ⓘ Stadhuis, Grote Markt, (05) 531 7251.

STRATEGICALLY situated beside the River Scheldt, the little town of Oudenaarde has suffered at the hands of many invaders, and little remains of the old town. The 16th-century Stadhuis has survived, and is adorned with beautiful stonework. The interior is open to visitors and is famous for an exquisitely carved oak doorway and its outstanding collection of tapestries – one of the finest in the country.

Oudenaarde was once a centre of tapestry manufacture and its products were bought by monarchs across Europe. Today, visitors can see tapestries being made at the Huis de Lalaing, a workshop near the Grote Markt.

### THE YPRES SALIENT

The Ypres Salient was the name given to a bulge in the line of trenches that both the German and British armies felt was a good place to break through each others' lines. This led to large concentrations of men and four major battles including Passchendaele in July 1917, in which hundreds of thousands of men died. Today, visitors can choose to view the site with its vast cemeteries and monuments by car or guided tour.

**View of the battlefield at Passchendaele Ridge in 1917**

# Street-by-Street: Ghent ⑲

A S A TOURIST DESTINATION, the Flemish city of Ghent has long been over-shadowed by its neighbour, Bruges. In part this reflects their divergent histories. The success of the cloth trade during the Middle Ages was followed by a period of stagnation for Bruges, while Ghent became a major industrial centre in the 18th and 19th centuries. The resulting pollution coated the city's antique buildings in layers of grime from its many factories. In the 1980s Ghent initiated a restoration programme. The city's medieval buildings were cleaned, industrial sites were tidied up and the canals were cleared. Today, it is the intricately carved stonework of its churches and antique buildings, as well as the city's excellent museums and stern, forbidding castle that give the centre its character.

**Bell on display in the Belfort**

**★ Het Gravensteen**
*Ghent's centre is dominated by the thick stone walls and imposing gatehouse of its ancient Castle of the Counts.*

**★ Museum voor Sierkunst**
*This elegant 19th-century dining room is just one of many charming period rooms in the decorative arts museum. The collection is housed in an 18th-century mansion and covers art and design from the 1600s to the present.*

**Graslei**
*One of Ghent's most picturesque streets, the Graslei overlooks the River Leie on the site of the city's medieval harbour. It is lined with perfectly preserved guildhouses; some date from the 12th century.*

To Ghent
St-Pieters

**Korenmarkt**
*This busy square was once the corn market; the commercial centre of the city since the Middle Ages. Today, it is lined with popular cafés.*

---

**STAR SIGHTS**

★ St Baafskathedraal

★ Het Gravensteen

★ Museum voor Sierkunst

### Museum voor Volkskunde
*A row of humble white-washed cottages house the excellent folk museum. Exhibits here include everyday objects from the late 19th century.*

**VISITORS' CHECKLIST**

240,000. 🚆 *Sint Pieters.*
🚌 *Sint Pieters.* 🚊 *Korenmarkt.*
🛈 *Botermarkt 17a, (09) 266 5232.* 🆆 *www.gent.be*

### Stadhuis
*Visitors can view this throne room in the town hall, which displays the 1780 coronation throne of Joseph II.*

### ★ St Baafskathedraal
*Dating from the 1200s, this magnificent Gothic cathedral was built over several hundred years.*

VRIJDAG MARKT

ANGE MUNT

ONDERSTRAAT

KAMERSTRAAT

HOOGPOORT

BELFORISTRAAT

POELJEMARKT

KAPITTELSTRAAT

St. Niklaaskerk

**The Belfort** is one of the city's great landmarks and, together with the adjacent Lakenhalle (cloth hall), was a centre of medieval trade.

| 0 metres | 50 |
| 0 yards | 50 |

**KEY**

- - - Suggested route

# Exploring Ghent

**Charles V's coat of arms**

THE HEART OF Ghent's historic centre was originally built during the 13th and 14th centuries when the city prospered as a result of the cloth trade. Ghent was founded in the 9th century when Baldwin Iron-Arm, the first Count of Flanders, built a castle to protect two important abbeys from Viking raids. Despite constant religious and dynastic conflicts, Ghent continued to flourish throughout the 16th and early 17th centuries. After 1648, the Dutch sealed the Scheldt estuary near Antwerp, closing vital canal links, which led to a decline in the fortunes of both cities. By the 19th century there was a boom in cotton spinning, and the wide boulevards in the south of the city reflect the affluence of the factory owners. Today, textiles still form a big part of Ghent's industry.

The Gothic turrets of Sint-Niklaaskerk seen from St Michael's Bridge

## Getting around

Ghent is a large city with an excellent bus and tram system. The main rail station, St Peters, adjoins the bus station from where several trams travel to the centre every few minutes. However, many of Ghent's main sights are within walking distance of each other. Canal boat trips are also available.

### 🔓 St Baafskathedraal

St Baafsplein. **(** (09) 225 1626.
❍ *daily.* **Adoration of the Mystic Lamb** ❍ *Apr–Oct: daily; Nov–Mar: Sun–Fri.* 🖼

Built in several stages, St Baafskathedraal has features representing every phase of Gothic style, from the early chancel through to the later nave, which is the cathedral's architectural highlight. The cavernous nave is supported by slender columns and has a soft dappled light filtering through the windows. In a small side chapel one of Europe's most remarkable paintings is on display, Jan van Eyck's polyptych *Adoration of the Mystic Lamb* (1432). Van Eyck is noted for his attention to detail, but is also universally respected as the first painter to master the art of working with oils. His use of colours and tones is so realistic that even today, hundreds of years after the work was completed, the skin of his characters looks real enough to touch. The cover screens of this seminal work feature portraits of the donor – Joos Vijd – and his wife below an Annunciation scene. The inside is stunning. Here, God the Father, John the Baptist and the Virgin Mary are pictured on the upper level in radiant tones, while the Lamb, the symbol of Christ's sacrifice, is the centrepiece below.

### 🏛 Stadhuis

Botermarkt 1. **(** (09) 266 5111.
🖼 ✔ *May–Oct: 3pm Mon–Thu. Tours depart from the Tourist Office.*

The Stadhuis façade displays two different architectural styles. Overlooking Hoogstraat, the older half dates from the early 16th century, its tracery in the elaborate Flamboyant Gothic style. The plainer, newer part, which flanks the Botermarkt, is a characteristic example of post-Reformation architecture. The statues in the niches on the façade were added in the 1890s. Among this group of figures it is possible to spot the original architect, Rombout Keldermans, who is shown studying his plans.

The building still serves as the city's administrative centre. Guided tours allow a glimpse at a series of large rooms. Perhaps the most fascinating of these is the Pacification Hall, which was once the Court of Justice and the site of the signing of the Pacification of Ghent (a treaty between Catholics and Protestants against Hapsburg rule) in 1576.

The tiled floor forms a maze in the Pacification Hall in Ghent's Stadhuis

**Views of Graslei and 16th-century guildhouses along the River Leie**

### 🏯 Graslei

The Graslei runs along the River Leie and is the eastern side of the Tussen Bruggen, once Ghent's main medieval harbour. The quay possesses a fine set of guildhouses. Among them, at No. 14, the sandstone façade of the Guildhouse of the Free Boatmen is decorated with finely detailed nautical scenes, while the late 17th-century Corn Measurers' guildhouse next door is adorned by bunches of fruit and cartouches. The earliest building here is the 12th-century *Spijker* (Staple House) at No. 10. This simple Romanesque structure stored the city's grain supply for several hundred years until a fire destroyed the interior.

### ♠ Het Gravensteen

Sint-Veerleplein. 📞 (09) 225 9306, 269 3730. ◯ daily. ● 1 & 2 Jan, 25 & 26 Dec. 🧷

Once the seat of the counts of Flanders, the imposing stone walls of Het Gravensteen (or the Castle of the Counts) overlook the city centre. Parts of the castle date back to the late 1100s, but most are later additions. Up to the 14th century the castle was Ghent's main military stronghold, and from then until the late 1700s it was used as the city's jail. Later, it became a cotton mill.

From the gatehouse, a long and heavily fortified tunnel leads up to the courtyard, which is overseen by two large buildings, the count's medieval residence and the earlier keep. Arrows guide visitors round the interior of both buildings, and in the upper rooms there is a spine-chilling collection of medieval torture instruments.

### 🏛 Museum voor Sierkunst

Jan Breydelstraat 5. 📞 (09) 267 9999. ◯ Tue–Sun. 🧷

This decorative arts museum has a wide-ranging collection contained within an elegant 18th-century townhouse. The displays are arranged in two sections, beginning at the front with a series of lavishly furnished period rooms that feature textiles, furniture, and artifacts from the 17th to the 19th centuries. At the back, an extension completed in 1992 focuses on modern design from Art Nouveau to contemporary works, and includes furniture by Victor Horta (*see p78*), Marcel Breuer and Ludwig Mies van der Rohe. One highlight is an Art Nouveau room designed by the noted Belgian artist Henry van der Velde.

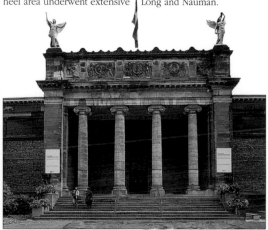

**Sofa at Sierkunst Museum**

### 🏯 The Patershol

North of the Kraanlei are the quaint little lanes and low brick houses of the Patershol, a district that developed in the 17th century to house the city's weavers. This once down-at-heel area underwent extensive refurbishment in the 1980s and is now one of the trendiest parts of town, with upmarket restaurants, cafés and shops.

### 🏛 Museum voor Schone Kunsten

Citadelpark. 📞 (09) 240 0700. ◯ Tue–Sun. 🧷

Ghent's largest collection of fine art is displayed in this Neo-Classical building dating from 1902. Inside, a rotunda divides the collection, with the older works in a series of rooms on the right and 19th- and 20th-century art to the left. The medieval paintings include the *Bearing of the Cross* by Hieronymus Bosch (1450–1516). There are also works by Rubens (*see pp14–15*), Anthony van Dyck (1599–1641) and Jacob Jordaens (1593–1678).

The museum is closed for renovations until September 2006. In the meantime, some of the Old Masters can be seen at the cathedral and at the Museum voor Sierkunst on Jan Breydelstraat.

### 🏛 Stedelijk Museum voor Actuele Kunst (SMAK)

Citadelpark. 📞 (09) 222 1703. W www.smak.be.

This museum includes works by Belgian and international contemporary artists, such as Bacon, Beuys, Broodthaers, Long and Nauman.

**The grand, Neo-Classical façade of the Museum voor Schone Kunsten**

# Street-by-Street: Bruges ⑳

**Traditional organ grinder**

WITH GOOD REASON, Bruges is one of the most popular tourist destinations in Belgium. An unspoilt medieval town, Bruges' winding streets pass by picturesque canals lined with fine buildings. The centre of Bruges is amazingly well preserved. The town's trade was badly affected when the River Zwin silted up at the end of the 15th century. It was never heavily industrialized and has retained most of its medieval buildings. As a further bonus Bruges also escaped major damage in both world wars.

Today, the streets are well maintained: there are no billboards or high rises, and traffic is heavily regulated. All the major attractions are located within the circle of boulevards that marks the line of the old medieval walls.

**View of the Rozenhoedkaai**
*A charming introduction to Bruges is provided by the boat trips along the city's canal network.*

**Onze Lieve Vrouwekerk**
*The massive Church of Our Lady employs many architectural styles. It took around 200 years to build, and its spire is Belgium's tallest.*

**Hans Memling Museum**
*Six of the artist's works are shown in the small chapel of the 12th-century St Janshospitaal, a city hospital that was still operating until 1976.*

0 metres     100
0 yards     100

### ★ The Markt
*Medieval gabled houses line this 13th-century market square at the heart of Bruges, which still holds a market each Saturday.*

VISITORS' CHECKLIST

119,000.  Stationsplein.  Stationsplein, Markt.  Burg 11, 8000 Bruges, (050) 44 8686.  www.brugge.be

**Oude Griffie, or Old Recorder's House**

**Blind Donkey Alley**
*This narrow, arched alley leads from the Burg to the 18th-century Vismarkt.*

**Heilig Bloed Basiliek**

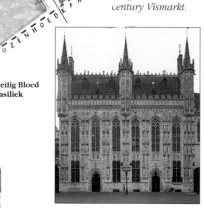

### ★ Stadhuis
*One of the oldest and finest town halls in Belgium, this was built between 1376 and 1420. Inside, the beautifully restored Gothic hall is noted for its 1385 vaulted ceiling.*

**Groeninge Museum**
*(see pp118–19)*

**Arentshuis Museum**

**Gruuthuse Museum**
*(see pp116–17)*

### The Belfort
*Built in the 13th century, the Belfort or Belfry is a stunning octagonal tower where the city's medieval charter of rights is held.*

KEY

– – – Suggested route

STAR SIGHTS

★ The Markt

★ Stadhuis

# Exploring Central Bruges

**B**RUGES DEVELOPED around a 9th-century fortress, built to defend the coast against the Vikings. Despite the vagaries of successive invasions by the French, between the 14th and 16th centuries Bruges became one of northern Europe's most sophisticated cities. Today, it owes its pre-eminent position to the beauty of its historic centre, whose narrow cobbled lanes and meandering canals are lined by an ensemble of medieval buildings. These are mostly the legacy of the town's heyday as a centre of the international cloth trade, which flourished for two hundred years from the 13th century. During this golden age, Bruges' merchants lavished their fortunes on fine mansions, churches and a set of civic buildings of such extravagance that they were the wonder of northern Europe.

**Bell maker in market**

Bruges' medieval buildings reflected in the River Dijver

## Getting Around
The centre of Bruges is compact, and as most major sights are near each other, it is easiest to walk around. However, the bus service is useful for getting from the railway station to the centre. Half-hour boat trips along the canals leave from several jetties. From March to November, boats depart twice every hour.

## The Vismarkt
Braambergstraat. ⬭ *daily.*
From the Burg an attractive arched path called the Alley of the Blind Donkey (Blinde Ezelstraat) leads to the open-air fish market with its elegant 18th-century colonnades. Fish is still sold here early each morning and business is brisk.

## 🏛 The Burg
The Burg, a pleasant cobbled square a few metres from the Markt, was once the political and religious focus of Bruges. It is also the site of the original fort around which the city grew. Some of the most imposing civic buildings are located here. The beautiful sandstone Stadhuis or town hall has a façade dating

from 1375, and is adorned with turrets and statues. In contrast, the Proostdij or Provost's House was built of grey stone in 1662 in the Baroque style and boasts an ornate entrance.

## 🏛 Stadhuis
Burg 12. 🎧 *(050) 44 8111.*
⬭ *daily.* 🔲
The intricately carved façade of the Stadhuis was completed in 1375, but the niche statues are modern effigies of the counts and countesses of Flanders. These were added in the 1960s to replace those destroyed by the French army over a century before. The building is still used as a town hall. It is also a popular venue for Bruges weddings. Inside, a staircase leads up from the spacious foyer to the beautiful Gothic Hall, which is open to visitors year round. This magnificent parliamentary chamber was built around 1400. Immaculately restored, the ceiling boasts some lavish woodcarvings including 16 beautiful corbels (brackets) bearing representations of the seasons and the elements. A series of paintings around the hall was completed in 1895, each portraying a key event in the city's history.

In an adjacent building is the Renaissance Hall, which houses a massive wood, marble and alabaster chimney designed by Lanceloot Blondeel. The chimney is one of the best sculptural works of 16th-century Flanders.

## ⛪ Heilig Bloed Basiliek
Burg 10. 🎧 *(050) 44 8111, 33 3767.*
⬭ *daily.* ● *Mon (in winter).*
The Basilica of the Holy Blood holds one of the most sacred reliquaries in Europe. The basilica divides into two distinct sections, the lower part being the evocative St Basil's chapel with its plain stone-pillared entrance and arches. The upper chapel was rebuilt in the 19th century after the French destroyed it in the 1790s. Here, brightly coloured decorations surround a silver tabernacle of 1611 which houses a sacred phial, supposed to contain a few drops of blood and water

washed from the body of Christ by Joseph of Arimathea. The phial was brought here from Jerusalem in 1150, and is still the object of great veneration. The church also has a museum that houses paintings, vestments and other artifacts.

## The Markt

The Markt is Bruges' main square and marketplace (a market has been held on this site since the 10th century). It is an impressive open space lined with 17th-century houses and overlooked by the Belfort on one side. The oldest façade on the square (dating from the 15th century) belongs to the Huis Bouchotte, which was the home of Charles II of England during part of his exile from 1656–7.

In the middle is a statue of Pieter de Coninck and Jan Breidel, two 14th-century guildsmen who led a rebellion against the French in 1302. Known as the *Bruges Matin*, they led Flemish soldiers to attack the French at dawn on May 18, 1302, killing almost all of them. This bloody uprising paved the way for a form of independence for the Low Countries' major towns. Rights such as the freedom to trade were subsequently enshrined in the towns' charters until the 15th century.

## The Belfort

Markt. ◯ daily. 🖼
The Markt is dominated by the belfry, whose octagonal belltower rises 83 m (272 ft) above the square. Built between the 13th and 15th centuries, the belfry is Bruges' most celebrated landmark as it was used to store the town's charter, and is therefore a constant reminder of the city's past as a centre of trade. Inside the tower a winding staircase leads up, past the chamber where the town's rights and privileges were stored, to the roof, where the views across Bruges are delightful.

**Bruges' Belfort or belltower overlooking the Markt**

## Groeninge Museum

See pp118–19.

## Arentshuis Museum

Dijver 16. 📞 (050) 44 8763. ◯ Apr–Sep: daily; Oct–Mar: Wed–Mon. 🖼
The Arentshuis Museum is housed in a genteel, 18th-century mansion overlooking the Dijver Canal. The interior is divided into two sections, with the ground floor devoted to a delightful selection of antique lace. Bruges was a centre of Belgian lace making and, although there were a few local factories, most of the work was done by women toiling in their own homes. The beautifully presented collection focuses on needlepoint and bobbin lace, with several fine examples of Bruges floral or Duchesse lace as well. Upstairs is the work of Frank Brangwyn (1867–1956), a painter and sculptor who was born in Bruges of Welsh parents. Most of Brangwyn's life was spent in Britain, but he bequeathed this collection to Bruges, as well as his drawings, furniture and carpets. Among his work, the dark and powerful canvases depicting industrial scenes are perhaps the most diverting.

**Statue of Breidel and Pieter de Coninck**

## Concertgebouw

't Zand. 📞 (050) 17 6999.
Built as part of the celebrations for Bruges' European City of Culture, this terracotta concert hall features a 28-m (92-ft) tower that offers great views.

## Gruuthuse Museum

See pp116–17.

## Onze Lieve Vrouwekerk

Mariastraat. ◯ Apr–Sep: Tue–Fri & Sun; Oct–Mar: Tue–Sat. 🖼 during services. 🖼 mausoleum only.
The Church of Our Lady took over two hundred years to build, starting in 1220, and incorporates a variety of styles. The interior, with its white walls, stark columns and black-and-white tiled floor has a medieval simplicity, while the side chapels and pulpit are lavishly decorated in the Baroque manner.

One of the church's artistic highlights is Michelangelo's sculpture *Madonna and Child* (1504–5), at the end of the southern aisle. This marble statue was imported by a Flemish merchant, and was the only one of the artist's works to leave Italy during his lifetime. In the choir there are fine paintings by Pieter Pourbus including a *Last Supper* (1562), and the carved mausoleums of the Burgundian prince Charles the Bold and his daughter Mary.

**The soaring spire of the Church of Our Lady**

# Gruuthuse Museum

**Facial fireguard**

THE GRUUTHUSE MUSEUM occupies a large medieval mansion close to the Dijver Canal. In the 15th century, it was inhabited by the merchant (or Lord of the Gruuthuse) who had the exclusive right to levy a tax on the "Gruit", an imported mixture of herbs added to barley during the beer-brewing process. The mansion's labyrinthine rooms, with their ancient chimneypieces and wooden beams, have survived intact and nowadays hold a priceless collection of fine and applied arts. There are tapestries, wood carvings, furniture and even a medical section devoted to cures of everyday ailments such as haemorrhoids. The authentic kitchen and original 1472 chapel transport visitors back to medieval times.

**2nd Floor**

**1st Floor**

**Façade of the Gruuthuis**
*The museum's Gothic façade, with its elegant tower, stepped gables and fine stone windows, was built in the 15th century.*

**Ground Floor**

★ **Charles V**
*This incredibly life-like terracotta and wood bust of Haps-burg king Charles V was carved in 1520 and is attributed to German sculptor Konrad Meit.*

**Entrance**

---

**STAR EXHIBITS**

★ **Charles V bust**

★ **Chapel**

**The Seven Free Arts**
*Dating from around 1675, this exquisite tapestry depicts the "free arts", which included music.*

## GALLERY GUIDE

*Laid out over three floors, the
collection is organized into
types of object from glassware,
porcelain and ceramics to
medical instruments in a
series of 22 numbered rooms.
Visitors may view the rooms
in sequence from 1–22 and
get a good sense of the
original uses and layout of
the house in doing so.*

**★ Chapel**

*Built in 1472, this oak-
panelled chapel on the
museum's second floor
overlooks the high altar
of the church next door.*

## KEY

- ☐ Glassware, porcelain and ceramics
- ☐ Kitchen
- ☐ Chapel
- ☐ Musical instruments
- ☐ Coins
- ☐ Tapestries
- ☐ Tools, weights and measures
- ☐ Entrance hall
- ☐ Textiles and lace
- ☐ Household implements
- ☐ Renaissance works
- ☐ Baroque works
- ☐ Reliquary and furniture
- ☐ Medical instruments
- ☐ Great Hall
- ☐ Weaponry

**House on the Southern Bridge at Minnewater**

### 🏛 Hans Memling Museum

Mariastraat 38, 8000 Bruges.
☎ (050) 44 8771. ⏱ Tue–Sun. ▨
This small museum (a former
13th-century hospital) contains
the works of Hans Memling
(1430–94), one of the most
talented painters of his era.
Among them, *The Mystical
Marriage of St. Catherine*
(1479), the central panel of a
triptych, is superb. The former
wards also house a collection
of paintings and furniture
related to the hospital's history.

### ⛪ Sint Salvator-Kathedraal

St Salvatorskof 1, 8000 Bruges.
☎ (050) 33 61 88. ⏱ Apr–Sep:
daily. ● 1 Jan, 25 Dec. ▨
Built as a parish church from
the 12th and 15th centuries,
this large, yellow-brick building became Bruges' cathedral
in 1788 when the French army
destroyed the existing one. The
interior is enormous and quite
plain except for a handsome
set of Brussels' tapestries hanging in the choir, and a 1682
organ adorned with angels.

**Pale brick tower of St Salvator-
Kathedraal in Bruges**

### 🌿 Minnewater

Just south of the Begijnhof,
Minnewater is a peaceful
park with a lake populated
by ducks and swans. Swans
have been here since 1448
when Maximilian of Austria
ordered they be kept in mem-
ory of his councillor, Pierre
Lanchais, who was beheaded
by the Bruges citizens.

Once this was a bustling
harbour which connected to
the canal network and the sea.
Today, Minnewater can be
visited by one of the tourist
barges that take visitors on a
tour of Bruges by canal. It is
also a popular spot for walkers
and picnickers who may view
the pretty 15th-century lock
gate and house and the 1398
tower (Poedertoren).

### 🏠 Begijnhof

Wijngaardplein 1, 8000 Bruges.
☎ (050) 36 01 40. ⏱ daily.
Béguines were members of
a lay sisterhood founded in
1245. They lived and dressed
as nuns but did not take vows
and were therefore able to
return to the secular world
at will. The begijnhof or
béguinage is the walled complex in a town that housed
the béguines. In Bruges, this
is an area of quiet tree-lined
canals faced by white, gabled
houses, with a pleasant green
at its centre. Visitors and locals
enjoy strolling here and may
visit the small, simple church
which was built in 1602. The
nuns who live in the houses
are no longer béguines, but
Benedictine sisters who moved
here in the 1930s. One of the
houses is open to visitors and
displays simple rustic furniture
and artifacts that illustrate the
women's contemplative lives.

# Groeninge Museum

**B**RUGES' PREMIER FINE ARTS museum, the Groeninge, holds a fabulous collection of early Flemish and Dutch masters, featuring artists such as the influential Rogier van der Weyden (1399–1464) and Jan van Eyck (d.1441). Hieronymous Bosch (1450–94), famous for the strange freakish creatures of his moral allegories, is well represented too, as are Gerard David (d.1523) and Pieter Brueghel the Younger (1564–1638). These early works are displayed on the ground floor of the museum, as well as a collection of later Belgian painters, most notably Paul Delvaux (1897–1994) and René Magritte (1898–1967). Originally built between 1929 and 1930, the museum is small and displays its collection in rotation, along with temporary exhibitions.

**Museum Façade**
*Originally built in 1930, the gallery was extended in 1994 to a design by architect Joseph Viérin. The old entrance is based on that of a Romanesque convent.*

**Last Judgement**
*Painted on three oak panels in the early 16th century, this detail from Hieronymous Bosch's famous tryptich depicts scenes of cruelty and torture. The strong moral tone of the work suggests that man's sinful nature has created a hell on earth.*

★ **The Moreel Triptych** *(1484)*
*This panel of the triptych, by German-born artist Hans Memling, was designed to adorn the altar in a Bruges church. It is said to be the first ever group portrait.*

### STAR PAINTINGS

★ **Virgin and Child with Canon by Jan van Eyck**

★ **The Moreel Tryptich by Hans Memling**

**Portrait of Bruges family** *(1645)*
*Jacob van Oost the Elder's focus on the affluence of this family overlooking their beloved city shows why he was Bruges' most popular artist of the Baroque period.*

1st Floor

Ground Floor

Main Entrance

## VISITORS' CHECKLIST

Dijver 12, 8000 Bruges. (050) 44 8750. Markt. 9:30am–5pm Tue–Sun (tickets sold until 4:30pm). 1 Jan, 25 Dec.

### Household Cares (1913)
*Rik Wouters used his wife Nel as the model for this statue, cast in bronze. The work's Fauvist style (see p15), is reflected in the bold planes that enhance the figure's anxious stance.*

### ★ Virgin and Child with Canon (1436)
*Jan van Eyck's richly detailed painting is noted for its realism. It shows van Eyck's patron, the canon, being presented to St Donatian by St George.*

### Serenity (1970)
*This unusually representative work by Paul Delvaux was commissioned by the museum, and retains elements of the artist's surrealist style.*

## GALLERY GUIDE
*The Groeninge is on one level with a two-storey extension. To the right of the main entrance there is a series of rooms displaying the early Flemish masters, and works from the 17th to 20th centuries. The extension, which is to the left of the main entrance, has temporary exhibitions on the ground floor, and work by the Bruges-born British artist Frank Brangwyn on the first floor.*

## KEY

- ☐ 15th and 16th centuries
- ☐ 17th to 19th centuries
- ☐ 19th and 20th centuries
- ☐ Frank Brangwyn
- ☐ Temporary exhibitions
- ☐ Non-exhibition space

# Exploring Northeast Bruges

IN THE HEIGHT OF THE summer and on holiday weekends, tourists pour into Bruges, and parts of the city centre often get too crowded for comfort. Fortunately, the narrow cobbled streets and picturesque canals to the northeast of the Markt never suffer from this, and this fascinating area remains one of the most delightful parts of Bruges. Streets of charming, medieval terraced houses are dotted with grand, yet elegant 18th-century mansions. The best approach is via Jan van Eyckplein, in medieval times the city's busiest harbour, from where it is a short stroll along Spinolarei and Potterierei streets to the many museums and churches that are found in this historic district.

**Statue of Jan van Eyck**

Lace-making skills on show at the Kantcentrum lace centre

The historic buildings and lovely canals of northeast Bruges

## ✠ Kantcentrum
Peperstraat 3. 📞 (050) 33 0072. 🕐 Mon–Sat. 🆓
The area from the whitewashed cottages to the east of Potterierei Street is one of several old neighbourhoods where the city's lace workers plied their craft. Mostly, the women worked at home, receiving their raw materials from a supplier who also bought the finished product.

Lace-making skills are kept alive at the Kantcentrum, the Lace Centre at the foot of Balstraat, where local women (and a few men) fashion lace in a variety of styles, both modern and traditional. It is a busy place, and visitors can see the lace-making demonstrations held every afternoon during the summer. Some of the finished pieces are sold in the Kantcentrum shop at very reasonable prices.

## 🏛 Brugse Brouwerij-Mouterijmuseum
Verbrand Nieuwland 10. 📞 (050) 33 0699. 🕐 daily. Call for details. 🆓
Up to World War I there were 31 breweries operating in Bruges. This brewery museum,

housed in a malthouse built in 1902, lies south of the lace centre and the Jerzalemkerk. On display are artifacts and documents that tell the centuries-old story of beer and brewing in the city. Next door to the museum, De Gouden Boom is a working brewery founded in 1584 that produces the noted beer Brugse Tripel and the spicy wheat beer (known as *bière blanche*), Brugs Tarwebier.

## ⛪ Jeruzalemkerk
Peperstraat. 🕐 Mon–Sat. 🆓
Next door to the Kantcentrum, the Jeruzalemkerk is Bruges' most unusual church. The present building dates from the 15th century, and was built on the site of a 13th-century chapel commissioned by a family of wealthy Italian merchants, the Adornes family, whose black marble tomb can be seen inside. Based on the design of the church of the Holy Sepulchre in Jerusalem, the structure possesses a striking tower with two tiers of wooden, polygon-shaped lanterns topped by a tin orb. Inside, the lower level contains a macabre altarpiece, carved with skulls and assorted demons. Behind the altar is a smaller vaulted chapel; leading

from this is a narrow tunnel guarded by an iron grate. Along the tunnel, a lifelike model of Christ in the Tomb can be seen at close quarters.

## ✠ The Kruispoort and the windmills
Medieval Bruges was heavily fortified. It was encircled by a city wall which was itself protected by a moat and strengthened by a series of massive gates. Most of the wall was knocked down in the 19th century, but the moat

The Jeruzalemkerk was built in 1497

has survived and so has one of the gates, the Kruispoort, a monumental structure dating from 1402 that guards the eastern approach to the city. The earthen bank stretching north of the Kruispoort marks the line of the old city wall, which was once dotted with some 20 windmills. Today, only three remain overlooking the canal. The first windmill, the Bonne Chieremolen, was brought here from a village in Flanders in 1911, but the second – St Janshuismolen – is original to the city, an immaculately restored structure erected in 1770. The northernmost mill of the three is De Nieuwe Papegai, an old oil mill that was relocated here in 1970.

**The massive Kruispoort is all that remains of Bruges' old city walls**

### 🛡 English Convent

Carmersstraat 85. **C** *(050) 33 2424.* ◯ *Mon–Sat.* 🎫 *obligatory.*
The English Convent was where dozens of English Catholics sought asylum following the execution of Charles I in 1642, and during Oliver Cromwell's subsequent rule as Lord Protector. The conventual buildings are not open to the public, but the nuns provide a well-informed tour of their beautiful church, which was built in the Baroque style in the 1620s. The interior has a delightful sense of space, its elegant proportions enhanced by its cupola, but the highlight is the altar, a grand affair made of around 20 types of marble.

### 🏛 Museum voor Volkskunde

Rolweg 40. **C** *(050) 33 0044.* ◯ *Tue–Sun.* 🎫
The Museum voor Volkskunde is one of the best folk museums in Flanders. It occupies

**These 17th-century almshouses house the Museum voor Volkskunde**

an attractive terrace of low, brick almshouses located behind an old neighbourhood café called the "Zwarte Kat" (Black Cat), which serves as the entrance. Each of the almshouses is dedicated to a different aspect of traditional Flemish life, with workshops displaying old tools. Several different crafts are represented here, such as a cobbler's and a blacksmith's, through to a series of typical historical domestic interiors.

### 🏰 Schuttersgilde St Sebastiaan

Carmersstraat 174. **C** *(050) 33 1626.* ◯ *Tue–Thu & Sat (May–Sep: also open on Fri).* 🎫
The Archers' guild (the Schuttersgilde) was one of the most powerful of the militia guilds, and their 16th- and 17th-century red-brick guildhouse now houses a museum.

The commercial life of medieval Bruges was dominated by the guilds, each of which represented the interests

**The St Sebastiaan guildhouse belonged to the archers**

of a particular group of skilled workmen. The guilds guarded their privileges jealously and, among many rules and customs, marriage between children whose fathers were in different guilds was greatly frowned upon. The guild claimed the name St Sebastian after an early Christian martyr, who the Roman Emperor Diocletian had executed by his archers. The bowmen followed orders – and medieval painters often show Sebastian looking like a pincushion – but miraculously Sebastian's wounds healed and he had to be finished off by a band of club-wielding assassins. The guildhouse itself is notable for its collection of paintings of the guild's leading lights, gold and silver trinkets and guild emblems.

### 🏛 Museum Onze Lieve Vrouw van de Potterie

Potterierei 79. **C** *(050) 44 8777* ◯ *Tue–Sun.*
Located by the canal in one of the quietest parts of Bruges, the Museum Onze Lieve Vrouw van de Potterie (Our Lady of Pottery) occupies part of an old hospital that was founded in 1276 to care for elderly women. There is a 14th- and 15th-century cloister, and several of the old sick rooms are now used to display a modest collection of paintings, the best of which are some realistic 17th- and 18th-century portraits of leading aristocrats. The hospital church is in excellent condition too; it is a warm, intimate place with fine stained-glass windows and a set of impressiv Baroque altarpieces.

# TRAVELLERS' NEEDS

# WHERE TO STAY

OR MOST OF the year, Brussels is primarily a business or political destination, and accommodation is often priced accordingly. The wide range of top hotels has one fine advantage for the visitor; weekend and summer deals make it possible even on a modest budget to stay in some of Europe's most luxurious establishments. The midrange of hotels is also well represented

**Métropole bellboy**

in the city, with period houses turned into stylish family-run hotels and chain hotels. To keep accommodation costs to a minimum, choose from Brussels' abundance of youth hostels and bed-and-breakfast options. *Choosing a Hotel* on pp128–9 will help you find at a glance the best hotels to suit your needs. A more detailed description of each hotel is listed on pp130–35.

**Hallway in the Hôtel Métropole on Place de Brouckère (see p132)**

## HOTEL LOCATIONS

WHILE BRUSSELS does not have a specific hotel area, there are clusters of hotels in various parts of the city. Centrally, the most fertile ground is between Place Rogier and Place de Brouckère, which is within walking distance of both the Upper and Lower Town and a short bus ride from most major sights. The streets to the west of the Grand Place are also well supplied for those who want to be in the historic centre of town, but road noise can be a problem at night. To the north, Place Ste-Catherine or the streets behind Avenue de la Toison d'Or also have plenty of options. Following the pattern of cities worldwide, hotels generally reduce in price the further they are from the centre. Bed-and-breakfast rooms are dispersed across the capital and can often be found in residential

districts at very good rates. When arriving in the city from abroad by train or plane, it is worth knowing that the Gare du Midi and the airport both have nearby hotel colonies, although the station surroundings are run down in places. The airport has principally attracted chain hotels, which often offer good value package deals with the national airlines, although sightseeing from here is inconvenient.

## ROOM RATES

HOTELS AT THE TOP end of the market offer exceptional standards of comfort and convenience to their largely corporate clients, and their prices reflect this. In general, prices are higher than in the rest of Belgium, but on a par with other European capitals. For a night in a luxury hotel, expect to pay €250 to €300 for a double room; the price for a room in the city averages in the €150 to €175 bracket.

**Façade of the Crowne Plaza Hotel, one of the hotel chain (see p131)**

However, there are numerous discounts available *(see Special Rates, p126)*.

Single travellers can often find reasonable discounts on accommodation, although few places will offer rooms at half the price of a double. It is usual to be charged extra if you place additional guests in a double room. Travelling with children is not the financial burden it might be in this child-friendly society *(see p127)*. Youth hostels cater very well to the budget student traveller and some also have family rooms.

## TAXES AND CHARGES

ROOM TAXES and sales taxes should be included in the cost of your room, so the price quoted should be what appears as the total. The price of car parking may be added. Some hotels offer free parking, others charge up to €17 a night. In hotels with no private car park, it is worth checking discounts for public parking facilities if these are located nearby. While many hotels are happy to allow pets, many will add a small nightly charge to the bill.

Breakfast is not always included in the price of a room, even in very expensive establishments. However, many hotels do offer excellent free breakfasts, so ask when you book. The fare usually consists of continental breakfasts, including good coffee, warm croissants and brioche rolls, preserves and fruit juice. Bear in mind that if the expensive place where you are staying is charging €20 for a morning meal, there will be plenty of places nearby offering equal quality for much less money. The usual price for a hotel breakfast ranges upwards from €2.50, but coffee and rolls are usually priced at around €6.20. Unusually, youth hostels also offer lunches and dinners at around €9.90 each.

Phone calls from hotel rooms can be extremely expensive, with unit charges of €.60 for even a local call not uncommon. To make a long-distance call, buying a phonecard and using the efficient public payphone service is several times less expensive. Hotel faxes or modem charges, when available, can also mount up.

Minibar charges are usually very high, although no more so than in any other western European city. Watching satellite or pay-TV stations can also be expensive. However, Belgium's advanced cable network and proximity to other countries means that there are usually more than 20 free channels to choose from including the BBC as well as French and German television.

## FACILITIES

IN A CITY with so many luxury hotels, fierce competition has led to ever more sophisticated gadgets and services for businesspeople. Several private phone lines, screened calls, free internet access, automatic check-out services, 24-hour news via Reuters, secretarial services, free mobile phones and even executive suites designed expressly for women

**A business traveller's room at the Hotel Alfa Sablon** *(see p132)*

are all on offer. Most of the top hotels also house extensive fitness facilities, including saunas and full gymnasiums, although there are few large swimming pools.

Brussels' reputation as a centre for fine dining is significantly enhanced by the hotel trade, with major hotels often offering several options, from expert gastronomy to excellent brasserie dining. For snacks and drinks, Brussels' hotels are known for their old-style, entertaining bars with piano music for those guests who prefer not to venture into the city at night. A handful have nightclub facilities where lively crowds meet for cocktails and dancing.

As one of Europe's major centres for the convention trade, Brussels is not short of meeting and function rooms, with the big hotels offering dozens of spaces for anything from conferences to society weddings and even relatively modest hotels offering good-sized rooms for business seminars and the like. Many

more expensive hotels have serviced apartments on offer; these can be useful for the greater freedom they provide.

**19th-century courtyard of the Conrad International** *(see p135)*

## HOW TO BOOK

ROOMS ARE available in Brussels at most times of the year, but you should book several days in advance to ensure that you get the place you want. In mid- and top-range hotels, a credit card is the usual way to book, giving card details as a deposit; in smaller hotels, bookings can often be made simply by giving your name and details of the day and time of arrival.

The **Tourist Office** offers a free, same-day reservation service on-site. It also publishes a practical guide to Brussels hotels, updated annually, which is available on request. For booking by telephone, **Belgian Tourist Reservations** is a free service for visitors and very helpful.

**Bar of the Hotel Arenberg, decorated with a cartoon mural** *(see p131)*

View of the Grand Place from a room at Auberge Saint-Michel *(see p130)*

## SPECIAL RATES

BRUSSELS IS AN exceptional destination, in that relatively few people come for the weekend or in July and August, meaning that often remarkable deals can be acquired at these times.

The cost of staying in one of the top hotels over the weekend or at off-peak times can plummet by as much as 65 per cent (for example, from €300 to €100 for a double room), so checking before booking about any special deals may save a large sum of money. A few hotels also offer discounts for guests who eat in their restaurants.

Some reservation services charge a small fee, but they can usually find competitively priced accommodation. Any deposit given is deducted from the final hotel bill.

Many travel agents also offer packages for visiting Brussels or Belgium, with accommodation working out less expensively than a custom-booked break.

Another option worth looking into is to check with your airline about possible discounts through its reservation services, and to find out about frequent-flyer bargains for affiliated hotels.

Bellboy at the Conrad International

## DISABLED TRAVELLERS

HOTELS IN Brussels and the rest of Belgium take the needs of disabled travellers seriously. Many have one or more rooms designed with wheelchair-bound guests in mind. Bear in mind that many hotel buildings in Brussels are historic and therefore may not be suitable. Most staff, however, will be helpful. It is wise to ask in advance whether the hotel can cater to travellers with special needs. Most hotels will allow the visually handicapped to bring a guide dog onto the premises, although again it is best to make sure that this is the case before you arrive.

## YOUTH ACCOMMODATION

BRUSSELS HAS several central, excellent youth hostels, with modern facilities, reasonably priced food and more privacy than is usually associated with hostel stays. Perhaps the best are the **Jacques Brel**, close to Place Madou, and the **Sleep Well**, which has disabled access. A bed in a four-person room should cost in the region of €19, rising to around €26 for a single room. Breakfast is sometimes included or costs from €2.50, with lunch and dinner for a charge of around €9.90. If you are not a member of the International Youth Hostel Foundation, rates will rise by €2.50 extra per night; membership cards, priced €12.40, are available at most hostels.

---

**The Hilton Brussels, formerly the Albert Premier Rogier** *(see p130)*

Joining is worthwhile when seeing the rest of Belgium, as there are over 30 hostels around the countryside.

## GAY AND LESBIAN ACCOMMODATION

THERE ARE NO specifically gay or lesbian hotels in the city, but same-sex couples should have few problems finding welcoming accommodation. The **Tels Quels** association is the best source of information about suitable lodging, and also has a documentation centre covering most aspects of gay life in the city.

## TRAVELLING WITH CHILDREN

CHILDREN ARE welcome at all hotels in Brussels. Most allow one or two under-12s to stay in their parents' room without extra charge; indeed, some hotels will extend this

principle to under-16s and under-18s. When travelling with children, it is worth reserving in advance as the hotel will find the room that best suits your needs. Families planning a long stay in Brussels should consider renting a suite or a self-catering apartment, which are economical.

## SELF-CATERING APARTMENTS

THERE IS NO shortage of self-catering accommodation in Brussels, with many places available for a short stay as well as by the week or month. A few are attached to hotels as suites, with the rest run by private companies. Prices start at around €300 per week, for a fairly basic but furnished one- or two bed-room apartment, to €990 or more for more luxurious lodgings. Contact the Belgian Tourist Reservations or visit the Tourist Office for a detailed list of suggestions.

## BED-AND-BREAKFAST

BED-AND-BREAKFAST, also called *chambre d'hôte*, accommodation can be a very pleasant alternative to staying in a cheap hotel, and rooms can often be found even in the centre of town. You may come across a bargain by wandering the streets, but the easiest way to find bed-and-breakfast lodgings is through the Tourist Office or one of the capital's specialist agencies.

**The interior of the George V hotel** *(see p130)*

# Choosing a Hotel

THE HOTELS AND HOSTELS on the following pages have all been inspected and assessed specifically for this guide. This chart highlights some of the factors that may affect your choice. During the week, Brussels is Europe's top business destination, and hotels with office facilities are included here; but sight-seeing travellers may find weekend discounts. For more information on each entry, see pp 130–35. They are listed by area and appear alphabetically within their price categories.

| Hotel | Price | Number of Rooms | Business Facilities | Restaurant | Garden | Quiet Location | Period Decor | Weekend Discounts |
|---|---|---|---|---|---|---|---|---|
| **THE LOWER TOWN** (see pp130–32) | | | | | | | | |
| Barry | € | 32 | | | | | | ● |
| Auberge Saint-Michel | €€ | 15 | | | | | ■ | ● |
| George V | €€ | 16 | | | | | | |
| Ibis Brussels City | €€ | 236 | ■ | | | | | |
| La Légende | €€ | 26 | | | | ● | ■ | |
| La Madeleine | €€ | 52 | | | | | | ● |
| Les Eperonniers | €€ | 21 | | | | | ■ | |
| Matignon | €€ | 37 | | ● | | | | |
| Mozart | €€ | 47 | | | | | ■ | ● |
| Noga | €€ | 19 | ● | | | ● | | |
| Welcome | €€ | 15 | | ● | | | ■ | |
| Windsor | €€ | 35 | ■ | | | | | ● |
| Arenberg NH | €€€ | 155 | ■ | ● | | ● | | |
| Art Hotel Siru | €€€ | 101 | ■ | ● | | | ■ | |
| Atlas | €€€ | 88 | ■ | | | | | ● |
| Citadines St. Catharine | €€€ | 169 | | | ■ | | | ● |
| Crowne Plaza | €€€ | 356 | | ● | | ● | ■ | ● |
| Dome | €€€ | 125 | ■ | ● | | | ■ | ● |
| Hilton Brussels City | €€€ | 285 | | | | | ■ | ● |
| Ibis off Grand Place | €€€ | 184 | | | ■ | | | |
| Queen Anne | €€€ | 60 | | | | | | ● |
| Vendôme | €€€ | 106 | ■ | ● | | | | ● |
| Aris | €€€€ | 55 | | | | | | ● |
| Bedford | €€€€ | 319 | ■ | ● | | | | ● |
| Novotel off Grand Place | €€€€ | 136 | ■ | ● | | | | ● |
| Radisson SAS | €€€€ | 281 | ■ | ● | ■ | | | ● |
| Amigo | €€€€€ | 174 | ■ | ● | | | ■ | ● |
| Carrefour de L'Europe | €€€€€ | 63 | ■ | ● | | | | ● |
| Métropole | €€€€€ | 410 | ■ | ● | ■ | | ■ | ● |
| Plaza | €€€€€ | 193 | ■ | ● | | | ■ | ● |
| Sheraton Towers | €€€€€ | 533 | ■ | ● | ■ | | | ● |
| | | | | | | | | |
| **THE UPPER TOWN** (see pp132–33) | | | | | | | | |
| Les Bluets | € | 10 | | | | | | |
| Argus | €€ | 42 | ■ | | | ● | | ● |
| Sabina | €€ | 24 | | | | ● | ■ | |
| Dixseptième | €€€€ | 24 | ■ | | ■ | ● | ■ | ● |
| Hilton | €€€€ | 434 | ■ | ● | ■ | | | ● |
| Le Sablon | €€€€ | 32 | | | | ● | | ● |
| Sofitel | €€€€ | 175 | ■ | | ■ | | ■ | ● |
| Stanhope | €€€€ | 50 | ■ | ● | ■ | ● | ■ | ● |
| Astoria | €€€€€ | 118 | ■ | ● | | | ■ | ● |
| Dorint | €€€€€ | 212 | ■ | ● | ■ | | | ● |
| Jolly Grand Sablon | €€€€€ | 193 | ■ | ● | | | ■ | ● |
| Méridien | €€€€€ | 224 | ■ | ● | | | | ● |
| Renaissance Brussels Hotel | €€€€€ | 257 | ■ | ● | | ● | | ● |
| Royal Windsor | €€€€€ | 266 | ■ | ● | | | ■ | ● |

**Price categories** for a double room (not per person), including service:

€ up to €62
€€ €62–112
€€€ €112–174
€€€€ €174–248
€€€€€ over €248

**WEEKEND DISCOUNTS**
Substantial drops in the room rate at weekends.

**RESTAURANT**
Hotel contains a dining room or restaurant serving lunch and dinner for hotel guests.

**BUSINESS FACILITIES**
Conference rooms, desks, fax, internet and computer service for guests.

**PERIOD DECOR**
Historic features, furniture and art decorate the public and private rooms.

**QUIET LOCATION**
Quiet residential neighbourhood or quiet street in a busy area.

| | | NUMBER OF ROOMS | BUSINESS FACILITIES | RESTAURANT | GARDEN | QUIET LOCATION | PERIOD DECOR | WEEKEND DISCOUNTS |
|---|---|---|---|---|---|---|---|---|
| **GREATER BRUSSELS** (see pp 134–35) | | | | | | | | |
| De Boeck's | €€ | 36 | | ■ | | ● | | ● |
| Les Tourelles | €€ | 21 | ■ | | | ● | ■ | ● |
| Sun | €€ | 22 | | | | ● | | |
| Abbey | €€€ | 47 | ■ | | | | | |
| Alfa Louise | €€€ | 40 | | | ■ | | | |
| Château Gravenhof | €€€ | 26 | ■ | | ■ | ● | ■ | |
| Holiday Inn City Centre | €€€€ | 201 | ■ | ● | | | | ● |
| Manos Stéphanie | €€€€ | 55 | | | ■ | ● | | ● |
| NH Brussels City Centre | €€€€ | 246 | ■ | ● | | | | ● |
| President WTC | €€€€ | 302 | ■ | ● | ■ | ● | | ● |
| Sofitel | €€€€ | 125 | ■ | ● | ■ | ● | | ● |
| Bristol Stéphanie | €€€€€ | 142 | ■ | ● | | | ■ | ● |
| Conrad International | €€€€€ | 269 | ■ | ● | ■ | | | ● |
| Gresham Belson | €€€€€ | 135 | ■ | | | | | ● |
| Hyatt Regency Brussels | €€€€€ | 99 | ■ | | | | ■ | ● |
| Montgomery | €€€€€ | 63 | ■ | ● | | ● | ■ | ● |
| Sheraton | €€€€€ | 304 | ■ | ● | | | | ● |
| | | | | | | | | |
| **ANTWERP** (see p135) | | | | | | | | |
| Firean | €€€ | 15 | | ● | | | | |
| Hilton | €€€€€ | 211 | | ● | | | | ● |
| | | | | | | | | |
| **BRUGES** (see p135) | | | | | | | | |
| de Pauw | €€ | 8 | | ● | | | | |
| 't Bourgoensch Hof | €€€ | 22 | | ● | | | | |
| Hotel de Tuilerieen | €€€€€ | 45 | | | | | | |
| | | | | | | | | |
| **GHENT** (see p135) | | | | | | | | |
| Erasmus | €€ | 11 | | | | | | |
| Gravensteen | €€€ | 49 | | | | | | ● |

## THE LOWER TOWN

### Barry

Place Anneessens 25, 1000 Brussels.
 (02) 511 2795. ⓕ (02) 514 1465.
@ hotel.barry@skynet.be *Rooms:*
*32.* 🛏 🎲 📺 📶 🍽 💶 *AE,*
*DC, MC, V.* €

Basic but comfortable hotel in an
early 20th-century building on a
slightly rundown square, south
of the Bourse and close by the
Anneessens metro station. Breakfast
is included in the already very low
prices. A 10 per cent discount
operates at weekends.

### Auberge Saint-Michel

Grand Place 15, 1000 Brussels.
**Map** 2 D3. ⓒ (02) 511 0956. ⓕ
(02) 511 4600. *Rooms: 15.* 🛏 🎲
📺 📶 💶 *AE, DC, MC, V.* €€

This former ducal mansion has a
peerless Baroque façade and stunning views of the square and Town
Hall. Unfortunately, not all the
rooms face on to the Grand Place;
Room 22 has the best view. Service
is excellent, but the noise from the
square may be a little intrusive.

### George V

Rue 't Kint 23, 1000 Brussels. **Map** 1
B3. ⓒ (02) 513 5093. ⓕ (02) 513
4493. @ reservations@george5.com
*Rooms: 16.* 🛏 🎲 🍽 📺 📶 📶
🛏 💶 *AE.* €€

One of the city's few examples of
English-inspired 19th-century architecture, the George V is just a short
stroll from the Bourse. The hotel
retains a degree of old-world charm.
Recent changes have made rooms
more comfortable, and those for
three and four people are among
the cheapest per person in Brussels.

### Ibis Brussels City

Rue Joseph Plateau 2, 1000 Brussels.
ⓒ (02) 513 7620. ⓕ (02) 514 2214.
*Rooms: 236.* 🛏 🎲 📺 📶 📶 🍽
🛏 📶 🍽 🍽 💶 *AE, DC, MC, V.*
€€

One of the attractions of this bland
but good-value hostelry just off
Place Ste-Catherine was its proximity to the 12th-century Black
Tower, now built into the walls of
the Novotel Brussels City next door.
The location is still convenient.

### La Légende

Rue du Lombard 35, 1000 Brussels.
**Map** 1 C3. ⓒ (02) 512 8290.
ⓕ (02) 512 3493. ⓦ www.hotella
legende.com *Rooms: 26.* 🛏 🎲
📺 🛏 📶 💶 *AE, DC.* €€

This reasonably priced and tourist-
friendly hotel is very close to the
Grand Place, and offers great value
in central Brussels. Its charmingly
dishevelled 18th-century buildings
are arranged around a pleasant
central courtyard. The rooms are
clean and functional, although costs
rise for rooms with bathrooms and
a TV. Breakfast is included.

### La Madeleine

Rue de la Montagne 20–22, 1000
Brussels. **Map** 2 D3. ⓒ (02) 513
2973. ⓕ (02) 502 1350. *Rooms: 52.*
🛏 🎲 📺 🍽 📶 💶 *AE, DC, MC,*
*V.* €

This friendly, basic hotel, usefully
located near the Grand Place, is
fêted by many Belgians for its
Parisian charms. Slightly shabby
furniture and frumpy decor char-
acterize the modern public areas,
but the rooms are perfectly decent.

### Les Eperonniers

Rue des Eperonniers 1, 1000 Brussels.
**Map** 2 D3. ⓒ (02) 513 5366. ⓕ
(02) 511 3230. @ leseperonniers@
skynet.be *Rooms: 21.* 🛏 🎲 📺 🛏
💶 *AE.* €€

The location, on a bustling street
near the Grand Place, is a great
bonus for this small and very basic
hotel. Low prices make it a
favourite with young travellers on
a budget. Many of the rooms have
showers, which for a small extra
fee are recommended. Breakfast is
not included.

### Matignon

Rue de la Bourse 10, 1000 Brussels.
**Map** 1 C2. ⓒ (02) 511 0888. ⓕ
(02) 513 6927. *Rooms: 37.* 🛏 🎲
📺 📶 🛏 🍽 🍽 🍽 💶 *AE, DC,*
*MC, V.* €€

The beautiful, 19th-century Belle
Epoque façade conceals a recently
renovated, family-owned hotel in
an excellent location opposite the
Bourse. The spot is a noisy one, but
the rooms are comfortable. Five
multi-occupancy suites provide
great-value accommodation.

### Mozart

Rue du Marché-aux-Fromages 23, 1000
Brussels. **Map** 2 D3. ⓒ (02) 502 6661.
ⓕ (02) 502 7758. @ hotel.mozart@
skynet.be *Rooms: 47.* 🛏 🎲 📺
📶 🛏 💶 *AE, DC, MC, V.* €€

On a street festooned with fast-food
outlets, this plain building has the
advantage of being a short walk
from the Grand Place. This hotel
is a decent option for those on a
budget, with pleasant oak-beamed
rooms, all with fridges. Breakfast is
included and service is helpful.

### Noga

Rue du Béguinage 38, 1000 Brussels.
ⓒ (02) 218 6763. ⓕ (02) 218 1603.
@ info@nogahotel.com *Rooms: 19.*
🛏 📺 🍽 🛏 🛏 🛏 📶 📶 💶
*AE, DC, V.* €€

This smart hotel on a quiet street
in the Ste-Catherine area is at the
top end of the cut-price accommodation market. The modern rooms
are cosy and in excellent condition. A games room with billiard
table is also on site.

### Welcome

Rue du Peuplier 5, 1000 Brussels.
ⓒ (02) 219 9546. ⓕ (02) 217
1887. @ info@hotelwelcome.com
*Rooms: 15.* 📺 🛏 🛏 📶 📶 🍽
💶 *DC, MC, V.* €€

The self-styled "smallest hotel in
Brussels" offers simple but tasteful
rooms in a sidestreet opposite
Ste-Catherine metro station.
The friendly owners keep their
establishment in immaculate
condition and offer guests a 5
per cent discount at the hotel's
restaurant, the excellent Truite
d'Argent *(see p153)*.

### Windsor

Place Rouppe 13, 1000 Brussels.
**Map** 1 C4. ⓒ (02) 511 2014.
ⓕ (02) 514 0942. *Rooms: 24.* 🎲
📺 💶 *AE, DC, MC, V.* €€

This is a cheerful and clean hotel
about 15 minutes' walk from the
town centre, with an appealing
19th-century stucco façade. Two
people can stay here for two
nights and still splash out on a
meal at Comme Chez Soi, the
Michelin three-star restaurant across
the street, for the cost of a night in
a mid-priced hotel *(see p149)*.

### Arenberg NH

Rue d'Assaut 15, 1000 Brussels. **Map**
2 D2. ⓒ (02) 501 1616. ⓕ (02) 501
1818. @ nhgrandplacearenberg@
nhhotels.be *Rooms: 155.* 🛏 🎲 🛏
📺 🍽 🛏 🍽 🍽 🛏 📶 🍽
💶 *AE, DC, MC, V.* €€€

This charming hotel on a quiet
street between the cathedral
and Place de la Monnaie has
recently been restored.

### Art Hotel Siru

Place Rogier 1, 1210 Brussels. **Map** 2
D1. ⓒ (02) 203 3580. ⓕ (02) 203
3303. *Rooms: 101.* @ art.hotel.siru
@skynet.be 🛏 📺 🍽 🛏 🛏 📶
🍽 🍽 💶 *AE, DC, MC, V.* €€€

Built on the site where 19th-century
poets and lovers Paul Verlaine and
Arthur Rimbaud once stayed, the

Siru was transformed in the late 1980s into one of Brussels' most distinctive hotels. Over 100 Belgian artists were invited to refurbish it, turning every room into a mini art gallery. Some would say that the hotel offers a better survey of contemporary Belgian art than any of the city's museums.

## Atlas

Rue du Vieux Marché-aux-Grains 30, 1000 Brussels. **Map** 1 C2. ☎ (02) 502 6006. ☒ (02) 502 6935. @ info@atlas-hotel.be ⬜ www.atlas-hotel.be **Rooms:** 88. ⬚ ① ⬚ ⬚ ⬚ ⬚ ⬚ ⬚ ⬚ ⬚ ⬚ AE, DC, MC, V. €€€

This comfortable modern hotel is off the fashionable Rue Dansaert. Rooms are spacious if slightly lacking in character. The relaxed atmosphere makes this hotel popular with businesspeople who prefer a more intimate establishment.

## Citadines St. Catharine

Quai aux Bois à Bruler 51, Brussels. **Map** 1 C1. ☎ (02) 221 1411. ☒ (02) 221 1599. @ stecatharine@citadines.com **Rooms:** 169 ⬚ ① ⬚ ⬚ ⬚ ⬚ ⬚ AE, DC, V. €€€

This apartment-hotel on Place Ste-Catherine offers studios and apartments at very competitive prices. The stark modern exterior is echoed in the functional decor. There is a peaceful courtyard and well-appointed rooms compensate for the initial lack of homeliness. The apartments are particularly good for long-term visitors.

## Crowne Plaza

Rue Gineste 3, 1210 Brussels. **Map** 2 E1. ☎ (02) 203 4011. ☒ (02) 203 5555. ⬜ www.crowneplaza.com **Rooms:** 356. ⬚ ⬚ ⬚ ⬚ ⬚ ⬚ ⬚ ⬚ ⬚ ⬚ ⬚ ⬚ AE, DC, MC, V. €€€

Built by a disciple of Victor Horta in 1910, this elegant building near Place Rogier was Grace Kelly's hotel of choice when she stayed in Brussels. Art Nouveau still features strongly in the interior here. The hotel combines period elegance with modern convenience, and 30 of the rooms are furnished in lavish Second Empire style. Expensive in high season.

## Dome

Boulevard du Jardin Botanique 12–13, 1000 Brussels. **Map** 2 E1. ☎ (02) 218 0680. ☒ (02) 218 4112. @ dome@skypro.be **Rooms:** 125. ⬚ ⬚ ⬚ ⬚ ⬚ ⬚ ⬚ ⬚ ⬚ ⬚ ⬚ ⬚ AE, DC, MC, V. €€€

This elegant edifice is the work of architect Alban Chambon, who also designed the Métropole. Built in 1902, at the height of the Art Nouveau movement, the Dome failed to stand the test of time, finally closing in the 1960s. Its fortunes changed, however, in 1990, with a launch combining the original Art Nouveau façade with a modern wing and minimalist decor. Each room has been individually decorated and all are spacious and comfortable.

## Hilton Brussels City

Place Rogier 20, 1000 Brussels. **Map** 2 D1. ☎ (02) 203 3125. ☒ (02) 203 4331. @ ras.brusselscity@hilton.com **Rooms:** 285. ⬚ ① ⬚ ⬚ ⬚ ⬚ ⬚ ⬚ €€€

Before World War II, this attractive Art Deco establishment had ambitions to become one of Brussels' best hotels. After the war it went into steady decline, becoming a comfortable establishment for budget travellers. Acquired by the Hilton Group in 2001, the Brussels has been fully refurbished.

## Ibis off Grand Place

Rue du Marché-aux-Herbes 100, 1000 Brussels. **Map** 2 D3. ☎ (02) 514 4040. ☒ (02) 514 5067. **Rooms:** 184. ⬚ ① ⬚ ⬚ ⬚ ⬚ ⬚ AE, DC, MC, V. €€€

This reliable, functional and professional chain hotel near the Grand Place has little to delight visitors but nothing to offend. With a sister hotel near Place Ste-Catherine, the chain is less expensive than similar hotels. Breakfast is not included.

## Queen Anne

Boulevard Emile Jacqmain 110, 1000 Brussels. **Map** 2 D1. ☎ (02) 217 1600. ☒ (02) 217 1838. **Rooms:** 60. ⬚ ① ⬚ ⬚ ⬚ ⬚ ⬚ ⬚ AE, DC, MC, V. €€€

This family-run hotel on a main road, a short walk from the city centre is relaxed, friendly and very good value for money. Once a three-star hotel, the Queen Anne has lost its accolade but little of its charm, with sizeable rooms, a warm welcome, a homely atmosphere and a good night's sleep guaranteed.

## Vendôme

Boulevard Adolphe Max 98, 1000 Brussels. **Map** 2 D1. ☎ (02) 227 0300. ☒ (02) 218 0683. ⬜ www.hotel-vendome.be **Rooms:** 106. ⬚ ① ⬚ ⬚ ⬚ ⬚ ⬚ ⬚ ⬚ ⬚ ⬚ ⬚ AE, DC. €€€

The Vendôme is a comfortable modern hotel north of Place de Brouckère catering mainly to business people. Each generously sized and tasteful room comes with an en-suite bathroom. The hotel feels less anonymous than any similar establishment.

## Aris

Rue du Marché-aux-Herbes 78–80, 1000 Brussels. **Map** 2 D3. ☎ (02) 514 4300. ☒ (02) 514 0119. ⬜ www.arishotel.be **Rooms:** 55. ⬚ ① ⬚ ⬚ ⬚ ⬚ ⬚ DC, MC, V. €€€€

Housed in a late 19th-century building with an attractive stone façade, this comfortable and efficient hotel is ideal for families. Situated right next to the Grand Place and only a few minutes' walk from the Îlot Sacré with its many restaurants, it offers a duplex room for four people at very reasonable rates. Otherwise, prices are rather expensive, although breakfast is included. There are considerable discounts to be had for weekend bookings.

## Bedford

Rue du Midi 135, 1000 Brussels. **Map** 1 C3. ☎ (02) 512 7840. ☒ (02) 507 0010. @ info@hotelbedford.be **Rooms:** 319. ⬚ ① ⬚ ⬚ ⬚ ⬚ ⬚ ⬚ ⬚ ⬚ ⬚ ⬚ ⬚ AE, DC, MC, V. €€€€

Incongruously situated towards the rundown end of central Brussels, the Bedford is an efficient hotel that does what all hotels should: it keeps on improving. The rooms are excellent and the service is impeccable. Although the weekday price seems a little high, there is a 50 per cent reduction at weekends. The Grand Place is just a short walk away.

## Novotel off Grand Place

Rue du Marché-aux-Herbes 120, 1000 Brussels. **Map** 2 D3. ☎ (02) 514 3333. ☒ (02) 511 7723. ⬜ www.novotel.com **Rooms:** 136. ⬚ ⬚ ⬚ ⬚ ⬚ ⬚ ⬚ ⬚ ⬚ ⬚ ⬚ AE, DC, MC, V. €€€€

This extremely successful mid-market chain hotel, a stone's throw from the Grand Place, is good for families and groups. A sofa bed is installed in each room and children under 16 have free accommodation. Breakfast is not included. There is a well-equipped children's play area next to the breakfast room. Single travellers should be aware that the room rate is not reduced.

## Radisson SAS Hotel

Rue du Fossé-aux-Loups 47, 1000 Brussels. **Map** 2 D2. **C** (02) 219 2828. **FAX** (02) 219 6262. **W** www. radisson.com *Rooms: 281.* 🛏 1 🛗 TV 🎦 Y 🍴 🛎 📶 🔆 🍴 ⚑ 🏨 P Y 🍴 ⚑ *AE, DC, MC, V.* €€€€€

Built around a 12th-century section of the city walls, this Art Deco-inspired hotel near the Galéries St-Hubert is among the city's most impressive, with comfortable rooms tastefully decorated in Asian, Italian or Scandinavian styles. Services for guests include a personal answer-phone and free mobile phones. If required, tours around the city, as well as golfing trips, can be organized by the hotel. The hotel also has its own restuarant, the 2-star Michelin Sea Grill, which is among Brussels' finest *(see p153)*.

## Amigo

Rue de l'Amigo 1–3, 1000 Brussels. **Map** 1 C3. **C** (02) 547 4747. **FAX** (02) 513 5277. **W** www.hotelamigo. com *Rooms: 174.* 🛏 1 🛗 24 TV Y 🔆 🛎 🔆 🎦 🔆 🍴 ⚑ P Y 🍴 ⚑ *AE, DC, MC, V.* €€€€€

This elegant six-storey hotel occupies the site of a 16th-century prison, only a minute's stroll from the Grand Place. The luxurious rooms, recently renovated, are decorated in the style of the Spanish Renaissance, which was popular during the reign of the French king Louis XV. The Amigo offers a range of excellent facilities and an extremely friendly, helpful service in what is primarily a business hotel. The marble bath-rooms are suavely charming if slightly cramped. There is also a good choice of restaurants. Breakfast is included in the price of the room. Rates from Friday through Sunday nights inclusive are reduced by half.

## Carrefour de l'Europe

Rue du Marché-aux-Herbes 110, 1000 Brussels. **Map** 2 D3. **C** (02) 504 9400. **FAX** (02) 504 9500. **@** info@carrefoureurope.net *Rooms: 63.* 🛏 24 TV 🔆 Y 🛎 🔆 🔆 Y 🍴 ⚑ *AE, DC, MC, V.* €€€€€

This business-oriented hotel is in a modern building near the Grand Place and the Gare Centrale. The rooms are uniformly decorated but comfortable; the double glazing, important in this busy city, ensures that the worst of the city's noise is kept at bay.

## Métropole

Place de Brouckère 31, 1000 Brussels. **Map** 1 D2. **C** (02) 217 2300. **FAX** (02) 218 0220. **W** www.metropolehotel. be *Rooms: 410.* 🛏 1 🛗 24 TV Y 🔆 🛎 🔆 🍴 Y 🍴 ⚑ *AE, DC, MC, V.* €€€€€

Located on the busy, crowded but central Place de Brouckère, this Belle Epoque masterpiece dates from 1895 and inside recalls the city in its Art Nouveau heyday. The period lift offers a wonderful view of the richly decorated lobby with its high ceilings, gilt cornices and crystal chandeliers. The modern rooms are comfortable if a touch less characterful. The bar is splendidly decorated with Corinthian columns, palm plants and roomy sofas. The room price includes a good continental breakfast.

## Plaza

Boulevard Adolphe Max 118–126, 1000 Brussels. **Map** 2 D1. **C** (02) 278 0100. **FAX** (02) 278 0101. **W** www.leplaza-brussels.be *Rooms: 193.* 🛏 1 🛗 TV 🔆 Y 🔆 🛎 🔆 🔆 🍴 P Y 🍴 ⚑ *AE, DC, MC, V.* €€€€€

The quarters of choice for senior German officers during World War II, this classic 1930s building on a rather downbeat street off Place de Brouckère has been resurrected after a 20-year closure. Combining old-fashioned style with state-of-the-art facilities, period features include chandeliers and Murano glassware. Several rooms are tailored to busi-nesswomen, and have been deco-rated in a gently relaxing pastel pale turquoise with hairdryers and extra-special toiletries.

## Sheraton Towers

Place Rogier 3, 1210 Brussels. **Map** 2 D1. **C** (02) 224 3111. **FAX** (02) 224 3456. **W** www.sheraton.com/brussels *Rooms: 533.* 🛏 🛗 24 TV Y 🔆 🛎 🔆 🔆 🍴 P Y 🍴 ⚑ *AE, DC, MC, V.* €€€€€

Even among the looming sky-scrapers that rear over Place Rogier, there is no mistaking the twin towers of the capital's biggest hotel. The emphasis here is firmly on comfort, with large rooms deco-rated in understated brown and deep red tones. This is a luxurious and relaxing environment for businesspeople to work, rest or play with ease. Some rooms have private offices, and all have well-equipped work stations. The indoor swimming-pool on the 30th floor has spectacular views over the city.

## Les Bluets

Rue Berckmans 124, 1060 Brussels. **C** (02) 534 3983. **FAX** (02) 543 0970. **W** www.geocities.com/ les_bluets/angl1/html *Rooms: 10.* 🛏 TV 🔆 🔆 *AE, DC, MC, V.* €

This charming late-19th-century hotel is non-smoking throughout. The decor features antique furniture, lots of plants and caged birds. Rooms are simply furnished and breakfast is included in the already reasonable price.

## Argus

Rue Capitaine Crespel 6, 1050 Brussels. **Map** 2 D5. **C** (02) 514 0770. **FAX** (02) 514 1222. **W** www.hotel-argus.be *Rooms: 42.* 🛏 1 TV Y 🔆 P 🔆 *AE, DC, MC, V.* €€

Handily placed between the Porte de Namur and Place Louise, this tasteful, quiet hotel makes a good base for exploring the whole city. The rooms are clean and comfortable. Prices drop further at weekends and through-out July and August.

## Sabina

Rue du Nord 78, 1000 Brussels. **Map** 2 F2. **C** (02) 218 2637. **FAX** (02) 219 3239. **W** www.hotel sabina.be *Rooms: 24.* 🛏 1 TV 🔆 🍴 P Y 🔆 *AE, DC.* €€

This friendly and well-kept hotel occupies an elegant 19th-century building. Inside, authentic wood panelling and fireplaces enhance the peaceful atmosphere. The hotel is located on a quiet street in the residential area around Place Madou. It is also close to Brussels' main attractions and the European government institutions.

## Dixseptième

Rue de la Madeleine 25, 1000 Brussels. **Map** 2 D3. **C** (02) 517 1717. **FAX** (02) 502 6424. **@** info@ledixseptieme.be **W** www.ledixseptieme.be *Rooms: 24.* 🛏 1 TV 🔆 🔆 🔆 🔆 *AE, DC, MC, V.* €€€€

Built in the 17th century as the home of the Spanish ambassador, this small, peaceful hotel offers a calming break from the bustling Ilôt Sacré. Each room is named after a Belgian artist, and enthusiasts can refresh their painting knowledge thanks to the art library in the lounge. Many of the rooms are authentically decorated in Baroque style with parquet flooring throughout, and flamboyant crystal chandeliers in the public areas. A splendid Louis XVI staircase connects some of the rooms, several of which look out over a private courtyard.

## Hilton

Boulevard de Waterloo 38, 1000 Brussels. **Map** 2 E5. (02) 504 1111. FAX (02) 504 2111. W www.hilton.com **Rooms:** 434. 24 TV Y AE, DC, MC, V. €€€€

In addition to the usual features – crisp service, business facilities and large, comfortable rooms – the Hilton offers personal security guards and such facilities for Japanese visitors as Japanese speakers, newspapers and kimonos. The lobby is decorated with a large golden frieze depicting the Grand Place. The hotel also houses the Michelin-starred restaurant Maison de Boeuf.

## Le Sablon

Rue de la Paille 2–8, 1000 Brussels. (02) 513 6040 FAX (02) 511 8141. W www.hotellesablon.be **Rooms:** 32. 1 TV Y AE, DC, MC, V. €€€€

This calm, refined hotel boasts a great location near the Place du Grand Sablon, which is noted for its appealing antique shops and enticing cafés. An attractive late 19th-century façade houses a light, inviting contemporary interior. There is a garden and a sauna, and the four large, split-level suites are particularly comfortable.

## Sofitel

Avenue de la Toison d'Or 40, 1050 Brussels. **Map** 2 E5. (02) 514 2200. FAX (02) 514 5744. W www. accorhotels.com **Rooms:** 175. TV AE, DC, MC, V. €€€€

Dwarfed by the looming 1960s-built Hilton on the opposite side of the street, this relatively discreet branch of the upmarket French chain easily holds its own in terms of elegance. The most impressive features are the English-style bar and library with its comfortable leather chairs. It is also possible to escape from the bustle of the city in the Sofitel's beautiful garden. Inside the rooms, king-size beds and a quiet, comfortable atmosphere attract plenty of admirers. The hotel does not have its own restaurant but is within a short walk of a selection of Brussels' finest.

## Stanhope

Rue du Commerce 9, 1000 Brussels. **Map** 2 F4. (02) 506 9111. FAX (02) 512 1708. W www.summit hotels. com **Rooms:** 50. 1 TV AE, DC, MC, V. €€€€

The Stanhope represents a luxurious Belgian vision of traditional upper-class historic British hospitality. The hotel has taken over three adjacent townhouses to deliver its elegant old-world service, which includes chauffeur-driven cars, afternoon tea and newspapers pushed under the door in the mornings. The rooms have marble bathrooms, handmade furniture and paintings on the walls. Breakfast is included. There are very good rates at weekends.

## Astoria

Rue Royale 103, 1000 Brussels. **Map** 2 E2. (02) 227 0505. FAX (02) 217 1150. W www.sofitel.com **Rooms:** 118. 1 TV Y AE, DC, MC, V. €€€€€

This opulent Belle Epoque masterpiece recalls the capital's glory days of the early 20th century, when such famous statesmen as Eisenhower and Churchill were among its most distinguished guests. The lobby, staircase, wood-panelled lift and furnishings are all original. The recently renovated rooms retain their individual character, and each is triple-glazed. The Pullman bar is in a former Orient Express carriage.

## Dorint

Boulevard Charlemagne 11–19, 1000 Brussels. **Map** 3 B2. (02) 231 0909. FAX (02) 231 3371. W www.dorint.be **Rooms:** 212. 1 TV Y AE, DC, MC, V. €€€€€

Situated near the European government complex, the Dorint is favoured by visiting journalists, diplomats and politicians. The hotel offers ISDN lines, translation cabins and a bar with a Reuters terminal updating news 24 hours a day. Try the fitness club with its Turkish bath, sauna and solarium, or take a stroll in the tranquil Oriental garden. For a taste of Brussels' culture, contemporary works by local photographers hang in the rooms.

## Jolly Grand Sablon

Rue Boedenbroeck 2–4, 1000 Brussels. **Map** 2 D4. (02) 512 8800. FAX (02) 512 6766. W www.jollyhotels.it **Rooms:** 193. 1 TV Y AE, DC, MC, V. €€€€€

With an unbeatable location on the southern edge of the Place du Grand Sablon, this Italian chain's flagship Brussels hotel offers impeccable service and grand rooms. The façade is an unobtrusive addition to the wonderful Baroque masterpieces all around it. Good weekend rates.

## Méridien

Carrefour de l' Europe 3, 1000 Brussels. (02) 548 4211. FAX (02) 548 4080. W www.meridien.be **Rooms:** 224. 1 24 TV Y AE, DC, MC, V. €€€€€

This luxurious modern hotel is very close to the Grand Place but is also opposite the Gare Centrale, which can be, to some tastes, a slightly seedy area. The hotel is decorated in modern style and has a plush lobby featuring a large brass chandelier; this is a popular meeting place with a comfortable atmosphere that is enhanced by a regular pianist. The rooms are furnished in English Victorian style. The hotel manages to cater to both business travellers and families, with corporate facilities such as multilingual staff.

## Renaissance Brussels Hotel

Rue de Parnasse 19, 1050 Brussels. (02) 505 2929. FAX (02) 505 2555. **Rooms:** 257. 1 TV Y AE, DC, MC, V. €€€€€

The first luxury hotel to establish itself near the European Parliament, just a few minutes from the Palais Royal, the former Archimède was taken over by Renaissance in 2001. Each bedroom is large and well equipped. Guests also have access to the world-class Academy Gym next door.

## Royal Windsor

Rue Duquesnoy 5, 1000 Brussels. **Map** 2 D3. (02) 505 5555. FAX (02) 505 5500. W www.warwickhotels. com **Rooms:** 266. 24 TV Y AE, DC, MC, V. €€€€€

This characterful deluxe hotel near the Grand Place has small but exquisite facilities. The sumptuous French-styled bedrooms are reckoned to be Brussels' most expensive per square metre. However, the wonderful marble bathrooms make up for the lack of space. Other facilities include a restaurant with a glorious circular stained-glass window in its ceiling.

## GREATER BRUSSELS

### De Boeck's

Rue Veydt 40, 1050 Brussels.
(02) 537 4033. FAX (02) 534 4037. @ deboecks@hotel.skynet.be
**Rooms:** 36. AE, DC. €€

De Boeck's is a converted turn-of-the-century townhouse on a quiet street not far from Avenue Louise. The pleasant rooms have a family feel and many cared-for touches. Breakfast is included. The city centre is easily accessible by the 93 or 94 tram. There is a weekend discount on the already very reasonable daily rate.

### Les Tourelles

Avenue Winston Churchill 135, 1180 Brussels. (02) 344 9573. FAX (02) 346 4270. @ info@lestourelles.be
**Rooms:** 21. AE, MC, V. €€

Les Tourelles' fake medieval towers and rustic cottage façade stand out among the modern villas and stucco townhouses of Avenue Winston Churchill. Inside, the wood-heavy decor has an old-fashioned feel, while the hotel's atmosphere retains the personal idiosyncracies that hotel schools have, weirdly, done their best to stamp out. This family-friendly place also offers an evening babysitting service.

### Sun

Rue du Berger 38, 1050 Brussels.
**Map** 2 E5. (02) 511 2119.
FAX (02) 512 3271. @ sunhotel@skynet.be **Rooms:** 22. AE, DC, MC, V. €€

If a firm mattress is essential to your slumber, then this comfortable, homely establishment near Porte de Namur will suit you. Although the quiet street on which it stands may be a little run down, this small hotel is spotlessly clean and popular, with light-green decor and a glass mural in the breakfast room.

### Abbey

Kerkeblokstraat 5, 1850 Grimbergen.
(02) 270 0888. FAX (02) 270 8188.
@ info@hotelabbey.be **Rooms:** 47. AE, DC, MC, V. €€€

This modern, villa-style hotel just north of the city is a pleasant alternative to staying near the airport. It is popular with businesspeople in town for an event at the Heysel Exhibition Centre. The rooms are large and well appointed, with massage showers in the bathrooms.

### Alfa Louise

Avenue Louise 212, 1050 Brussels.
**Map** 2 D5. (02) 644 2929.
FAX (02) 644 1878. @ info@alfalouise.be **Rooms:** 40. AE, DC, MC, V. €€€

This is one of the most spacious hotels in the city. All of the Alfa's rooms are extremely large, with a sizeable desk and a pleasant sitting area, while the bathrooms come with hairdryer and bathrobes. Many also have individual terraces. The city centre is a 10-minute tram-ride away (on the 93 or 94). The hotel does not possess its own fitness facilities, but there is a health centre nearby, with gym and pool.

### Château Gravenhof

Alsembergsesteenweg 676, 1653 Dworp. (02) 380 4499.
FAX (02) 380 4060. W www.gravenhof.be **Rooms:** 26. AE, DC, MC, V. €€€

For those visitors to Brussels who prefer a quieter location, this 18th-century manor house is ideal. Located in handsome grounds in a leafy village, not far south of the city, the hotel is close to a golf course and equestrian facilities. Perhaps because it is not in the city proper, Château Gravenhof attracts more convention clients than overnight visitors, which may explain the relatively low prices on offer. Period fittings and furniture create an atmosphere of relaxed gentility, and the luxurious feel of the place represents extremely good value for money.

### Holiday Inn City Centre

Chaussée de Charleroi 38, 1060 Brussels. (02) 533 6666. FAX (02) 538 9014. W www.holidayinn.com
**Rooms:** 201. AE, DC, MC, V. €€€€

The Holiday Inn's flagship Brussels branch is not exactly in the city centre, but it is close to Avenue Louise and the major sights are a short ride away on the 91 or 92 trams. The building is modern and the rooms have all the comforts of a business-oriented hotel, including a safe, room service and a trouser press. Triple-glazing makes the rooms surprisingly quiet, while the firm queen-size double beds (in some rooms) ensure a good night's sleep. The service is polite.

### Manos Stéphanie

Chaussée de Charleroi 28, 1060 Brussels. (02) 539 0250. FAX (02) 537 5729. W www.manoshotel.com
**Rooms:** 55. AE, DC, MC, V. €€€€€

This charming, friendly hotel resides in a converted townhouse, whose Parisian flavour is popular with visiting actors and well-heeled French families. While all rooms are well-appointed and spacious, some are larger than others: the split-level room 103 is particularly enticing. Breakfast is included. There is no restaurant, but a chef is available every evening until 10:30pm for room service orders.

### NH Brussels City Centre

Chaussée de Charleroi 17, 1060 Brussels. (02) 539 0160. FAX (02) 537 9011. @ nhbrusselscitycentre@nh-hotels.com **Rooms:** 246. AE, DC, MC, V. €€€€

This hotel has been recently refurbished, with the installation of a maritime-themed bar, Deck 17, the most obvious sign of restored pride. The rooms are all to three-star standard and the staff will make your stay as pleasant as possible.

### President WTC

Boulevard du Roi Albert II 248, 1000 Brussels. **Map** 2 D1. (02) 203 2020. FAX (02) 203 2440.
@ wtc.info@presidenthotel.be
**Rooms:** 302. AE, DC, MC, V. €€€€

The best of the three President hotels in Brussels, this business-oriented establishment near the World Trade Centre is the hotel of choice for conference organizers. The sky-blue and white rooms are fresher than in most business hotels, and the Jacuzzi, sunbeds and table-tennis tables are added benefits for the traveller in need of relaxation.

### Sofitel

Bessenveldstraat 15, 1831 Diegem.
(02) 713 6666. FAX (02) 721 4345. @ ho548@accor-hotels.be
**Rooms:** 125. AE, DC, MC, V. €€€€€

This smart, professional establishment is part of an upmarket French chain. The lobby and public spaces are discreetly luxurious with deep comfortable armchairs and sofas. The rooms are large with inviting king-size double beds. Efficient triple-glazing excludes the noise from the nearby Brussels National Airport. The open-air swimming pool, surrounded by the hotel's gardens, is a rare treat.

## Bristol Stéphanie

Avenue Louise 91–93, 1050 Brussels. **Map** 2 D5. (02) 543 3311.
FAX (02) 538 0307. W www.bristol.be
**Rooms:** 142.
AE, DC, MC, V. €€€€€

Norwegian entrepreneur Olav Thon turned the Bristol Stéphanie into a sophisticated homage to his native land. The large rooms and suites are decorated in chalet-style, with wooden floors, and some also have kitchen facilities. The hotel offers baby-sitting, as well as conference facilities and room service, and there is a heated indoor pool.

## Conrad International

Avenue Louise 71, 1050 Brussels. **Map** 2 D5. (02) 542 4242. FAX (02) 542 4200. W www.conradhotels.com **Rooms:** 269.
AE, DC, MC, V. €€€€€

Combining old-fashioned elegance with business conveniences (such as multi-line phones, modem and fax in the room, and 12 meeting rooms), this palatial establishment is perhaps the best of Brussels' luxury hotels. Former US President Bill Clinton is among the hotel's many celebrity guests. Even the standard rooms are huge, often featuring a mezzanine. There are two good restaurants here: Café Wiltcher and La Maison de Maître.

## Gresham Belson

Chaussée de Louvain 805, 1140 Brussels. (02) 708 3100. FAX (02) 708 3166. W www.ryan-hotels.com
**Rooms:** 135.
AE, DC, MC, V. €€€€€

This efficient hotel is conveniently located between Brussels National Airport and the Grand Place, and is only five minutes' drive from the EC headquarters. Facilities are especially good for business visitors, with fax and computer points in many rooms. Transport to and from the airport is included.

## Hyatt Regency Barsey

Avenue Louise 381, 1050 Brussels. (02) 649 9800. FAX (02) 640 1764. **Rooms:** 99.
AE, DC, MC, V. €€€€€

Awarded four stars by the Belgian authorities, the Barsey employed top French interior designer Jacques Garcia to provide an opulent feel for its loyal visitors, who are mostly businessman. The public rooms are decorated in traditional English style, with 19th-century antique furniture and silk drapery. Many of the rooms have views out over a private garden.

## Montgomery

Avenue de Tervuren 134, 1150 Brussels. **Map** 4 E4. (02) 741 8511. FAX (02) 741 8500. @ hotel@montgomery.be
**Rooms:** 63.
AE, DC, MC, V. €€€€€

Despite the futuristic façade, this luxurious hotel near the European institutions has a resolutely old-fashioned atmosphere. The rooms are decorated in three themed styles: Oriental, English and New England. Each room has a well-equipped office area with internet and fax connections. The hotel is a member of the Leading Small Hotels of the World group.

## Sheraton

Brussels National Airport, 1930 Zaventem, (02) 725 1000. FAX (02) 710 8777. W www.sheraton.com/brussels **Rooms:** 304.
AE, DC, MC, V. €€€€€

The Sheraton is the only hotel in Belgium to have its own airport, as Belgian critics never tire of joking. While the airport is not exclusively reserved for Sheraton guests, the hotel's on-site presence makes it improbably convenient for short-stay guests. A 24-hour business centre is available for those who want to work till departure.

## ANTWERP

## Firean

Karel Oomsstraat 6, 2018 Antwerp. (03) 237 0260. FAX (03) 238 1168. W www.firean.com **Rooms:** 15.
AE, DC, MC, V. €€€

A small, family-run hotel with a warm atmosphere. Trams run from outside the hotel, housed in an Art Deco building in a residential neighbourhood, to the city centre. Breakfast is included.

## Hilton

Groenplaats, 2000 Antwerp. (03) 204 1212. FAX (03) 204 1213. W www.antwerp.hilton.com **Rooms:** 211.
AE, DC, MC, V. €€€€€

Situated at the heart of the Old Town, behind a listed Baroque façade, the Hilton has large, well-equipped rooms. Facilities include a sauna and a solarium.

## BRUGES

## de Pauw

Sint-Gilliskerkhof 8, 8000 Bruges. (050) 33 7118. FAX (050) 34 5140. W www.hoteldepauw.be
**Rooms:** 8.
MC, V. €€

This family-run hotel, located in a quiet side street, offers great value for money and a warm, friendly service.

## 't Bourgoensch Hof

Wollestraat 39, 8000 Bruges. (050) 33 1645. FAX (050) 34 6378. W www.bourgoensch-hof.be
**Rooms:** 15.
MC, V. €€€

The rooms at this cosy hotel in the heart of the city centre are decorated in Flemish style, and some have romantic views of the canal. Breakfast is included.

## Hotel de Tuilerieen

Dijver 7, 8000 Bruges. (050) 34 3691 FAX (050) 34 0400. W www.hoteltuilerieen.com **Rooms:** 27.
AE, DC, MC, V. €€€€€

This canalside hotel occupies a beautiful 15th-century mansion, close to some of the city's best museums and tourist attractions. The hotel also offers a heated swimming pool, sauna, jacuzzi and solarium. Childminding available.

## GHENT

## Erasmus

Poel 25, 9000 Ghent. (09) 224 2195. FAX (09) 233 4241. @ hotel.erasmus@proximedia.be **Rooms:** 11.
AE, MC, V. €€

An immaculate family-run hotel with a lovely wood-beamed lounge and rooms with stone fireplaces. There is also a small, private garden.

## Gravensteen

Jan Breydelstraat 35, 9000 Ghent. (09) 225 1150. FAX (09) 225 1850. W www.gravensteen.be
**Rooms:** 49.
AE, MC, V. €€€

Housed in a 19th-century mansion, the Gravensteen has been refurbished in the Second Empire style.

# WHERE TO EAT

**Thai chef in Brussels**

IT IS ALMOST impossible to eat badly in Brussels. Some say one can eat better here than in Paris, and even meals in the lower- to mid-price bracket are always carefully prepared and often innovative. Venues range from top gastronomic restaurants to unpretentious local taverns where you can find generous servings of local specialities. If you tire of Belgian fare, try the variety of excellent local seafood and the range of ethnic cuisine that reflects the city's lively cultural diversity. The listings on pp146–53 give a detailed description of all the selected restaurants and the key features of each restaurant are summarized on pp144–5.

**Brasserie Horta in Centre Belge de la Bande Dessinée (see p146)**

## WHERE TO EAT

THE BELGIAN love affair with dining out makes for an astonishing concentration of restaurants and eateries: a 10-minute stroll from almost anywhere in Brussels should bring you to a decent, and often almost undiscovered, tavern or brasserie. However, superb dining is to be had without leaving the Ilôt Sacré, the area around the central Grand Place, where many very good and surprisingly reasonable restaurants abound. Beware the tourist traps around the Grand Place that make their living from gulling unwary visitors into spending far more than they intended to. The impressive displays of seafood adorning the pavements of Rue des Bouchers northwest of the Grand Place and Petite Rue des Bouchers can promote rather touristy restaurants, but those on pp146–7 are recommended.

## TYPES OF CUISINE

ELSEWHERE IN the city centre is a wealth of quality fish restaurants, especially around the former fish market at Place Ste-Catherine, while the city's trendiest eateries can be found on Rue Dansaert and in the Place Saint-Géry district. If you are planning to explore other parts of Brussels, or if you are staying outside the city centre, you will find plenty of good Belgian fare on offer in the southern communes of Ixelles and Saint-Gilles, and in Etterbeek, where the European Commission buildings are located. Ixelles also boasts the largest concentration of Vietnamese and Southeast Asian cuisine, especially around Chaussée de Boondael. This student area in the Matonge district is also home to several African restaurants, serving food from the Congo (formerly Zaire), Senegal and Rwanda.

North of the city centre, in the communes of Schaerbeek and Saint-Josse, Turkish and North African communities have sprung up, and excellent Moroccan and Tunisian cuisine is commonplace. There is also a growing trend for "designer couscous", with Belgian restaurateurs exploiting the popularity of North African food in spectacularly ornate venues, often featuring ethnic music in the evenings.

Spanish and Portuguese restaurants can be found in the Marolles district and in Saint-Gilles, reflecting the wave of immigration in the 1950s and 1960s when many southern Europeans chose to settle in Brussels. The city is also liberally sprinkled with Greek restaurants, although many veer on the over-touristy side. A better bet are the modern Latin American eateries.

### VEGETARIANS

DESPITE A MARKED upturn in recent years, Brussels is far from being a vegetarian-friendly city, since there are only a handful of specialist vegetarian restaurants (see p153). However, those who eat fish will find mainstream restaurants cater generously to their needs; Brussels is very strong on fish and seafood. Also, the traditional dish, stoemp, mashed potatoes

**Façade of the popular brasserie La Belle Epoque (see p147)**

mixed with root vegetables, is a classic vegetarian speciality. North African restaurants usually offer vegetarian couscous options, and there are plenty of Italian options for cheese-eaters. Indian restaurants are few and far between, but most offer vegetable curries. Vegans may struggle, particularly in European restaurants.

## How Much to Pay

M OST RESTAURANTS, taverns and cafés display a menu in the window and the majority take credit cards. Prices usually include VAT (21 per cent) and service (16 per cent), although it is worth checking the latter before you tip. A meal at the city's most luxurious restaurants can cost up to €150 per head, but you can eat superbly for around €50 per head (including wine) and a hearty snack in a tavern should cost no more than €15. The mark-up level on wine can be very high, especially in most Mediterranean restaurants and in obviously touristic areas, but most taverns do a reasonable *vin maison* and serve myriad varieties of beer.

Service in all but the most expensive restaurants can be erratic by British and US standards. But beneath the sometimes grumpy exterior, you will often find warmth and an earthy, cheerfully self-deprecating sense of humour that is unique to Belgium. There are no hard and fast rules, but some diners leave an additional tip of up to 10 per cent if they are especially

The exotic interior of the Blue Elephant, Thai restaurant *(see p151)*

satisfied with the quality of the meal and the service. Note that some restaurants cannot take service on a credit card slip, and this, plus the tip, will have to be paid in cash, as do other gratuities in the city.

Stall selling freshly made snacks in Saint-Gilles at the weekend

## Dining on a Budget

M ANY RESTAURANTS offer bargain, fixed-price or rapid lunchtime menus for under €12.50, plus reasonably priced dishes of the day. Even the city's most expensive

eateries have similar deals, meaning you can sample haute cuisine for less than €37. In the evening, look out for set menus with *vin compris* (wine included), which are often a way to save a large part of the dining bill.

At the other end of the scale, Brussels has most of the usual fast-food outlets, and sandwiches are sold at most butchers or delicatessens *(traiteurs)*, usually with tuna, cheese or cold meat fillings. Some of the latter offer sit-down snacks too. Alternatively, take advantage of Belgium's national dish, *frites/frieten* (French fries, hand-cut and double-fried to ensure an even crispiness). There are *Friteries/Frituurs* all over town, serving enormous portions of French fries with mayonnaise and dozens of other sauces, plus *fricadelles* (sausages in batter), lamb kebabs, fish cakes or meatballs. Inevitably, these establishments vary in quality; one sure bet is Maison Antoine on Place Jourdan in Etterbeek, where they have been frying for over half a century.

Brussels' sizeable Turkish community means that kebab, gyros and pitta restaurants are ubiquitous, especially in Saint-Josse and on the gaudy Rue du Marché aux Fromages, just off the Grand Place. Perhaps a better bet is the nearby L'Express, a Lebanese takeaway specializing in chicken and felafel pittas, generously crammed with fresh salad.

Most cafés and taverns offer *petite restauration* (light meals) on top or instead of

Interior of Scheltema, a Belle Epoque brasserie *(see p153)*

**Entrance of the historic tavern In 't Spinnekopke** *(see p146)*

a regular menu. These simple, traditional snacks include croque monsieur, shrimp croquettes, chicory baked with ham and cheese, salads, spaghetti bolognaise and *américain* (raw minced beef with seasoning). Do not be fooled by the word "light" – most of these dishes will keep you going from lunchtime well into the evening.

Healthy breakfasts and light lunches with an emphasis on organic food are the staple of Le Pain Quotidien/Het Dagelijks Brood *(see p155)*, a fashionable Belgian chain where customers are seated all together around a large wooden table: trying this out is highly recommended if breakfast is not included in your hotel accommodation. For snackers who are sweet-toothed, waffle stands or vans appear on almost every corner, while cafés and taverns offer a tempting variety of waffles (topped with jam, cream or chocolate). Pancakes *(crêpes)* are just as popular – and filling – although you can cut down the calories with a savoury wholewheat pancake at one of the city's crêperies.

Ethnic food can also work out at a very reasonable price; large portions of couscous, pizzas and African specialities are often to be found at good rates in student areas and at stands throughout the city.

**Open-air tables outside fish restaurants in Rue des Bouchers**

## OPENING TIMES

Since time-consuming business lunches are still very much part of the culture in Belgium, most restaurants are open for lunch from noon until 2 or 3pm. Dinner is generally served from 7pm onwards and last orders are taken as late as 10pm. You are more likely to find late-night restaurants, serving until midnight, in the side streets of downtown Brussels; only a handful provide meals after 1am. Breakfast bars usually open around 7am. For details of café and bar opening times, see pp154–5.

## MAKING A RESERVATION

When visiting one of the city's more celebrated restaurants, it is always wise to book in advance. The listings indicate where booking is advisable. If you are planning to go to the legendary Comme Chez Soi, you should reserve weeks ahead rather than hope for a last-minute cancellation. Trendy designer restaurants are often crowded in the evening, but usually take reservations well in advance.

## READING THE MENU

Menus at most restaurants are written in French, sometimes in Flemish and French. Some, especially in tourist areas, may have explanations in English. Dishes of the day or suggestions are often illegibly scribbled on

**The Art Nouveau interior of Comme Chez Soi, often praised as Brussels' best restaurant** *(see p149)*

**The 16th-century cellar of 't Kelderke in the Grand Place** *(see p147)*

blackboards. Fortunately, most waiters speak at least a little English. You may find a food dictionary useful. For details of some of the most popular Belgian specialities, see pp140–41. The phrasebook on pp189–91 also gives translations of many menu items.

## ETIQUETTE

BRUSSELS IS LESS relaxed than, say, Amsterdam and, although casual or smart-casual dress is acceptable in most restaurants, you will probably feel more at home dressing up for upmarket places. A few formal restaurants will insist on a jacket and tie for men. The dress code for women is more flexible, but smartness is appreciated.

## CHILDREN

IN GENERAL, Brussels is family-oriented and child-friendly, perhaps because Belgian children tend to be restrained and well behaved in restaurants. Many establishments have children's menus, although they are not always a bargain, and several offer free meals for children under 12. High-chairs should be available on request, and some restaurants have inside play areas, including some of the big hotels, where children are usually welcome. On the outskirts of Brussels or near one of the city's many parks, eateries can offer extensive outside playgrounds. Ethnic restaurants, in particular Vietnamese, Greek and the

less formal Italian ones, tend to be especially accommodating. They do not always have children's menus, but are happy for adults to share their meal with youngsters. Children are usually allowed in cafés and in bars although they are forbidden to drink alcohol. Some restaurants may be too formal for children to feel comfortable.

## SMOKING

BRUSSELS IS STILL very much a smokers' city. Although a new law requests all but the smallest establishments to provide non-smoking areas plus ventilation, many do not conform to this regulation. If you are truly averse to cigarette smoke, make sure you ask about arrangements when reserving, or before you take a seat. Many cafés and taverns can be very smoky, and some locals do not take kindly to

**Place settings at the restaurant La Truffe Noire** *(see p149)*

being asked to put out a cigarette. Smokers should know that most restaurants do not sell cigarettes.

## DISABLED FACILITIES

FACILITIES FOR the disabled are poor in Brussels, although there have been some recent improvements. The cobbled streets and hilly areas may well be difficult to negotiate, but most people are very helpful and will go out of their way to help those with difficulty walking or in a wheelchair. There is a limited number of restaurants with ramps and ground-floor bathrooms, so do check the extent of the access before making a reservation or taking a seat. A list of restaurants and cafés with disabled facilities is published by a Flemish charity; contact AWIPH at Rue de la Rivelaine 21, 6061 Charleroi (071 205 711).

## USING THE LISTINGS

Key to symbols in the listings on pp144–53:

¶☺¶ fixed price menu, either at lunch or for dinner.
**V** vegetarian dishes a speciality
⚹ childrens' portions
& wheelchair access to all or part of the restaurant
outdoor eating
good wine list
live music on some nights of the week
★ highly recommended
credit cards accepted
*AE* American Express
*DC* Diners Club
*MC* Master Card/Access
*V* VISA

Price categories for a three-course meal for one, including cover charge, service and half a bottle of wine or other drinks:

€ up to €25
€€ €25–37
€€€ €37–50
€€€€ €50–62
€€€€€ over €62

# A Glossary of Belgian Dishes

**French fries served with mayonnaise**

Belgians love food, and the quality of their cooking is matched only by the vast size of their portions. The Flemish and the Walloons each have their own style of cooking, both readily available in Brussels. With its lively history of invasions from around Europe, the culinary traditions of Holland, Spain and Austria have occasionally filtered into both cuisines. Walloon (Belgian-French) food is similar to French provincial cuisine – hearty and spicy, with rich dishes throughout the menu. Flemish cuisine is often simpler, featuring some substantial stews and traditional cooking. Many regions of Belgium have their specialities, such as Ardennes pâté and Liège sausage, but Brussels is truly the culinary heart of the country, and the city contains many fine restaurants to suit every budget. Most menus in the tourist areas will offer explanations in English but if not, usually the waiter will try to assist.

**Moules marinières, sweated in wine and onion, served in a tureen**

**Steaming waffles freshly made on a stand, a familiar scent in the city**

## SNACKS

Some of the most famous Belgian food is snack food, and with the amount of chip vans and waffle stands dotted around Brussels, you need never go hungry. Perhaps not appealing to all taste buds, but authentically Belgian, are the *caricole* stands, offering steaming hot, ready to eat buttered sea snails.

**Frites**
Thinly cut potato chips (French fries) are twice-fried and usually served in a cardboard cone, accompanied by a dollop of mayonnaise.

**Gaufres**
Waffles made of sweet batter, "toasted" in a waffle iron and served with syrup, chocolate or dusted with icing sugar.

**Speculoos**
Sugared ginger biscuits, often baked in patron saint-shaped moulds, served with coffee.

**Smoutebollen**
Sugared doughnuts.

**Caricoles**
Salted, boiled and buttered sea snails wrapped in paper.

**Pistolets**
Round oval-shaped bread breakfast rolls, with a hard crust and fluffy white interior.

## SOUPS

Soup in Belgium is often a hearty meal in itself, served in large tureens accompanied by freshly baked bread. Vegetable soups with a stock base are particularly common, using ingredients such as carrot, cauliflower, cabbage or green peas, often mixed. Vegetarians, however, should be warned; green pea soup often includes pork and spicy sausage as well as potatoes.

**Waterzooi**
A stew of chicken or fish simmered in their stock, with cream and often white wine, and served with puréed vegetables.

**Bisque de homard**
Lobster poached in reduced seafood stock with brandy.

## FISH AND SEAFOOD

Most of the fish served in Brussels comes straight from the Ostend coast, which, on a direct route less than 90 km (55 miles) away, means that it is fresh every day. At the turn of the 20th century, the port of Brussels extended as far north as the Eglise Ste-Catherine, with a huge covered fish market behind the church. This area is still the centre of a bustling trade in seafood; although the market has long since vanished, the surrounding streets and alleys are filled with terraced fish restaurants.

The Belgians' love of seafood extends further than the national dish, *moules et frites*. Ostend sole, eels in green sauce, lobster in season and crispy shrimp croquettes are just some of the favourites. While the city's more formal establishments tend to be expensive, there are plenty of simple eateries offering the day's catch at very low prices.

**Moules**
Mussels, traditionally served in copper tureens, cooked in white wine and onions, with a side order of *frites*.

**Marinated herring**

**Hareng**
Herring, prepared in a variety of ways: roll-mop, fried, steamed, marinated in vinegar or smoked.

**Langouste**
Spiny lobster, brought in fresh from Ostend; when it is available much will be made of it in lavish seafood displays and on daily "specials" menu boards.

**Huîtres**
Oysters, swallowed raw or served *au gratin*; covered with breadcrumbs, bacon, herbs and cheese and grilled.

**Anguilles au vert**
Eels, commonly served with green herbs such as thyme or parsley, and cooked in butter.

**Sole Ostendaise**
Fresh sole fillet served with lemon and butter.

## MEAT

ALTHOUGH HAPPY to use poultry in soups and lighter dishes, Belgians use their abundant supplies of red meat to create hearty main meals, often marinated in cream sauces or alcohol.

**Choesels**
Very fresh sweetbreads in cream sauces are a Brussels speciality.

**Ragôut d'agneau**
Lamb braised for hours with chicory, onions and herbs.

**Gentse stoverij**
Ghent's long-standing culinary legacy takes the form of a beer and beef stew with mustard.

**Ardennes pâté**
A coarse pork pâté often flavoured with garlic.

**Bloedpens**
Black pudding with chopped bacon.

**Lapin**
Rabbit will be seen in many guises, but it is most traditionally served with prunes soaked in brandy, or with beer and mustard.

**Carbonnades flamandes**
A popular Flemish dish for centuries, fillets of beef are braised very slowly in gueuze beer, or occasionally kriek, cherry fruit beer.

**Faisan à la Brabançonne**
Pheasant roasted with braised chicory, herbs and bacon.

Carbonnade of beef

## VEGETABLES

VEGETABLES are often treated as accompaniments to the main meat or fish course, although some can be served as dishes in their own right.

*Witloof*, chicory wrapped in ham and braised *au gratin*

**Choux de Bruxelles**
The Brussels sprout is served young, fresh and dripping with crispy lardons and butter.

**Witloof/Chicon**
Chicory, a favourite vegetable all over Brussels, is often served with ham and cheese.

**Jets de houblon**
Young Belgian hop shoots are braised to make a tender side dish.

**Stoemp**
Coarse mash of potatoes and vegetables (usually carrots or cabbage) served with sausage.

## DESSERTS

ALMOST ANY DESSERT wished for can be found in restaurants in Brussels, from chocolate cake, mousses and profiteroles, to the classic French dishes, *tarte tatin* (upside-down apple cake) and *crème caramel*. Second only to the reputation of Belgium's chocolatiers is that of its pastry- and cakemakers. Using the same fine ingredients, and techniques honed since the 18th century, pastry chefs create concoctions as breathtakingly good-looking as they are delicious to eat.

**Profiteroles**

Shelves of fresh cream and chocolate cakes in a pâtisserie

A common way to finish off a meal, however, is with cheese, served before or instead of dessert. Often mild and uncured, local cheeses are made in the damp, fertile, cattle-grazing land of Wallonia and delivered fresh to the city.

**Herve**
A soft runny cheese, often served in bowls, with bread.

**Tartine de fromage blanc**
This soft cheese open sandwich is eaten with radishes.

Tarte tatin, upside-down apple cake made with fresh fruit

## BELGIAN CHOCOLATE

Belgian chocolate is considered by many to be the finest in the world. The chocolate manufacturing industry took off during the 1880s, aided by the acquisition of the Belgian Congo (*see p36*), which meant easy access to Africa's cocoa plantations. Traditionally Belgian chocolates, known as *pralines*, are filled with cream, nuts or a high-quality soft dark chocolate and covered with milk or white chocolate. Plain chocolate has a high cocoa content, usually at least 70 per cent. Belgian chocolate houses have passed down their recipes over generations, the contents of which are highly guarded and secret. Some of the renowned *"grandes maisons de chocolat"* include Mary, Neuhaus, Godiva, Léonidas and Wittamer. Ideal for a gift, buying chocolates is a treat; individually picked, they are often packaged in crêpe tissue in a finely decorated box.

Belgian chocolates wrapped in a typical luxury gift box

# Belgian Beer

**Gambrinus, legendary Beer King**

**B**ELGIUM MAKES MORE beers, in a greater mix of styles and flavours, than any other country in the world. The Belgian citizen drinks on average 100 litres (200 pints) a year, and even small bars will stock at least 20 varieties. The nation's breweries produce over 400 different beers. The cheerful peasants in Brueghel the Elder's 15th-century medieval village scenes would have been drinking beer from their local brewery, many of which had been active since the 11th century, as every small town and community produced its own beer. By 1900 there remained 3,000 private breweries throughout Belgium. Today, more than 100 still operate, with experts agreeing that even large industrial concerns produce a fine quality beer.

**Detail from *The Wedding Dance* by Pieter Brueghel the Elder**

## TRAPPIST BEERS

**Chimay label with authentic Trappist mark**

**Label for Westmalle Trappist beer**

**T**HE MOST REVERED of refreshments, Belgium's Trappist beers have been highly rated since the Middle Ages when monks began brewing them. The drink originated in Roman times when Belgium was a province of Gaul, Gallia Belgica. Beer was a private domestic product until the monasteries took over and introduced hops to the process. Today's production is still controlled solely by the five Trappist monasteries, although the brewers are mostly laymen. Trappist beers are characterized by their rich, yeasty flavour. They are very strong, ranging from 6.2 to 11 per cent in alcohol content by volume. The most celebrated of the 20 brands is Chimay, brewed at Belgium's largest monastic brewery in Hainaut. This delicate but potent bottled beer has three different strengths, and is best kept for many years before drinking. The strongest Trappist beer is Westvleteren, from Ypres.

**Chimay served in its correct glass**

## LAMBIC BEERS

**M**ADE FOR CENTURIES in the Senne Valley around Brussels, the unique family of lambic beers are made using yeasts naturally present in the air to ferment the beer, rather than being added separately to the water and grain mix. Containers of unfermented wort (water, wheat and barley) are left under a half-open roof in the brewery and wild airborne yeasts, only present in the atmosphere of this region of Belgium, descend to ferment it. Unlike the sterility of many breweries and officially exempt from EU hygiene regulations, lambic cellars are deliberately left dusty and uncleaned in order for the necessary fungal activity to thrive. Matured in untreated wooden casks for up to five years, the lambic is deliciously sour to drink, with a moderate strength of 5 per cent alcohol.

Young and old lambic beers are blended together to produce the variant of gueuze. A tiny bead, distinctive champagne mousse and a toasty, slightly acid flavour, are its main characteristics. Bars and restaurants lay down their gueuze for up to 2 years before it is drunk.

**Lambic cherry beer**

**Brewer sampling beer from the vat at a brewery outside Brussels**

## SPECIALITY BELGIAN BEERS

| Duvel | Chimay | Brugse Tripel | De Verboden Frucht | Kwak |

SPECIALITY BEERS are common in Belgium, where the huge variety of brands includes unusual tastes and flavours. Fruit beers are a Brussels speciality but are available throughout the country. The most popular, kriek, is traditionally made with bitter cherries grown in the Brussels suburb of Schaerbeek; picked annually, these are added to the lambic and allowed to macerate, or steep. The distinctive almond tang comes from the cherry stone. Raspberries are also used to make a framboise beer, or frambozen.

For a characterful amber ale, Kwak is good choice. Strong beers are also popular; apart from the Trappist beers, of which Chimay is a popular variety, the pilseners De Verboden Frucht (meaning "forbidden fruit") and Duvel ("devil") are almost as strong as red wine. Brugse Tripel, from Bruges, is also popular. Even Belgium's best-sellers, Jupiler and Stella Artois, are good quality beers.

**Fruit beer mat of Chapeau brewery**

*The façade of a beer emporium in Brussels*

## BLANCHE BEERS

BELGIUM'S REFRESHING wheat beers are known as "blanche", or white beers, because of the cloudy sediment that forms when they ferment. Sour, crisp and light, they are relatively low in alcohol at 5 per cent. Blanche is produced in the western region of Hoegaarden, after which the best-known blanche is named. Many people now serve them with a slice of lemon to add to the refreshing taste, especially on warm summer evenings.

**Hoegaarden**

## HOW TO DRINK BELGIAN BEER

THERE ARE NO snobbish distinctions made in Belgium between bottled and casked beer. Some of the most prestigious brews are served in bottles, and, as with casks, bottles are often laid down to mature. The choice of drinking glass, however, is a vital part of the beer-drinking ritual. Many beers must be drunk in a particular glass, which the barman will supply, ranging from goblets to long thin drinking tubes. Beers are often served with a complementary snack; cream cheese on rye bread and radishes are a popular accompaniment.

**The traditional drinkers' snack of** *fromage blanc* **on rye bread**

# Choosing a Restaurant

THE RESTAURANTS IN THIS GUIDE have been selected for their good value, exceptional food and interesting location. This chart highlights some of the factors which may influence your choice. Entries are listed in alphabetical order within price category, starting with the least expensive. The more detailed listings on pp146–53 are arranged by type of cuisine. Information on cafés and bars is on pp154–55.

| | | PAGE | CREDIT CARDS | HIGHLY RECOMMENDED | TABLES OUTSIDE | CHARACTER SETTING | ETHNIC | FIXED-PRICE MENU | CHILD FRIENDLY |
|---|---|---|---|---|---|---|---|---|---|
| **THE LOWER TOWN** | | | | | | | | | |
| **Brasserie Horta** (Belgian) | € | 146 | ● | | | ■ | | | ● |
| **Chez Léon** (Belgian) | € | 146 | ● | | ● | | | ■ | ● |
| **El Papagayo** (Latin American) | € | 152 | | | ● | ■ | | ■ | |
| **La Grande Porte** (Belgian) | € | 146 | ● | | | ■ | | | |
| **Le Petit Chou de Bruxelles** (Belgian) | € | 146 | ● | | | ■ | | | |
| **Al Barmaki** (Lebanese) | €€ | 151 | ● | | | | ● | | |
| **Auberge des Chapeliers** (Belgian) | €€ | 146 | ● | | | ■ | | | |
| **Aux Paves de Bruxelles** (Belgian) | €€ | 146 | ● | | ● | | | | |
| **Bij den Boer** (Seafood) | €€ | 153 | ● | ■ | | | | ■ | ● |
| **Brasserie de la Roue d'Or** (Belgian) | €€ | 146 | ● | ■ | | ■ | | | |
| **Cantina Cubana** (Latin American) | €€ | 152 | ● | ■ | | ■ | ● | ■ | |
| **Casa Manuel** (Portuguese) | €€ | 152 | ● | | ● | | | | |
| **Chez Patrick** (Belgian) | €€ | 146 | ● | ■ | | ■ | | | |
| **Domaine de Lintillac** (French) | €€ | 148 | | | | ■ | | | |
| **In't Spinnekopke** (Belgian) | €€ | 146 | ● | | ● | ■ | | | |
| **Kasbah** (Moroccan) | €€ | 150 | ● | ■ | ● | | ● | ■ | ● |
| **L'Achepot** (Seafood) | €€ | 153 | ● | | ● | | | | ● |
| **La Marée** (Seafood) | €€ | 153 | ● | ■ | | | | | |
| **La Rose Blanche** (Belgian) | €€ | 147 | ● | | ● | | | | |
| **Rugantino** (Italian) | €€ | 149 | ● | ■ | ● | | | | |
| **'t Kelderke** (Belgian) | €€ | 147 | ● | ■ | | | | | |
| **Aux Armes de Bruxelles** (Belgian) | €€€ | 147 | ● | | ● | | | ■ | |
| **Aux Marches de la Chapelle** (French) | €€€ | 148 | ● | | | ■ | | ■ | |
| **Bonsoir Clara** (French) | €€€ | 148 | ● | | | ■ | | | |
| **La Taverne du Passage** (Belgian) | €€€ | 147 | ● | ■ | ● | ■ | | | |
| **Le Pou qui Tousse** (Sardinian) | €€€ | 150 | ● | | | ■ | | | |
| **La Truite d'Argent** (Seafood) | €€€€ | 153 | ● | ■ | ● | ■ | | ■ | |
| **L'Ogenblik** (French) | €€€€ | 149 | ● | ■ | | ■ | | | |
| **Scheltema** (Seafood) | €€€€ | 153 | ● | | ● | | | | |
| **Comme Chez Soi** (French) | €€€€€ | 149 | ● | ■ | | ■ | | | ● |
| **Sea Grill** (Seafood) | €€€€€ | 153 | ● | ■ | | | | | |
| | | | | | | | | | |
| **THE UPPER TOWN** | | | | | | | | | |
| **La Pirogue** (African) | € | 150 | | | ● | | ● | | |
| **Entrée des Artistes** (French) | €€ | 148 | ● | | ● | ■ | | ■ | ● |
| **Au Vieux Saint-Martin** (Belgian) | €€ | 147 | ● | | | | | | ● |
| **La Porte des Indes** (Indian) | €€€ | 151 | ● | ■ | | ■ | ● | ■ | |
| **L'Estrille du Vieux Bruxelles** (Belgian) | €€€ | 147 | ● | | | ■ | | | |
| **Chez Moi** (Belgian) | €€€€ | 147 | ● | | ● | | | ■ | |
| **L' Ecailler du Palais Royal** (Seafood) | €€€€€ | 153 | ● | ■ | | | | | |
| | | | | | | | | | |
| **GREATER BRUSSELS** | | | | | | | | | |
| **Dolma** (Vegetarian) | € | 153 | ● | | | | | ■ | ● |
| **Gri Gri** (African) | € | 150 | ● | ■ | ● | | ● | ■ | ● |
| **Hông Hoa** (Vietnamese) | € | 150 | | | | ■ | ● | ■ | ● |
| **La Cantonnaise** (Chinese) | € | 151 | | ■ | | | ● | | ● |
| **Le Pacifique** (Vietnamese) | € | 151 | ● | ■ | | | ● | | ● |

**Price categories** for a three-course meal for one, including cover charge, service and half a bottle of wine or other drinks:
€ up to €25
€€ €25–37
€€€ €37–50
€€€€ €50-62
€€€€€ Over €62

**CREDIT CARDS**
Establishment accepts a combination of major credit cards.

**HIGHLY RECOMMENDED**
The quality of the dishes, decor and service are especially highly commended.

**TABLES OUTSIDE**
Outdoor dining facilities and service in summer.

**CHARACTER SETTING**
Unusually attractive interior decor and/or street setting and atmosphere.

**ETHNIC**
Exotic world cuisine of a high standard from outside Europe.

| | | PAGE | CREDIT CARDS | HIGHLY RECOMMENDED | TABLES OUTSIDE | CHARACTER SETTING | ETHNIC | FIXED-PRICE MENU | CHILD FRIENDLY |
|---|---|---|---|---|---|---|---|---|---|
| L'Ouzerie (Greek) | € | 151 | ● | | | | | | |
| L'Ouzerie du Nouveau Monde (Greek) | € | 151 | ● | ● | ● | | | | |
| Poussières d'Etoiles (Vietnamese) | € | 151 | | | ● | | ● | ● | ● |
| Shanti (Vegetarian) | € | 153 | ● | ● | | | ● | ● | |
| Tsampa (Vegetarian) | € | 153 | | | ● | | | | |
| Au Brabançon (Belgian) | €€ | 146 | ● | ● | | | | | |
| Aux Anges (Italian) | €€ | 149 | ● | | ● | ● | | | |
| Ile de Gorée (African) | €€ | 150 | | | ● | | ● | | ● |
| Kocharata (Bulgarian) | €€ | 152 | | | | | | | |
| La Belle Epoque (Belgian) | €€ | 146 | ● | | ● | | | ● | ● |
| La Citronnelle (Vietnamese) | €€ | 151 | ● | | ● | | ● | ● | |
| La Danse des Paysans (Belgian) | €€ | 147 | ● | ● | ● | | | | |
| Le Grain de Sel (French) | €€ | 148 | ● | ● | ● | ● | | | |
| Les Ateliers de la Grande Ile (Russian) | €€ | 152 | ● | | | | | | |
| La Maison de Thaïlande (Thai) | €€ | 151 | ● | ● | ● | | ● | ● | |
| Medina (African) | €€ | 150 | ● | | | ● | ● | | ● |
| Mon Village (Belgian) | €€ | 147 | ● | | | | | | ● |
| Sahbaz (Turkish) | €€ | 151 | ● | | | | | | |
| Tierra del Fuego (Latin American) | €€ | 152 | ● | | ● | ● | | ● | |
| Volle Gas (Belgian) | €€ | 147 | ● | ● | ● | | | | ● |
| Amadeus (French) | €€€ | 148 | ● | | ● | ● | | | |
| A'mbriana (Italian) | €€€ | 149 | ● | | | | | ● | |
| La Brouette (Belgian) | €€€ | 147 | ● | | | | | ● | |
| La Fin de Siècle (Italian) | €€€ | 149 | ● | ● | ● | ● | | | |
| La Scala (Italian) | €€€ | 149 | ● | | | | | | |
| Le Doux Wazoo (French) | €€€ | 148 | ● | | | | | ● | |
| Le Fils de Jules (French) | €€€ | 148 | ● | | ● | ● | | | |
| Le Forcado (Spanish) | €€€ | 152 | ● | ● | ● | | | | |
| Le Pain et le Vin (French) | €€€ | 148 | ● | | ● | | | | |
| Les Amis du Cep (French) | €€€ | 149 | ● | | ● | | | ● | |
| Les Brasseries Georges (French) | €€€ | 149 | ● | ● | ● | | | | ● |
| Les Jardins de Bagatelle (African) | €€€ | 150 | ● | | ● | ● | ● | ● | ● |
| Osteria delle Stelle (Italian) | €€€ | 150 | ● | ● | | ● | | ● | |
| Blue Elephant (Thai) | €€€€ | 151 | ● | ● | | | ● | ● | ● |
| La Truffe Noire (French/Italian) | €€€€€ | 149 | ● | | ● | ● | | | |
| **ANTWERP** | | | | | | | | | |
| 't Zolderke (French) | €€ | 148 | ● | | | | | ● | |
| De Matelote (Seafood) | €€€€€ | 153 | ● | ● | | | | ● | |
| **BRUGES** | | | | | | | | | |
| Den Dyver (Belgian) | €€€ | 147 | ● | ● | ● | | | ● | |
| de Karmeliet (Belgian) | €€€€ | 147 | ● | ● | ● | | | ● | |
| 't Bourgoensche Cruyce (Belgian) | €€€€ | 148 | ● | ● | ● | | | | |
| **GHENT** | | | | | | | | | |
| Pakhuis (French) | €€ | 148 | ● | | | | | ● | |
| 't Bulske Vol (Belgian) | €€€ | 147 | ● | ● | | | | ● | |

## BELGIAN

Although Belgium is a relatively new European state, its culinary traditions date back to the Middle Ages, when the dukes of Burgundy ruled over the Low Countries. To this day Burgundian is a synonym for hearty extravagance, of which the Belgians are inordinately fond. Authentic Belgian cooking is very rooted in peasant traditions, including warming winter stews such as *waterzooi* (chicken or fish stewed with cream), or *carbonnades* (beef casseroled in beer) as well as the national vegetable, chicory. Slow cooking in beer is also an integral part of Belgian cuisine. Dieting is not, and never will be, compatible with rich Belgian food.

Most of the restaurants in this section offer authentic versions of Belgian dishes, usually at relatively affordable prices. While some pay great attention to presentation, lesser establishments are often more rewarding; this is a cuisine robust enough to cope with a few rough edges and dated decor.

### Brasserie Horta

Rue des Sables 20. **Map** 2 E2.
 (02) 217 7271.  AE, DC, MC, V.  10am–6pm daily.   

The Comic Strip Centre's restaurant is worth a visit to see the airy, high-ceilinged Art Nouveau brasserie designed by Victor Horta. Admire the cartoons of Tintin, the Smurfs and Lucky Luke while sampling cheap, hearty portions of chicken-stuffed vol-au-vents, spicy meatballs, *waterzooi*, beef stewed in beer and home-made *frites*. The bar is open during restaurant hours.

### Chez Léon

Rue des Bouchers 18. **Map** 2 D2.  (02) 513 0426.  AE, DC, MC, V.  11:30am–11pm daily.    

It may be more a fashionable factory-style diner than an intimate dining experience, but this casual haunt near the Grand Place provides unquestionable value for money in an expensive area (and has been doing so since 1893). It also offers a wide range of *moules-frites* dishes and a free menu for children under 12.

### La Grande Porte

Rue Notre-Seigneur 9. **Map** 1 C4.
 (02) 512 8998.  MC, V.  noon–3pm, 6pm–2am Tue–Fri; 6pm–2am Sat.  

This late-night spot in the Marolles area combines French *chanson* background music and an artfully chaotic interior adorned with finds from the flea market on Place du Jeu de Balle. Enjoy quality versions of basic Belgian fare such as *stoemp*, meatballs in tomato sauce or the traditional chicory grilled with cheese and, in winter, onion soup.

### Le Petit Chou de Bruxelles

Rue du Vieux-Marché-aux-Grains 2. **Map** 1 C2.  (02) 502 6037.  noon–10pm daily.  Wed & Thu in winter.  

Despite the dingy glass-fronted interior and non-existent decor, this café near Place Ste-Catherine is well worth the visit, especially for a full meal outside normal eating hours. Old-fashioned cooking includes home-made pork rillettes and horse steaks. In summer, the renovated outdoor terrace is pleasant.

### Auberge des Chapeliers

Rue des Chapeliers 3. **Map** 2 D3.
 (02) 513 7338.  AE, DC, MC, V.  noon–2pm, 6:30–11pm daily (until midnight on Sat).  

This 17th-century building near the Grand Place houses a cosy, split-level eatery with several dining sections and, unusually, a non-smoking area. The menu features sizeable helpings of classic Belgian dishes: mussels in a variety of preparations, black pudding Brussels-style *(boudin)*, rabbit cooked in kriek beer with cherries, and marinated herring fillets.

### Au Brabançon

Rue de la Commune 75. **Map** 3 A1.
 (02) 217 7191.  AE, MC, V.  noon–2:30pm, 7–9:30pm Mon–Sat.  Sun.  

This tiny St-Josse restaurant is a haven for lovers of authentic Belgian specialities. The formidable septuagenarian owner loves to cook offal, including brains and sweetbreads. The faint-hearted can opt for creamy chicken *waterzooi* or Marolles-style meatballs once they have deciphered the handwritten menu. As with much Belgian food, this is not an establishment for slimmers or vegetarians.

### Aux Pavés de Bruxelles

Rue Marché-aux-Fromages 1–3. **Map** 2 D3.  (02) 502 0457.  AE, DC, MC, V.  noon–2:30pm, 7–11pm Mon–Fri; 7pm–midnight Sat.  Sun.  

At this old-fashioned eatery in a 17th-century house near the Grand Place, good prices and a sturdy emphasis on red meat keep the place packed for lunch and dinner. While Argentine steaks and spare ribs are house specialities, the mussel dishes should satisfy non-carnivores and fish-eating vegetarians.

### Brasserie de la Roue d'Or

Rue des Chapeliers 26. **Map** 2 D3.
 (02) 514 2554.  AE, DC, MC, V.  noon–12.30am daily.  mid-Jul–mid-Aug.  

This upmarket Art Nouveau brasserie with Surrealist murals excels in modernism. The great-value menu blends Belgian and French cuisine: eel in mustard sauce, pig's trotter vinaigrette, prawn croquettes, snails in garlic butter and home-made *frites*. Pierre Wynants, the chef of Michelin three-star Brussels restaurant Comme Chez Soi, is an enthusiastic visitor.

### Chez Patrick

Rue des Chapeliers 6. **Map** 2 D3.
 (02) 511 9815.  AE, DC, MC, V.  noon–3pm, 6–10pm Tue–Sat.  

Despite its popularity with tourists and expats, the family-run Chez Patrick has remained quintessentially Bruxellois since it opened in 1931. Wooden benches and white tiles give the dining room a spartan, functional feel and the daily specials are scribbled on to mirrors on the walls. Beer cuisine figures large, but you can also tuck into *choucroute* (cabbage and sausage hotpot) or chicken *waterzooi*.

### In 't Spinnekopke

Place du Jardin aux Fleurs 1. **Map** 1 B2.  (02) 511 8695.  AE, DC, MC, V.  noon–3pm, 6–11pm Mon–Fri; 6pm–midnight Sat.   

This former coaching inn at the end of Rue Chartreux is popular with canny tourists and local politicians alike. Enjoy Belgian fare and creative beer cuisine in 18th-century decor: the restaurant's name means "In the spider's head" and, while spider is not on the menu, exotic dishes include guinea-fowl in raspberry beer and calf's head with vinaigrette. There is a huge choice of small cottage-industry beers.

### La Belle Epoque

Avenue Houba de Strooper 188.
 (02) 478 9647.  AE, DC, MC, V.  noon–11pm Sun–Thu; noon–midnight Fri & Sat.     

One of the best restaurants near the Atomium, this hospitable 1920s brasserie offers French and Italian cuisine as well as Belgian classics. Dishes include eels in herbs, rabbit in gueuze beer and *osso bucco* (stewed veal in wine and tomatoes).

## La Danse des Paysans

Chaussée de Boondael 441. ☎ *(02) 649 8505.* ★ ☒ *MC, V.* ⏲ *noon–3pm, 6:30–11:30pm Mon–Fri; 6:30–11:30pm Sat.* 🍴 €€

In the heart of the university area, this rustic restaurant is a perfect spot to sample authentic beer cooking such as scampi stew with white beer and lamb in pastry with mint and the blanche beer Duvel.

## La Rose Blanche/ De Witte Roos

Grand Place 11. **Map** 2 D3. ☎ *(02) 513 6479.* ☒ *AE, DC, MC, V.* ⏲ *10am–11pm daily.* 🍴 €€

One of the best places for traditional Belgian cuisine, this Baroque tavern serves mussels in beer, roast salmon with Faro beer, chicken in kriek and even waffles with an Ardennes brew called La Chouffe. The popular three-course menu is centred around three different types of beer, with a bottle of each included in the set price.

## Mon Village

Rue Champ de la Couronne 6. ☎ *(02) 478 3579.* ☒ *AF, DC, MC, V.* ⏲ *noon–3pm, 7–11:30pm Tue–Sat.* €€

At this informal restaurant close to Parc de Laeken, the owner also does the cooking, and favourites include chicken cooked in strong Duvel beer and rillettes prepared with white beer.

## 't Kelderke

Grand Place 15. **Map** 2 D3. ☎ *(02) 513 7344.* ★ ☒ *AE, DC, MC, V.* ⏲ *noon–2am daily.* €€

This reasonably priced restaurant in a 17th-century cellar feels genuine despite its commercial location. Speedy waiters proffer huge pots of mussels and good-sized portions of traditional Belgian food. Waffles with a topping of whipped cream make a fine ending to a meal. No reservations are accepted, so queues are not uncommon.

## Volle Gas

Place Fernand Cocq 21. ☎ *(02) 502 8971.* ★ ☒ *MC, V.* ⏲ *11am–1am Mon–Sat.* 🍴 🎵 ▣ 🍴 €€

There has been a restaurant here, on the pleasant square opposite Ixelles town hall, since 1849. The current occupant is a traditional Brussels establishment, serving mussels, *waterzooi* and superb *stoemp royal* (with bacon, sausages and eggs).

## Au Vieux Saint-Martin

Place du Grand Sablon 38. **Map** 2 D4. ☎ *(02) 512 6476.* ☒ *MC, V.* ⏲ *noon–midnight daily.* 🍴 €€€

A truly professional establishment with crisp modern decor, swift and courteous waiters, this restaurant also boasts a contemporary art collection. The accomplished menu features regional specialities like *stoemp*, rabbit in kriek and *filet américain*, prepared to a recipe conceived by the restaurant's founder in the 1920s.

## Aux Armes de Bruxelles

Rue des Bouchers 13. **Map** 2 D2. ☎ *(02) 511 5550.* ☒ *AE, DC, MC, V.* ⏲ *noon–11pm Tue–Sun.* ⏺ *mid-Jun–mid-Jul.* 🍴 🍴 €€€

This friendly restaurant was a favourite of Belgian chanson legend Jacques Brel. Some critics complain that its charm has faded a little in recent years, but the restaurant still offers classic, high-quality cuisine including lobster, mussels, poached cod, veal and, in season, game. The freshly made shrimp croquettes are a must. It is important to reserve in advance.

## Den Dyver

Dijver 5, Bruges. ☎ *(050) 33 6069.* ★ ☒ *AE, V.* ⏲ *noon–2pm, 6:30–9pm Thu–Tue.* ⏺ *Thu lunch.* ▣ 🍴 €€€

This excellent restaurant, located close to the Markt, specializes in Flemish beer cooking. There is no drinks list, and diners are automatically served a glass of the beer that features in their dish.

## La Brouette

Boulevard Prince de Liège 61, Anderlecht. ☎ *(02) 522 5169.* ☒ *DC, MC, V.* ⏲ *noon–2:30pm, 7–9:30pm Tue–Sun.* ⏺ *Sat lunch, Sun eve.* 🍴 ☒ *DC, MC, V.* 🍴 €€€

A restaurant with a well-deserved Michelin star, La Brouette is a jewel off the beaten track. Chef Hermann Dedapper, a top sommelier, provides gourmet food and an innovative menu in an unpretentious setting.

## La Taverne du Passage

Galerie de la Reine 30. **Map** 2 D2. ☎ *(02) 512 3731.* ★ ☒ *AE, DC, MC, V.* ⏲ *noon–midnight daily.* ⏺ *Jun–Jul: Wed & Thu.* 🍴 €€€

This Belgian brasserie has an alluring Art Deco interior and 70 years' worth of culinary expertise. Housed in the elegant Galerie de la Reine, between Rue des Bouchers and Rue du Marché aux Herbes, it features roasts carved at your table, as well as shrimp croquettes, steak tartare and mussels. The waiters are helpful and efficient; this is a popular choice with families. Relax on the terrace in the arcade and watch the world go by under the Art Deco roof.

## L'Estrille du Vieux Bruxelles

Rue de Rollebeek 7. **Map** 2 D4. ☎ *(02) 512 5857.* ☒ *AE, DC, MC, V.* ⏲ *noon–2pm, 7–10pm Mon–Fri; noon–3pm, 7–10:30pm Sat & Sun.* 🍴 €€€

Just off the Place du Grand Sablon and housed in an elegant 16th-century building, this cosy tavern specializes in meat grilled over an open fire in the main room. Homely dishes include beef stew, rabbit with plums and gueuze beer, eel in herbs and, in season, game. The background music is usually classical or jazz.

## 't Buikske Vol

Kraanlei 17, Ghent. ☎ *(09) 225 1880.* ★ ☒ *AE, V.* ⏲ *noon–2pm, 7–9:30pm Mon, Tue, Thu; 7–9:30pm Fri & Sat.* ▣ 🍴 €€€

The trendy Patershol district is home to many upscale restaurants, and this is one of the best. The beautifully prepared dishes range from river fish *waterzooi* to sweetbreads with rabbit.

## Chez Moi

Rue du Luxembourg 66. ☎ *(02) 280 2666.* ☒ *DC, MC, V.* ⏲ *noon–3pm, 7–10pm Mon–Fri.* 🍴 ▣ 🍴 €€€€

Close to the European Parliament, this welcoming restaurant is popular with Eurocrats at lunch, but quieter and more romantic in the evening. The menu offers fish and game with good vegetable side dishes.

## de Karmeliet

Langestraat 19, Bruges. ☎ *(09) 33 8259.* ★ ☒ *AE, DC, MC, V.* ⏲ *noon–1:30pm, 7–9:30pm Tue–Sun.* ⏺ *Tue lunch, Sun eve.* ▣ ▣ 🍴 🍴 €€€€

Impeccable service, lavish surroundings in the centre of town and exquisite Belgian/French cuisine have earned this restaurant in the heart of historical Bruges three Michelin stars. Try the rabbit with Rodenbach beer and the delicious thin omelettes.

## 't Bourgoensche Cruyce

Wollestraat 41, Bruges. [C] (050) 33
7926. ★ 🍽 AE, MC, V. 🕐 noon–
2pm, 7–9:15pm Thu–Mon. 🍴 📶
🟦 🟥 🍴 €€€€

This 19th-century wooden building
is the ideal place for a romantic,
canalside meal. The perfect setting
is matched by superior cuisine,
especially the seafood dishes.

### FRENCH

Perhaps unsurprisingly given its
proximity to France, Brussels has
a large number of extremely good
French restaurants, from grand
Parisian-style brasseries to modern
establishments serving nouvelle
cuisine. While the brasserie menus
sometimes overlap with their
Belgian counterparts, the nouvelle
cuisine places offer a lighter option
for those fed up with frites. Many
of the city's great French restaurants are expensive, but there are
plenty of bargains to be had,
especially at lunchtime or following
the set menus. Value for money is
almost universally guaranteed.

## Domaine de Lintillac

Rue de Flandre 25. **Map** 1 B1.
[C] (02) 511 5123. 🕐 noon–2pm,
7:30– 10pm Tue–Sat. 🍴 €€

This small restaurant serves nothing
but duck: wine-soaked pâté, sliced
breasts, *rillettes* cooked in lard and
pounded to a fine paste, confit, as
well as the gourmet *foie gras*. Each
of the tables has a toaster to ensure
your pâté toast is cooked to per-
fection. The main courses include
a marvellous cassoulet, with duck,
pork and goose cooked for hours in
duck fat, a rich wine tomato sauce
and haricot beans. For dessert, try
the excellent crème brulée. The rich
fare is not for those on a diet, but
is delicious for a special occasion.

## Entrée des Artistes

Place du Grand Sablon 42. **Map** 2 D4.
[C] (02) 502 3161. 🍽 AE, MC, V.
8am–2am daily. 🟥 📶 🍴 €€

The Grand Sablon can be an
unsatisfyingly expensive place to
eat, but this unassumingly trendy
brasserie is a happy exception.
Cinema posters and licence plates
decorate the walls and the well-
judged brasserie fare includes
toast with mushrooms, salmon
steaks and lobster. A *plat du jour*
at lunchtime costs around €7.

## Le Grain de Sel

Chaussée de Vleurgat 9. [C] (02) 648
1858. 🍽 MC. ★ 🕐 noon–3:15pm,
7:30–10:30pm Tue–Fri; 7:30–10pm
Sat. 🟦 lunch Sat. 🍴 🟦 📶 €€€

Tucked away in a townhouse near
Place Eugène Flagey in Ixelles, this
exquisite eatery is one of Brussels'
best-kept secrets. Book in advance
to ensure a spot on the rambling
rose-filled patio, then settle down
to a selection of light, fresh dishes
that make up the regularly changing
menu. Past dishes have included
cannelloni with goat's cheese and
spinach, scampi in creamy curry
sauce, pan-fried beef with rocket
and exquisite home-made ice
cream. The three-course menu
offers a wide selection of regular
dishes and daily suggestions.

## Pakhuis

Schuurkensstraat 4, Ghent. [C] (09)
223 5555. 🍽 AE, DC, MC, V.
🕐 noon–2:30pm, 6:30pm–midnight
Mon–Sat. 🟦 🍴 🟥 🍴 €€

This popular brasserie occupies a
huge, early-19th-century converted
warehouse. Its special attractions
are the oyster bar and the fresh
shellfish served daily.

## 't Zolderke

Hoofdkerkstraat 7, Antwerp. [C] (03)
233 8427. ★ 🍽 MC, V. 🕐 6–11pm
Mon–Fri, noon–midnight Sat & Sun.
📶 🍴 🟦 🟥 🍴 €€

The menu at this light and airy
French restaurant features old
classics such as steak in
peppercorn and *bearnaise* sauce
with fries, and meats such as boar
and deer when in season.

## Amadeus

Rue Veydt 13. [C] (02) 538 3427.
🍽 AE, DC, MC, V. 🕐 noon–3pm,
6:30pm–midnight Tue–Fri, Sun;
6pm–12:30am Mon & Sat. 🟦 🟥
📶 €€€

Near the Place Stephanie, off
Chaussée de Charleroi, this romantic
candle-lit restaurant and wine bar
was once the studio of 19th-century
French sculptor Auguste Rodin.
Diners come more for the ornate
mirrors and intimate corners than
the brasserie fare, which is
adequate but unremarkable by
Brussels standards. The wine list,
however, is top quality, and the
view of the entrance hall alone is
worth the trip.

## Aux Marches de la Chapelle

Place de la Chapelle 5. **Map** 1 C4.
[C] (02) 512 6891. 🍽 AE, MC, DC, V.
🕐 noon–2:30pm, 6–11pm Mon–Fri;
7pm–midnight Sat; noon–2:30pm,
7–10pm Sun. 🍴 🍴 🍴 €€€€

A Brussels institution, this stylish
restaurant with opulent Belle
Epoque decor and chandeliers is

a favoured gourmet haunt. Try the
excellent sauerkraut, poached egg
with grey shimps, or eel dishes.

## Bonsoir Clara

Rue Antoine Dansaert 22. **Map** 1 B2.
[C] (02) 502 0990. 🍽 AE, MC, V.
🕐 noon–2:30pm, 7–11:30pm
Mon–Fri; 7–midnight Sat & Sun.
🍴 🍴 €€€

Like most of the restaurants started
by young restaurateur Frederic
Nikolay, Bonsoir Clara is a great
place to eat in, rather than a great
place to eat. The city's fashionable
crowd are drawn by the prime
location on Brussels' trendiest
street, by the extravagant decor, a
confection of multicoloured quilt-
ing and garish mirror walls, and
by the chance to see and be seen.
The food is upmarket brasserie
cooking, with dishes including
seared tuna and caramelized duck
among the regular specialities.

## Le Doux Wazoo

Rue du Relais 21. [C] (02) 649 5852.
🍽 AE, DC, MC, V. 🕐 noon–2:30pm,
7–11pm Mon–Fri; 7–11:45pm Sat.
🕐 Mon pm. 🟥 🍴 🍴 €€€

A small, cheerful turn-of-the-
century bistro in the university
district, where the owners'
bohemian philosophy is applied
to the atmosphere rather than the
service. Confit of duck, roast lamb
with pepper purée or duck stew
are on the menu, all made with
quality local produce. The
restaurant's name translates as
"the sweet bird", although non-
natives might find this hard to
work out.

## Le Fils de Jules

Rue du Page 35. [C] (02) 534 0057.
🍽 AE, DC, MC, V. 🕐 noon–2:30pm,
7–11pm Mon–Fri; 7pm–midnight
Sat. 🟥 🟥 🍴 €€€

Brussels' only Basque restaurant
offers rich, imaginative cuisine and
fine wines from southwest France
in a plum spot near Ixelles' busy
Place du Châtelain. Dishes include
spiced squid, *foie gras* with a
compote of figs, and duck breast in
walnut sauce. While the cooking is
clearly Mediterranean, the setting
is a stylishly minimal blend of Art
Deco and the French modernist
designer Philippe Starck, who has
designed many of Europe's top
restaurants including the London
Conran chain. Reserve in advance.

## Le Pain et le Vin

Chaussée d'Alsemberg 812a. [C] (02)
332 3774. 🍽 AE, MC, V. 🕐 noon–
2:30pm, 7–10:30pm Mon–Fri;
7–10:30pm Sat. 🟥 🟥 €€€€

Eric Boschman is one of Belgium's most talented sommeliers, so it is no surprise that his restaurant on the southern tip of Brussels offers a splendid selection of French and New World wines at extremely reasonable prices. The good news is that it also offers light, imaginative French and modern Mediterranean cuisine, with an emphasis on fish, and a candle-lit garden.

## Les Amis du Cep

Rue Theodore Decuyper 136. **(** (02) 762 6295. **AE, MC, V.** noon–2pm, 7–10pm Tue–Sat. €€€

This refined restaurant housed in a Thirties villa in the residential Woluwe-Saint-Lambert district offers classic and modern French food. Most people choose the four-course "surprise menu" for two, but some may prefer to stick to the à la carte menu, which includes quail stew with *foie gras*, and *scallop tartare*. The lunch menu is fantastic value.

## Les Brasseries Georges

Ave Winston Churchill 259. **(** (02) 347 2100. ★ **AE, DC, MC, V.** 11:30am–midnight Sun–Thu; 11:30am–1am Fri & Sat. €€€

The first thing to notice here is the ostentatious pavement stall, piled high with tubs of oysters and lobsters. Inside, the brash, bustling brasserie has become one of southern Brussels' landmarks. The service is professional if a little brusque, which is understandable given the volume of custom. The extensive wine list includes several vintages by the glass, and menu staples vary from grilled tuna with herb butter to kidneys in mustard sauce, although the Georges' fame depends partly on the exquisitely fresh seafood platters.

## L'Ogenblik

Galerie des Princes 1. **Map** 2 D2. **(** (02) 511 6151. ★ **AE, MC, DC, V.** noon–2:30pm, 7pm–midnight Mon–Thu; 7pm–12:30am Fri & Sat. €€€€

In a little side street off the Rue des Bouchers, this classy but informal establishment masks its quality behind artfully faded Parisian-style bistro decor. The creative dishes, among them fillet of sea bass with aubergine caviar and calf sweetbreads with cheese-topped courgette, are prepared with impeccably fresh ingredients. Despite the central location, the lively crowd is mostly composed of well-heeled locals.

## Comme Chez Soi

23 Place Rouppe. **Map** 1 C4. **(** (02) 512 2921. ★ **AE, DC, MC, V.** noon–1:30pm, 7–9:30pm Tue–Sat. €€€€€

Brussels' best restaurant works hard to maintain its three Michelin stars, with head chef Pierre Wynants continually creating adventurous market-based dishes for those not satisfied by his legendary sole fillet with Riesling mousse. The game, *foie gras* and caviar are superlative, as is the Art Nouveau decor, although the intimacy can border on the cramped. Tables must be booked weeks in advance.

## La Truffe Noire

Boulevard de la Cambre 12. **(** (02) 640 4422. **AE, DC, MC, V.** noon–2pm, 7–10pm Mon–Fri; 7–10pm Sat. €€€€€

This gourmet restaurant is seventh heaven for truffle-lovers. The location – a townhouse on a quiet street near Bois de la Cambre – has a discreetly exclusive feel, heightened by the fresh, modern interior and the classical background music. Indulge in truffle-stuffed pigeon, truffle carpaccio, truffle purée or the extravagant six-course menu, which takes in all aspects of this delicious fungus.

### ITALIAN

Belgium has a sizeable Italian community, most of whom arrived in the 1950s to work in the mines of Wallonia. Many moved to Brussels, where they opened unpretentious trattorias or pizzerias. The bulk of the capital's Italian restaurants fall into this category, and are often unremarkable, though handy for those on a budget. Brussels also has several upmarket Italian restaurants, serving more accomplished and authentic food. These establishments tend to be rather formal, and booking is always advisable.

## Aux Anges

Rue Diderich 33–35. **(** (02) 539 3906. **MC, V.** noon–2pm Mon; noon–2pm, 7–11pm Tue–Sat. €€

This small hideout in the backstreets of St-Gilles is a must for couples, not least because of the half-veiled corner niche designed especially for two. The decor features statuettes of angels and Raphael reproductions, while the menu offers modern, sophisticated pasta dishes such as penne with *foie gras* and truffle oil. Light modern cuisine is also represented in the use of grilled polenta and macerated olive oils.

## Rugantino

Blvd Anspach 184–186. **Map** 1 C3. **(** (02) 511 2195. ★ **AE, MC, V.** noon–3pm, 6:30pm–midnight Mon–Fri; 6:30–11:45pm Sat. €€€

A short walk from the Grand Place, this airy, high-ceilinged trattoria has cream-coloured walls and flamboyant Art Deco motifs. The owner is from Abruzzi in Italy and the menu reflects his origins, with signature dishes including beef topped with rocket and Parmesan, rosemary roast lamb and pasta with spinach and ricotta.

## A'mbriana

Rue Edith Cavell 151. **(** (02) 375 0156. **AE, DC, MC, V.** noon–2:30pm, 7–10:30pm Wed–Mon; 7–10:30pm Sat. €€€

Exquisite Italian food and wine and a warm welcome have earned this slick modern eatery near Parc Montjoie a fine reputation, helped by the low prices of the fixed and lunch-time menus. Classic dishes include *carpaccio* of swordfish, beef with rocket and black lasagne with seafood and leeks. Much favoured by Eurocrats, the menu changes often but manages to buy both fresh and modern. Booking in advance is recommended.

## La Fin de Siècle

Avenue de l'Armée 3. **Map** 4 F4. **(** (02) 732 7434. ★ **V.** noon–2:30pm, 7–10:30pm Mon–Fri. €€€

Younger Eurocrats get business off their mind in this restfully Baroque restaurant, where candles and classical music ensure a harmonious ambiance. The creative, contemporary Italian menu includes linguine with scallops and truffle oil or smoked salmon with saffron and mascarpone. Its sister restaurant, Fin de Siècle, occupies a townhouse on Avenue Louise, with similar setting and dishes, but improved facilities for disabled travellers.

## La Scala

Chaussée de Wavre 132. **Map** 2 F5. **(** (02) 514 4995. **AE, DC, MC, V.** noon–2:30pm, 7–10pm Mon–Fri; 7–11pm Sat. €€€

One of the best Italian deals in town, this upbeat eatery has a popular fixed menu, which includes wine and coffee. Classical dishes include veal kidneys, *foie gras* with wild mushrooms and duck ravioli. Candle light and the owner's occasional tinklings on the piano provide plenty of romantic atmosphere.

## Le Pou qui Tousse

Vieille Halle aux Blés 49. **Map** 1 C3.
🄲 *(02) 512 2871.* 🄴 *AE, DC, MC, V.*
🄾 *noon–2pm, 6:30–10pm Mon,
Tue, Thu–Sat; noon–2pm Wed.*
⬤ *Sun.* €€€

Le Pou qui Tousse (the coughing
louse) is a pleasant, family-run
Sardinian restaurant just off Rue
de Lombard, where you can watch
the chefs prepare risotto with cut-
tlefish ink, grill Mediterranean fish
or toss seafood salad in an open-
plan kitchen. The walls are hung
with contemporary European art.

## Osteria delle Stelle

Avenue L. Bertrand 53–61.
🄲 *(02) 241 4808.* ★ 🄴 *AE, DC,
MC, V.* 🄾 *noon–3pm, 7–11pm
Mon–Sat.* 🍴 €€€

A hundred years ago, the northern
commune of Schaerbeek was one
of Brussels' most elegant districts,
and the splendid Art Nouveau
interior of this Italian brasserie
provides a poignant reminder of
former glories. A delightful place
to dine, fresh octopus salad, or sea
bass caught on a line accompany
gorgonzola polenta on the wide
menu. The all-you-can-eat buffet
of antipasti costs around just €15.
It is wise to reserve.

# NORTH AFRICAN AND
# CENTRAL AFRICAN

Whether the sharp, nutty tastes of
central Africa or a spicy couscous
from Morocco appeal, African
cooking is among the world's
most vibrant, and the sizeable
communities from the Democratic
Republic of Congo and North
Africa have brought plenty of
flavour to Brussels' dining scene.
The city's more enterprising
entrepreneurs have opened lavishly decorated "designer couscous"
eateries, although many feel these
are not entirely authentic. Central
African food can vary sharply, and
although the quality of the cooking is not always consistent, dishes
such as the peanut-based chicken
moambe and chicken yassa, made
with limes, are deliciously simple.
The relaxed atmosphere is great.

## Gri Gri

Rue Basse 16. 🄲 *(02) 375 8202.*
★ 🄴 *AE, DC, MC, V.*
🄾 *6:30–11pm Mon; noon–3pm,
6:30–11pm Tue–Fri; 6:30–11pm Sat.*
🍴 €

South of the city centre in the
district of Uccle, this small, brightly
decorated restaurant is an education
for those unfamiliar with central

African cooking. The starters
include spicy cod croquettes and
crispy meat samusas (deep-fried
mince-filled filo parcels) with a
sweet sauce. Kenyan-style scampi
with sweet curry and crocodile,
chicken yassa (in a lime sauce) or
stuffed crab are among the main
courses. On occasion, the owner
plays the drums for his customers.

## La Pirogue

Rue Sainte-Anne 18. **Map** 2 D4.
🄲 *(02) 511 3525.* 🄾 *3–10:30pm
Tue–Fri, noon–10:30pm Sat & Sun.*
€

If you find the cafés and restaurants on Place du Grand Sablon too
formal, then this is the perfect anti-
dote. Tucked away at the end of a
nearby quiet alley, it has an extensive and secluded outdoor seating
area where you can sip home-made
ginger beer or tamarind juice into
the early hours, or enjoy chicken
yassa (made with onions and lime),
spicy mutton chops or chicken in
peanut sauce. Given the location,
the prices are very low.

## Kasbah

Rue Antoine Dansaert 20. **Map** 1 C2.
🄲 *(02) 502 4026.* ★ 🄴 *AE, MC, V.*
🄾 *noon–3pm 6:30pm–midnight
daily.* 🆅 🍴 €€

The authentic ambiance in this
stylish Moroccan restaurant is the
perfect setting for the North African
food on offer. Located in a 19th-
century town house near to the
Bourse, the Kasbah's menu
includes such classic dishes as
lamb tajines, *merguez* sausages
and grilled couscous. There is also
a good selection of Moroccan
wines to choose from.

## Ile de Gorée

Rue Saint-Boniface 28. **Map** 2 E5.
🄲 *(02) 513 5293.* 🄾 *noon–
11:30pm, Tue–Sat, 3–11:30pm Sun.*
€€

One of the legacies of Belgium's
colonial past is an abundance of
Congolese, Senegalese and
Rwandan bars and eateries in the
capital. This upmarket restaurant
boasts traditional music, decor and
cuisine, including smoked chicken
wings, generous portions of couscous and spicy lamb. The service
is leisurely and relaxed.

## Medina

Avenue de la Couronne 2.
🄲 *(02) 640 4328.* 🄴 *AE, DC, MC, V.*
🄾 *noon–2:30pm, 6–11pm Tue–
Sun.* 🆅 €€

Moorish arches, high ceilings and
blue-and-white tiles give this pop-

ular Moroccan restaurant in Ixelles
a bright, airy feel. Lift the fun-
nelled clay tajine lid that arrives
over your food and the aroma of
lemons, onions and fruit floods
out, adding considerably to the
appeal of the couscous and tajines
that are the menu's mainstays.
Other specialities include pigeon-
stuffed pastries and orange and
cinnamon salad. A belly-dancer
performs at the weekend, much to
the delight of local patrons and
their families.

## Les Jardins de
## Bagatelle

Rue du Berger 17. **Map** 2 E5. 🄲 *(02)
512 1276.* 🄴 *AE, DC, MC, V.*
🄾 *noon–2pm, 7–11:30pm Tue–Sat.*
⬤ *Sat lunch.* 🍴 €€€

A turn-of-the-century Ixelles
townhouse houses one of the
capital's most eclectic restaurants,
where the leopard-skin chairs and
tropical plants are offset by stately
English porcelain. Equally lively,
the kitchen bursts with flavours
from across the globe. African and
French influences predominate,
with Congolese chicken, Louisana-
style prawns or salmon tartare
with a creamy lemon sauce.

# ASIAN AND
# PACIFIC RIM

Brussels has an enormous number
of both Chinese and Vietnamese
restaurants, ranging from drop-in
snack bars to veritable miniature
palaces. The Chaussée de
Boondael student area in Ixelles
has the best choice, with over 20
good restaurants. Lighter and more
pungent than Chinese cuisine,
Vietnamese food is simpler and
more homely than Thai. Its
emphasis on spicy soups and
pancakes can be a diversion in a
city of such rich food. Brussels'
Chinese restaurants may not be
entirely exceptional, but the city's
Thai restaurants, especially the
more expensive ones, are of high
quality. Those keen on low-priced
Indian food may be disappointed,
but, again, the more lavish dining
locations are excellent.

## Hông Hoa

Rue du Pont de la Carpe 10.
**Map** 1 C2. 🄲 *(02) 502 8714.*
🄾 *noon–11pm daily.* 🍴 €

There are only eight tables in this
cosy, crimson-walled restaurant
near the Halles St-Géry. Service
is fast and friendly and the food
includes pancakes stuffed with
pork and prawns, diced beef with
onions and crispy duck with fresh
slices of ginger.

## La Cantonnaise

Rue Tenbosch 110. 📞 *(02) 344 7042.*
🕐 *11:30am–3pm, 7–11pm Mon–Fri;
5–11pm Sat & Sun.* ★ 🔥 📶 🍴€

The owner of this deceptively plain
little restaurant off Chaussée de
Waterloo once ran a more formal
establishment, but realized that, by
reducing the number of tables and
dishes on offer, he could slash his
prices without compromising on
quality. The result is a restaurant
and take-away offering some of
the capital's tastiest Chinese food:
freshly cooked dim sum and spicy
beef and pork dishes are prepared
following recipes by the owner's
mother, who is a professional cook.

## Le Pacifique

Boulevard du General Jacques 115.
📞 *(02) 640 5259.* ★ 📶 *MC, V.*
🕐 *noon–3pm, 6:30–11pm
Wed–Mon.* 🔥 🍴€

Le Pacifique is an unpretentious,
hospitable Vietnamese restaurant in
the bustling Chaussée de Boondael
area of Ixelles, near the university.
The prices are geared to the
student market, but the cooking is
subtle and makes considerable use
of fresh herbs. Try clear, spicy soup
with scampi and lemon, chicken
and beansprout salad with mint
or the restaurant's signature dish,
pork-and-scampi stuffed pancakes.

## Poussières d'Etoiles

Chaussée de Boondael 437. 📞 *(02)
640 7158.* 🕐 *noon–2:30pm, 6:30pm–
11:30 daily.* 🔥 ♿ 📶 🎵 🍴€

Despite the kitschy decor – starry
skylights, twinkling twigs and
fluffy, feather-fringed lanterns – this
newish Vietnamese restaurant near
the university is a welcome addition
to the city's low-cost culinary
scene, attracting a trendy but laid-
back crowd. The range of dishes is
unusually small, with the emphasis
on quality produce rather than
diversity: fragrant seafood stew
with ginger and lime, caramelized
langoustines and chicken with
mushrooms and tangy ginger.
Portions are on the delicate side.

## La Citronnelle

Chaussée de Wavre 1377. 📞 *(02)
672 9843.* 📶 *AE, DC, MC, V.*
🕐 *noon–2:30pm, 6:30–10:30pm
Tue–Fri & Sun; 6:30–10:30pm Sat.*
📶 🍴€€

This Vietnamese restaurant in
Auderghem oozes charm whether
you sit in the plant-filled interior
or the pretty garden. Traditional
music plays in the background, and
the delicate dishes include crispy
duck with ginger, grilled scampi
with lemongrass and braised beef.

## La Maison de Thailande

Rue Middelbourg 22. 📞 *(02) 672
2657.* ★ 📶 *AE, DC, MC, V.*
🕐 *noon–2pm, 7–10pm Tue–Fri.*
🕐 *Tue lunch.* 🍴 📶 €€

Lauded for its refined, delicious
Thai cuisine, this restaurant in leafy
Watermael-Boitsfort is run by a
Thailand-obsessed Belgian photo-
grapher and his Thai wife. The
"discovery menu" offers five starters
and four main courses, offering a
surprising array of delicate dishes,
including fish and duck recipes.

## La Porte des Indes

Avenue Louise 455. **Map** 2 D5. 📞
*(02) 647 8651.* ★ 📶 *AE, DC, MC, V.*
🕐 *noon  2:30pm, 7–10:30pm daily.*
🕐 *Sun lunch.* 🍴 📶 €€€

Brussels is something of a wilder-
ness for curry-lovers, but this
upmarket Indian eatery provides
considerable consolation. Lavishly
decorated with antiques collected
by owner Karl Steppe, who also
runs the Blue Elephant, La Porte
des Indes serves delicate traditional cuisine from the Pondicherry
region. Both exotic and traditional
dishes are on offer, including Parsee
fish with mint and coriander
wrapped in banana leaf parcels and
beef Pondicherry style. Choose the
"Brass Plate" menu if you want to
sample several dishes. Traditional
drinks, including Indian beers, are
also on offer as well as the
ubiquitous sweet and sour lassi
and various native lager beers.

## Blue Elephant

Chaussée de Waterloo 1120. 📞 *(02)
374 4962.* ★ 📶 *AE, DC, MC, V.*
🕐 *noon–2:30pm, 7–10:30pm Sun–Fri;
7–11:30pm Sat.* 🍴 🔥 €€€€

This high-dining experience at the
Bois de la Cambre end of Chaussée
de Waterloo shares an owner with
the famous British restaurant of the
same name; both are run by the
Belgian nomad and antiques collector Karl Steppe. Thai paraphernalia
and exotic plants fill the dining
room without cluttering it, and the
subtly spicy food has the same
admirable clarity, combining sweet,
hot, sour and bitter tastes without
blurring them. The lunch menu,
at around €13, is wonderful.

### MEDITERRANEAN AND
### MIDDLE EASTERN

Like most European cities, Brussels
has some authentic Mediterranean
restaurants dotted about town.
Considering the size of the city's
Turkish population, Turkish restaurants have yet to make their mark,
but the number of good Lebanese

establishments is growing. Many
specialize in meze and Lebanese
kebabs, a quick way to eat well.
Greek restaurants have also had
a loyal following for decades.

## L'Ouzerie

Chaussée d'Ixelles 235. **Map** 2 E5.
📞 *(02) 646 4449.* 📶 *AE, MC, V.*
🕐 *7pm–midnight Mon–Sat (1am
Fri & Sat).* 📶 ♿ €

This informal eatery stands out for
the quality of its dishes and service.
The decor is refreshingly simple, as
is the menu, which avoids clichéd
moussaka or grilled lamb, focusing
instead on such traditional dishes
as spinach and cheese stuffed pastries, grilled peppers and aubergine
salad. L'Ouzerie can get crowded,
so it's worth booking in advance.

## L'Ouzerie du
## Nouveau Monde

Chaussée de Boondael 290. 📞 *(02)
649 8588.* ★ 📶 *AE, DC, MC, V.*
🕐 *noon–3pm, 6pm–midnight Sun–
Fri; 6pm–1am Sat.* 📶 📶 €

Along with L'Ouzerie, this authentic
Greco-Cretan restaurant has
breathed fresh life into Brussels'
Greek restaurant scene, with low
prices, delightful food and a warm
welcome. The emphasis is on meze
starters: grilled pepper salad, char-
grilled ribs, stuffed vine leaves,
spicy sausages, and Cypriot goat's
cheese; around four per person
should satisfy most appetites.

## Al Barmaki

Rue des Eperonniers 67. **Map** 2 D3.
📞 *(02) 513 0834.* 📶 *MC, V.*
🕐 *7pm–midnight Mon–Sat.*
📶 🍴 €€

A short walk from the Grand Place,
this cavernous eatery is probably
Brussels' best Lebanese restaurant.
Al Barmaki specializes in meze, an
assortment of small dishes that
include tabouleh (a pungent mint,
parsley and Bulgur wheat salad),
felafel and hummus, as well as
spicy sausages or chicken kebabs.

## Sahbaz

Chaussée de Haecht 102–104. 📞 *(02)
217 0277.* 📶 *MC, V.* 🕐 *11:30–3pm,
6pm–midnight Mon–Tue, Thu–Sun.*
📶 ♿ 🍴 €€

Brussels' oldest Turkish restaurant
opened in 1980, when a wave of
migrants from Turkey arrived in
the city. Now quite an institution,
a mixed crowd flocks to the little
restaurant to sample sheep's head
soup, oven-baked lamb, minced
meat in aubergine parcels and, for
vegetarians, crispy rolls stuffed
with sour goat's cheese. Turkish-
style omelettes and vegetable
pizzas are also on offer.

## SPANISH AND PORTUGUESE

Both Spanish and Portuguese cuisines adapt well to the Brussels food scene, as Belgium's fresh seafood and emphasis on quality ingredients reflect Mediterranean traditions. The Hapsburg dynasty ruled both Belgium and Spain for generations, and it was their diplomatic movements through the centuries that introduced these new schools of cookery to Brussels.

### Casa Manuel

Grand Place 34. **Map** 2 D3.
( (02) 511 4746. ⊠ AE, DC, MC, V. ◯ noon–2:30pm, 6:30–midnight daily. ⊞ ᕦ ♫ ¶❶ €€

A great place in the heart of town to escape the crowds, this unshowy restaurant has been serving Spanish and Portuguese specialities since 1960. Eat paella, calamaris, and prawns in garlic as you are serenaded by a guitarist and, occasionally, the tuneful head waiter.

### Le Forcado

Chaussée de Charleroi 192.
( (02) 537 9220. ★ ⊠ AE, DC, MC, V. ◯ noon–2pm, 7–10pm Tue–Sat. ⊞ ¶❶ €€€

The fado music, cool 18th-century tiles and Renaissance lanterns lend an authentic atmosphere to Brussels' best Portuguese restaurant. The food includes mushroom gratin with port, salt-cod croquettes, grilled red mullet and marinated pork with clams as well as the national dish, fish stew. For dessert, try the home-made cakes and pastries, many flavoured with cinammon which can also be found on sale at the restaurant's shop just around the corner.

## CENTRAL AND EASTERN EUROPE

Spicy, warming dishes are sometimes welcome in a city renowned for its haute cuisine. From blinis with smoked salmon and caviar to rich goulash and hearty casseroles, the range of Central and Eastern European authentic dishes is a wide one for such a small capital, and for the most part the dishes are very reasonably priced for the high quality on offer.

### Kocharata

Avenue Parc 4. ( (02) 537 4296. ◯ noon–1pm, 6pm–midnight Tue–Sun. €€

This simple restaurant, run by an elderly Bulgarian couple whose amiable welcome belies a canny business sense, has turned out substantial and good-value food for 30 years. It is tucked away in the heart of Saint-Gilles and has a loyal and ebullient following among locals and the city's east European community. Specialities include meatballs, kebabs, beetroot soup and a mountain goat's cheese served like a fondue.

### Les Ateliers de la Grande Ile

Rue de la Grande Ile 33. ( (02) 512 8190. ⊠ AE, DC, MC, V. ◯ 7:30pm–2am Tue–Sun. €€

This Russian eaterie is popular with large parties whose top priority is having fun without being told to keep the noise down. Copious quantities of speciality vodkas are next on the list, with the food a resolute third. Chicken Kiev is a favourite, not bad considering the speed at which it arrives. Table-thumping and sing-songs are regular here. This is the place to go if you want to let your hair down, but watch out for the hangover-inducing quaffability of the vodkas.

## LATIN AMERICAN

This exotic cuisine was brought to Brussels after World War II. Providing a light-hearted and less calorific cuisine to the native Belgian, South American restaurants are known for their warm, relaxed ambience and reasonable prices. Fresh ingredients and fine fillets of meat are priorities in the kitchens. The jazzy atmosphere is often accompanied by live salsa and pre-dinner cocktail menus can be innovative and sometimes seductively powerful.

### El Papagayo

Place Rouppe 6. **Map** 1 C4. ( (02) 514 5083. ◯ 4pm–2am Mon–Fri; 6pm–2am Sat & Sun. ⊞ ¶❶ €

Across the road from the majestic Comme Chez Soi, this Latino restaurant compensates for its slightly less refined cuisine with a relaxed and intimate atmosphere, perfect for relaxing in after a hard day's sightseeing. There are three floors, each with two or three tiny dining areas. The walls are unpainted brick and the innovative tables are converted iron sewing-machine stands. The South American food includes raw fish with lime, chili con carne, spicy pork stew and a wide range of salads. The cocktail menu is terrific. Unusually for Brussels, freshly made cock-

tails are on offer; exotic fruit juices and fruit pulp are poured over crushed ice and mixed with a powerful variety of spirits and tequilas, including gold tequila and Mexican brandies.

### Cantina Cubana

Rue des Grands-Carmes 6. **Map** 1 C3. ( (02) 502 6540. ⊠ MC, V. ★ ◯ Jun–Sep: 8pm–midnight daily; Oct–May: 7–11:30pm daily. €€

In a little street across the way from Manneken Pis, this small Cuban diner has brought a welcome taste of the Caribbean to central Brussels. Sway to the sound of traditional guitar in the background while admiring the photographs on the white-washed walls and the daily menu chalked up on a blackboard. The emphasis is on chicken, fish and pork dishes – chicken with coconut sauce, cod with salsa verde, spare ribs and pork with sour black bean sauce – as well as exotic fruit drinks and cocktails. Tropical fruit dishes are on offer for dessert, including mango sorbet and fruit crème brulée. The service is very friendly.

### Tierra del Fuego

Rue Berckmans 14. ( (02) 537 4272. ⊠ MC, V. ◯ 7–11pm Mon–Fri; 6:30pm–2am Sat–Sun. ⊞ ♫ €€

The bar-restaurant of Brussels' Latin-American cultural centre near Place Stéphanie is an accomplished blend of Old and New World cultures, with Spanish-style Moorish touches, offset by embossed ceiling stars and pictures of snow-capped peaks that recall South America's ancient Inca culture. The well-judged cuisine includes guacamole, marinated raw fish, burritos and Argentine beef, while you can relax after dinner with a Cuban cigar and South American coffees.

## FISH AND SEAFOOD

The tradition of seafood in Belgium is a long and illustrious one. With more Michelin-starred restaurants in the country than France, the centuries-old refinement of recipes and dishes owes something to the exceptional quality of fresh produce available from the ports. Even today fresh fish and shellfish are delivered to Brussels within two hours of the catch; sole, plaice and cod among the regular deliveries, with baskets of shrimps caught by horseback riders on the coast ferried daily to market. Both French and Flemish schools influence the cooking, which includes historic favourites such as Ostend sole and grilled lobster.

## Bij den Boer

Quai aux Briques 60. **Map** 1 C1.
**(** (02) 512 6122. ★ 🅔 AE, DC,
MC, V. ⬜ noon–2:30pm, 6–
10:30pm Mon–Sat. 🅱 🏃 ¶⦿¶
€€

This Flemish-run restaurant is
one of the most reasonably priced
and authentic brasseries on the
Vismarkt, or Old Fish Market.
The mirror panels and check
tablecloths give it a local, unpretentious feel, but the kitchen offers
accomplished versions of classic
fish dishes, including monkfish
with oysters.

## L'Achepot

Place Ste-Catherine 1. **Map** 1 C2.
**(** (02) 511 6221. 🅔 V.
⬜ noon–3pm, 6:30–10:30pm daily.
🅱 🏃 €€

The best reason to visit this
earthy but nonetheless stylish
bistro-tavern near the Vismarkt
is to try the poisson du jour (fish
dish of the day), a cheap, fresh
and invariably delicious meal
such as whiting in lemon and
butter with plain boiled potatoes.
The menu also features traditional
brasserie fare, including chicken
breast with tarragon sauce, goat's
cheese parcels and spare ribs.

## La Marée

Rue de Flandre 99. **Map** 1 B1.
**(** (02) 511 0040. ★ 🅔 AE, DC,
MC, V. ⬜ noon–2pm, 6:30–10pm
Wed–Sat; noon–2:30pm Sun.
🅱 €€

Simplicity is the hallmark of this
cosily unpretentious fish restaurant
located near Place Ste-Catherine.
The service is extremely professional and the pared-down, elegant
cooking puts many more expensive establishments to shame. Try
the fried cod with tartare sauce,
skate wings with butter or one of
eight varieties of stewed mussel
preparations. When in season,
plain grilled lobster is a highlight,
served with green herb sauce.

## La Truite d'Argent

Quai au Bois à Bruler 23. **Map** 1 C1.
**(** (02) 219 9546. ★ 🅔 AE, DC,
MC, V. ⬜ noon–2:30pm, 7–
11:30pm Mon–Fri; 7–11:30pm Sat.
🅱 🏃 ¶⦿¶ €€€€

This opulent but intimate restaurant in a 19th-century townhouse
is among the best restaurants on
the Vismarkt. The fresh, inventive
and uncluttered cuisine includes
beautifully presented millefeuille of
salmon, North Sea bouillabaisse,
six different preparations of
lobster, a splendidly nostalgic

prawn cocktail and steamed
monkfish with spinach. The
waiters go out of their way to
make you feel special, and the
wine list is varied and far from
overpriced.

## Scheltema

Rue des Dominicains 7. **Map** 2 D2.
**(** (02) 512 2084. 🅔 AE, MC.
⬜ 11:30am–3pm, 6pm–11:30pm
Mon–Thu; 11:30am–3pm, 6pm–
12:30am Fri & Sat. 🈹 €€€€

This superb Belle Epoque brasserie off Rue des Bouchers in the
heart of Brussels is a place for a
celebration, with a cheery atmosphere and upmarket fish cuisine.
Although the prices reflect the
central location and the proliferation
of tourists, the food is excellent
and generous, with reasonably
priced set menus. Dishes include
sole and scallops in champagne
vinaigrette, and lobster and
salmon grilled with orange.

## De Matelote

Haarstraat 9, Antwerp. **(** (03) 231
3207. ★ 🅔 AE, DC, MC, V.
⬜ noon–2pm, 7–10pm Mon–Sat.
⬜ Mon & Sat lunch, Jul. 🈳 🅥
¶⦿¶ €€€€€

Located in the old town, the cosy,
12-table De Matelote is reputed to
be Antwerp's best fish restaurant.
The menu varies daily and depending on the season, but typical
dishes include sea scallops cooked
with a stock of mushrooms and
sorrel and langoustines in a light
curry sauce. Reservations essential.

## L'Ecailler du Palais Royal

Rue Bodenbroeck 18. **Map** 2 D4.
**(** (02) 512 8751. ★ 🅔 AE, DC,
MC, V. ⬜ noon–2:30pm, 7–10:30pm
Mon–Sat. 🅱 🅿 €€€€€

Despite its awesome reputation
and a star location on Place du
Grand Sablon, this unshowy restaurant is the epitome of elegant
discretion. It specializes in French-
influenced fish and seafood, with
produce whose high quality lends
itself to simple preparations: monkfish with herb butter, lobster ravioli
and heavenly prawn croquettes.
The excellence, however, is reflected in the pricing: even a lunchtime dish of the day will set you
back around €25.

## Sea Grill

Rue du Fosse-aux-Loups 47. **Map** 2 D2.
**(** (02) 227 3120. ★ 🅔 AE, DC,
MC, V. ⬜ noon–2:30pm, 7–10:30pm
Mon–Sat. 🅢 Sat lunch. 🅱 🅿
€€€€€

When the Swedish hotel group
Radisson SAS hired French chef
Yves Mattagne to run the restaurant
at their new Brussels hotel in 1991,
they could never have anticipated
his success. Before the end of the
century, he had won two Michelin
stars and a reputation as the best
fish cook in Belgium. Mattagne's
classic dishes include sea bass
roasted in sea salt, crab with olive
oil and thyme, Breton lobster and
sumptuous seafood platters,
although the daily suggestions are
usually also worth careful attention. The decor is modern and
functional, but service is superb.

## VEGETARIAN

Because of the Belgian dedication
to red meat, Brussels is not a
haven for the vegetarian. Healthy
establishments, many located in
the student district of Chaussée
de Boondael, serve wholesome
dishes and often sell takeaways
and organic supplies.

## Dolma

Chaussée d'Ixelles 329. **Map** 2 E5.
**(** (02) 649 8981. 🅔 AE, DC, MC, V
⬜ noon–2pm, 7–9.30pm Mon–Sat.
🅥 🏃 ¶⦿¶ €

This eatery near Place Flagey
specializes in Tibetan dishes,
with a suitably ethnic decor. Its
hallmark is the reasonably priced
all-you-can-eat vegetarian buffet.
Snacks are on sale in the organic
shop just next door.

## Shanti

Avenue A. Buyl 68. **(** (02) 649 4096.
★ 🅔 AE, DC, MC, V. ⬜ noon–
2pm, 7–10pm Tue–Sat. 🅥 ¶⦿¶ €€

This Ixelles eatery is one of
Brussels' most popular vegetarian
restaurants, albeit not against that
much competition. The atmosphere is relaxed, with classical
music at lunchtime and jazz in
the evening. Try fragrant rice,
aubergine or tandoori fish.

## Tsampa

Rue de Livourne 109. **(** (02) 647
0367. ⬜ noon–2pm, 7–9:30pm
Mon–Sat. 🅥 🅱 🈹 ¶⦿¶ €

This plant-filled restaurant has an
organic produce shop at the front
and an Asian-inspired menu
drawing on Thai and Indian cuisine
in the rear dining area. Organic
wines are served with curries and
basmati rice and Tibetan-style
ravioli and cheese dishes, such
as deep-fried pastries stuffed with
sheep's cheese. With a lively
crowd composed of students and
the city's youth, the restaurant has
a cheery, bohemian atmosphere.

# Cafés and Bars

WITH A WATERING hole on almost every street offering world-famous quality ales, Brussels fully deserves its reputation as a paradise for beer-lovers. Taverns, cafés and bars all serve a range of at least twenty beers, as well as a handsome variety of continental coffees, herbal teas, fruit juice and spirits. Most establishments stay open from morning to midnight, and often later at weekends.

## CLASSIC CAFES

A DRINK ON the Grand Place is an essential part of any visit to Brussels, although costs can be high. Perhaps the best, and one of the best priced, is **Le Roy d'Espagne** (see p43), a huge two-tiered bar housed in the bakers' guildhouse with prime views from its terrace. The terraces at neighbouring La Brouette offer similar views, as does Le Cygne, where Karl Marx worked on *The Communist Manifesto* during the early 1840s.

Moments from the Grand Place lies **Au Bon Vieux Temps**, a quiet bar in a 17th-century building with the homely feel of an English pub. **Le Cirio**, near the Bourse, is a quintessential café from the 1900s, beloved by fans of Belle Epoque decor. Close by is **A la Mort Subite**, one of the capital's most celebrated establishments. Immense wooden tables, peeling mirrors and brusque service add to the appeal. Moving eastward to Place de Brouckère, the Hôtel Métropole contains a fabulous, opulent Belle Epoque bar, **The 19th**, as well as a heated outdoor terrace.

The Place du Grand Sablon is a favourite area for café-goers and those who want to catch the feel of the bustling city. The most upmarket spot here is **Au Vieux Saint-Martin**. **Les Salons du Sablon**, nearby, is a luxurious tea-room run by top chocolatiers Wittamer. This family-run business uses a century's worth of skill to create delicious confections.

## SPECIALIST BEER BARS

B EER BUFFS should head to **Chez Moeder Lambic**, near the town hall in St-Gilles. A small and chaotic bar with a few tables scattered outside on the pavement, it serves over 1,000 beers. The choice covers most of Belgium's 400 or so varieties, as well as exotic brews from overseas, many customers cope with the choice by picking a letter from the alphabetized menu.

## ART NOUVEAU

A FORMER haunt of Surrealist painter René Magritte, **Le Greenwich** is now the city's premier venue for chess enthusiasts; matches run around the clock. Also celebrated is **Les Fleurs en Papier Doré**, the meeting point for Belgian Surrealists in the late 1920s and still lively. **Café Falstaff**, opened in 1903 by the Bourse, has original Horta-designed furniture. South of Place du Grand Sablon, **Le Perroquet** attracts a young crowd, keen on its filled pittas. The best-known Art Nouveau bar, **De Ultieme Hallucinatie**, is nearby.

## COSMOPOLITAN

B RUSSELS HAS a thriving social scene for the young and fashionable, most of which takes place around Place St-Géry in the Lower Town. Trendy, but not pretentious or stuffy, the clutch of bars here are mostly modernist in design, with some restored historic features. **Zebra** is a tastefully minimal bare brick and metal bar with a huge terrace that attracts crowds on warm evenings. Opposite Zebra is **Mappa Mundo**, a two-storey oak-panelled drinking spot which offers light meals and a good beer selection. Nearby the cavernous **Beurs Café** attracts the artistic crowd with its DJ sets and hip sounds. **L'Archiduc** boasts a breathtaking Art Deco interior and live jazz performances (see p159).

(see p43)
(see p159)

---

## DIRECTORY

### CLASSIC

**Le Roy d'Espagne**
Grand Place 1. **Map** 2 D3.
( (02) 513 0807.

**Au Bon Vieux Temps**
Rue du Marché aux Herbes 12.
**Map** 2 D3. ( (02) 217 2626.

**Le Cirio**
Rue de la Bourse 18.
**Map** 1 C2. ( (02) 512 1395.

**A la Mort Subite**
Rue Montagne aux Herbes 7.
**Map** 2 D2. ( (02) 513 1318.

**Au Vieux Saint-Martin**
Place du Grand Sablon 38.
**Map** 2 D4. ( (02) 512 6476.

**Les Salons du Sablon**
Place du Grand Sablon 12.
**Map** 2 D4. ( (02) 512 3742.

### SPECIALIST BEER BARS

**Chez Moeder Lambic**
Rue de Savoie 68.
( (02) 539 1419.

### ART NOUVEAU

**Le Greenwich**
Rue des Chartreux 7.
**Map** 1 C2. ( (02) 511 4167.

**La Fleurs en Papier Doré**
Rue des Alexiens 55.
**Map** 1 C4. ( (02) 511 1659.

**Café Falstaff**
Rue Henri Maus 21.
( (02) 511 8789.

**Le Perroquet**
Rue Watteau 31. **Map** 2 D4.
( (02) 512 9922.

**De Ultieme Hallucinatie**
Rue Royale 316. **Map** 2 E2.
( (02) 217 0614.

### COSMOPOLITAN

**Zebra**
Place St-Géry 33–35.
**Map** 1 C2. ( (02) 511 0901.

**Mappa Mundo**
Rue Pont de la Carpe 2–6.
( (02) 514 3555.

**Beurs Café**
Rue Auguste Orts 28.
( (02) 550 0350.

# Light Meals and Snacks

BESIDES ITS TRADITIONAL taverns, luxurious patisseries and lively cafés, not to mention the celebrated chip and sticky waffle stands, Brussels is home to a growing number of fashionable quick lunch venues. Several ethnic restaurants also offer hearty, inexpensive snacks.

## BREAKFASTS

BRUSSELS WAS the birthplace of **Le Pain Quotidien,** the designer breakfast phenomenon, which now boasts chic outlets in New York, Munich and Paris. Wholesome breakfasts and lunches, featuring organic yogurt and wholemeal breads, are served around communal wooden tables. Founded in 1829, speculoo biscuit specialist **Dandoy** is an institution, popular with locals and visitors alike for coffee and homemade waffles. **La Maison de Paris** has delicious croissants.

## TAVERNS

THE TRADITIONAL refreshment of Belgian beer and shrimp or cheese croquettes can be found in the city's historic taverns. **Le Paon Royal** is an insight into true Brussels style. **Plattesteen** serves steaks and salads. Nearby **Mokafe** is an elegant café, perfect for a bowl of pasta or a *croque monsieur.*

## CHIP AND WAFFLE SHOPS

THE WARM SMELL of *frites* and sweet waffles is part of Brussels life. **Maison Antoine**, whose clients have included Johnny Hallyday and the Rolling Stones, is the most renowned *friterie*. **Fritland**, near the Grand Place, is also something of an institution.

## SANDWICHES AND SNACKS

MOST TAVERNS and butchers offer straightforward cheese, ham and salami sandwiches, but for *tartines* (British-style sandwiches) or baguettes (French bread), try the elegant **Lunch Company**. Belgian action star Jean-Claude van Damme favours the downtown **Au Suisse**, which has been in the business since 1873 and offers a large choice of fillings, plus its popular double hot-dog. The Flemish Cultural Centre, **De Markten**, sells filling and wholesome snacks.

## TEA ROOMS

BELGIUM IS NOTED for top-quality pastries and cakes, which easily rival its celebrated chocolates. **Au Flan Breton** has been baking fruit-filled cream pastries for nearly a century. Uptown, **Passiflore** serves heavenly chocolate concoctions. Ice-cream enthusiasts should head south to **Zizi's**, a family-run, traditional parlour.

## ETHNIC

MIDDLE EASTERN snacks and take-away food are very well priced at **Orientalia**. Lebanese **L'Express** is often lauded as the best pitta joint in Brussels. **L'Orfeo** has a good selection of pittas and fresh salads. Downtown, Chinese restaurant **Chaochow City** has a bargain lunch room. The Italian bistro **Intermezzo** serves excellent Italian pasta, with many non-meat sauces.

## VEGETARIAN

THE DELICIOUS quiches and salads at **Arcadi**, near the Galéries Saint-Hubert, are largely vegetarian. For organic vegan fare, **Den Teepot** is recommended; it offers a good daily dish or soup of the day, and vegan fruit tarts.

---

## DIRECTORY

### BREAKFASTS

**Dandoy**
Rue Charles Buls 14–18.
(02) 512 6588.

**La Maison de Paris**
Rue de Namur 89. **Map 2**
E4. (02) 511 1195.

**Le Pain Quotidien**
Rue Antoine Dansaert 16.
**Map 1** B1. (02) 502 2361.

### TAVERNS

**Mokafe**
Galerie du Roi 9.
(02) 511 7870.

**Le Paon Royal**
Rue du Vieux Marché aux Grains 6. **Map 1** C2.
(02) 513 0868.

### Plattesteen
Rue du Marché au Charbon 41. **Map 1** C3. (02) 512 8203.

### CHIP AND WAFFLE SHOPS

**Fritland**
Rue Maus.

**Maison Antoine**
Place Jourdan 1. **Map 3** B4. (02) 230 5456.

### SANDWICHES AND SNACKS

**Au Suisse**
73-75 Blvd Anspach.
(02) 512 9589.

**Orientalia**
129 Ch de Mons. **Map 1** A3. (02) 520 7575.

### The Lunch Company
Rue de Namur 16. **Map 2** E4. (02) 502 0976.

### TEA ROOMS

**Au Flan Breton**
Chaussée d'Ixelles 54. **Map 2** E5. (02) 511 8708.

**Passiflore**
Rue du Bailli 97.
(02) 538 4210.

**Zizi's**
Rue de la Mutualité 57a.
(02) 344 7081.

### ETHNIC

**Chaochow City**
Boulevard Anspach 89.
**Map 1** C3. (02) 512 8283.

### De Markten
Rue du Marché aux Grains 5. (02) 512 3475.

### L'Express
Rue des Chapeliers 8. **Map 2** D3. (02) 512 8883.

### Intermezzo
Rue des Princes 16.
(02) 218 0311.

### L'Orfeo
Rue Haute 20. **Map 1** C4.
(02) 512 6041.

### VEGETARIAN

**Arcadi**
Rue d'Arenberg 1b. **Map 2** D2. (02) 511 3343.

**Den Teepot**
Rue des Chartreux 66.
**Map 1** C2. (02) 511 9402.

# SHOPPING IN BRUSSELS

**B**RUSSELS IS an ideal place to shop for luxury goods, from its glorious chocolate shops to quirky market finds and cutting-edge fashion. Street markets are popular year round,

**Belgian chocolates**

or, if your tastes are more glitzy, head for Avenue Louise and Boulevard de Waterloo, where top designers are represented; for the original creations of the Antwerp Six and new-wave fashions, try Rue Antoine Dansaert. For specialist stores, including home decoration, go to rues Haute and Blaes. Many mainstream stores are located on Brussels' longest pedestrian shopping street, Rue Neuve. Other pockets of interest lie a short detour from downtown, in Uccle, St-Gilles and Ixelles.

**A colourful designer fashion boutique on Rue Neuve**

## OPENING HOURS

**T**HERE ARE NO set opening times in Brussels, but most places are open at least between 10am and 5pm.

Mainstream shops in arcades, malls and the Rue Neuve area typically open at 9.30am and close between 6 and 7pm. Late-night shopping runs at some places until 8pm on Friday. Otherwise it depends on where the shop is located and what it is selling.

Mondays and Wednesday or Saturday afternoons are the likeliest times for smaller shops to close (some shut for lunch daily), while many now open for part of Sunday (not supermarkets). For late-night purchases, the White Night chain stays open until 1am. From mid-July to mid-August, many specialist shops, cafés and restaurants close.

## HOW TO PAY

**C**ASH IS THE preferred method of payment, and a surprising number of shops will not accept credit cards, including most supermarkets and many smaller establishments.

At small shops discounts are sometimes given on the more expensive items when they are paid for in cash.

## VAT EXEMPTION

**N**ON-EU residents visiting Belgium are entitled to VAT refunds on purchases of over €125 spent in one store. Deducting VAT from the selling price gives a saving of 5.6 to 17.35 per cent. When shopping, look for the "Tax-Free Shopping" logo. After purchase ask for a Global Refund or Tax-Free Shopping Cheque. This will be stamped by customs on your way out of the EU, and refunds made on the spot at the airport. Customs often ask to see goods, so carry them as hand luggage.

## SALES

**S**ALES DATES IN Belgium are fixed by law. The summer sales run from July 1 to 31 and the January sales from the first weekday after New Year's Day until the end of the month. Discounts start at 10 per cent and gradually drop, reaching 40–50 per cent in the last week.

## DEPARTMENT STORES AND SHOPPING ARCADES

**T**HE MAIN department store in the city is **Inno**. It is not spectacular by British and American standards. Brussels' equivalent to Harrods toy department is Serneels on Place Louise, in the luxury Wiltshire shopping complex. Traditional men's outfitter Degand has recently started selling luxury gift items.

Rue Neuve contains mainstream stores, including popular Dutch stores – We for clothes and Blokker and Hema for household goods and toys – and French cut-price store Tati. There are three shopping malls at either end of the road: the Anspach and Monnaie Centres at Place de la Monnaie and City 2 at Place Rogier.

Window shopping in the city's numerous boutiques or arcades is a popular Sunday pastime. The best arcade is the recently renovated

**Galéries Saint-Hubert historic 19th-century shopping arcade**

**Browsers enjoying the Place du Jeu de Balle market in the sunshine**

Galéries Saint-Hubert which dates from 1847 *(see p47)*. It houses several jewellers, and luxury leather bag maker Delvaux, as well as chocolate shops and smart boutiques, including popular women's fashion designer Kaat Tilley.

Less conservative is the **Galéries d'Ixelles** to the north of the city centre, where a bustling collection of cafés thrives in the city's trendy Matonge district. A stone's throw away, Galéries Toison d'Or and the adjacent Galéries Louise are mostly full of chain and adults' high-street European fashion boutiques.

Downtown towards the Grand Place is the quaint **Galérie Bortier**, the place to visit for collectors of antiquarian books and maps.

## MARKETS

A TRIP TO Brussels must include the city's fabulous street markets, which offer anything from cheap flowers and food to second-hand bicycles and fine antiques.

Good for unusual fine antiques and a pleasant stroll is the weekend market on Place du Grand Sablon (from 9am, Saturday and Sunday). In the ancient Marolles district, the flea market on the Place du Jeu de Balle (daily, 7am to 1pm) is a colourful, eclectic affair.

Most spectacular is the huge vibrant market around Gare du Midi (Sundays, 6am to 1pm). with its mix of North African and home-grown delicacies.

It has a staggering blend of Moroccan and southern European treats, including oils, spices, and exotic herbs.

## BEST BUYS AND SPECIALIST SHOPS

F OR CHOCOLATE, choose from **Pierre Marcolini**'s edible sculptures and gateaux, or the internationally known fine chocolatiers **Wittamer** and **Godiva**. Their flagship stores are in the Place du Grand Sablon. Fine biscuit specialist **Dandoy** can be found just behind the Grand Place.

Serious collectors of comic-strip memorabilia should visit **Little Nemo** and **La Bande des Six Nez**.

**Elvis Pompilio's hats and bags**

At **Beer Mania**, speciality beers can be bought on the spot or delivered.

Milliner **Elvis Pompilio** produces hand-made hats at his pilot store. The best of Belgian fashion, including Dries Van Noten and Ann Demeulemeester, is on offer at upmarket store **Stijl**.

## BOOKSHOPS AND MAGAZINES

A BRANCH OF English book-store Waterstone's *(see p163)* sells English-language magazines, fiction and reference material. Nijinsky (15 Rue de Page) is great for second-hand English-language fiction. French store Fnac at the City 2 mall also has a good English-language section. For international papers, go to Librairie de Rome, 16 Rue Jean Stas.

*(see p47)* ... *(see p163)*

---

## DIRECTORY

### DEPARTMENT STORES AND SHOPPING ARCADES

**Inno**
Rue Neuve 111. **Map** 2 D2.
Avenue Louise 12. **Map** 2 D5.
[ (02) 211 2111.

**Galéries d'Ixelles**
Chaussée d'Ixelles. **Map** 2 E5.

**Galérie Bortier**
Rue de la Madeleine 17–19.
**Map** 2 D3.

### BEER

**Beer Mania**
Chaussée de Wavre 174–178.
**Map** 2 E5.
[ (02) 512 1788.

### CHOCOLATE

**Pierre Marcolini**
Place du Grand Sablon 39.
**Map** 2 D4.
[ (02) 514 1206.

**Godiva**
Grand Place 22.
**Map** 2 D3.
[ (02) 511 2537.

**Wittamer**
Place du Grand Sablon 6–12.
**Map** 2 D4.
[ (02) 512 3742.

**Dandoy**
Rue au Beurre 31. **Map** 2 D3.
[ (02) 511 0326.

### FASHION

**Elvis Pompilio**
Rue Pierres 29. **Map** 1 C3.
[ (02) 511 1188.

**Stijl**
Rue Antoine Dansaert 74.
**Map** 1 B2.
[ (02) 512 0313.

### CARTOONS

**Little Nemo**
Boulevard Lemonnier 25.
[ (02) 514 6804.

**La Bande des Six Nez**
Chaussée de Wavre 179.
**Map** 2 E5.
[ (02) 513 7258.

# ENTERTAINMENT IN BRUSSELS

**Ecran Total
Cinema poster**

WITHIN EASY REACH of London, Paris and Amsterdam, Brussels is an established stop on the international touring circuit, with regular visits from the world's best orchestras, soloists, rock bands and dance troupes. It is also a great place to experience Belgium's thriving cultural scene, which is especially distinguished in the fields of medieval music, jazz and contemporary dance. Brussels has several cinemas showing a wide range of films, including movies from the US and Europe (many in English). Professional theatre here is mostly performed in French or Flemish. Outside the city's major venues, the quality of entertainment can vary, but jazz and blues bars offer good free gigs.

The 19th-century interior of La Monnaie Opera House

## OPERA, CLASSICAL MUSIC AND DANCE

BRUSSELS' OPERA HOUSE, **La Monnaie**, has a unique claim to fame: on August 25, 1830, an aria in Auber's opera *La Muette de Portici* provoked the capital's citizens into rioting against their Dutch rulers, setting the country on the road to independence *(see pp34–5)*. Now the house is among Europe's finest venues for opera. Its current artistic director Antonio Pappano will join London's Royal Opera House when his contract runs out in 2003. The season runs from September to June, with tickets starting at €7.50. Most productions are sold out many months in advance.

Designed by Victor Horta in 1928, the **Palais des Beaux-Arts** is the capital's flagship cultural venue, with an exhibition space, a theatre, film archives, a small cinema and Brussels' largest auditorium for classical music *(see p60)*. Following sustained criticism

of the accoustics, the Art Nouveau hall has recently been renovated. The venue is home to the Belgian National Orchestra, which has grown in stature under Russian conductor Yuri Simonov. Again, the season runs from September to June, with tickets costing from €7.50 to €75.

In March, the city hosts a trend-making contemporary classical festival, *Ars Musica*, with an emphasis on new works and an impressively avant-garde feel. In the holiday season, the Brussels' Summer Festival offers concerts on the Grand Place as well as informal events in the Town Hall and the Palais des Beaux-Arts (see pp 62–7) nearby. In September and October, the Festival of Flanders is a gala-heavy event showcasing top Belgian artists as well as world-famous singers and conductors.

Over the past 15 years Belgium has won a reputation for being on the cutting edge of contemporary dance. Anne Teresa De Keersmaeker and her company Rosas put on regular performances, as do several other major Belgian companies, at the beautiful Art Deco **Kaaitheater** or the **Halles de Schaerbeek**, a 19th-century former market. Although Brussels has no ballet company of its own, it attracts major European touring companies including Jiri Kylian's outstanding Nederlands Dans Theater.

## ROCK AND JAZZ

ANTWERP MAY be the centre of Belgium's alternative rock scene, but Brussels has several superb venues for rock gigs. Big names such as Aerosmith and Céline Dion

Le Botanique cultural centre in Brussels' Rue Royale

perform at **Forest-National**, a modern arena southeast of the city centre. The **Ancienne Belgique** downtown is a medium-sized venue hosting hip or up-and-coming guitar bands, folk, Latin and techno acts; **Le Botanique**, the French-speaking Community's cultural centre, has a strong if intermittent roster of rock and electronic music, including a marvellous ten-day festival, *Les Nuits Botanique*, held at the end of September.

The best places to catch good jazz acts are **Travers**, a cramped, intimate bar frequented by most of the country's top players, and **Sounds**, a larger venue which places an equal emphasis on blues music. On Saturday and Sunday afternoons, it is worth stopping by **L'Archiduc**, a refurbished Art Deco bar in the centre of town where you can find jazz musicians in relaxed, informal mood.

## CINEMA

NORTH OF THE CITY, by the Heysel exhibition centre, the **Kinepolis** cinema is a state-of-the-art 28-screen multiplex which rivals US giants for consumer comfort. It screens all the Hollywood blockbusters and major French and British releases; one IMAX screen shows a selection of nature and adventure films. Parking is free.

In the centre of Brussels, the major cinema is **UGC/De Brouckère**, a modern 12-screen complex with a standard programme of mainstream releases. A second, smaller UGC is in Avenue de la Toison d'Or.

The **Arenberg/Galeries**, in the Galéries Saint-Hubert, is another quality cinema with comfortable auditoriums and an arthouse slant. From late June to September, it hosts "Ecran Total", a festival combining as yet unreleased films from around the world with established classics, often in remastered or "director's" versions. Perhaps the best of

Brussels' cinemas is the Musée du Cinéma, part of the Palais des Beaux-Arts complex. Home to one of the world's largest film archives, the museum shows classics, from Chaplin to Tarantino, for just €2. Silent films are accompanied by live piano music.

Tickets for most cinemas are around €6.20. Visit www.cinebel.be to find out which film is playing where.

## INFORMATION

THE PRINCIPAL SOURCE of entertainment information in English is *The Bulletin* magazine, which has comprehensive listings of forthcoming events in Brussels and the rest of Belgium. The magazine is published weekly and is available at newsstands throughout the country. Costing around €2.50, it has excellent coverage of news, travel ideas and a pot-pourri of information about life in the capital. The magazine's listings section, *What's On*, is also distributed free to hotels in the capital.

The company that publishes *The Bulletin* also owns an English-language website (www.xpats.com). The portal includes cultural information, news, weather reports and useful links for expats. The central **Tourist Information Office** *(see p162)* offers free maps, as well as information about arts and entertainment events, and publishes a calendar of major events. Advisors will assist in the booking of tickets.

French-speakers should try the monthly *Kiosque*, which offers capsule roundups of major arts events and a regular coupon with a variety of free ticket offers. Two daily papers, *Le Soir* and *La Libre Belgique*, publish cultural supplements on Wednesdays, with detailed arts and cinema listings. For Flemish-speakers, *Humo* or the daily newspaper *De Morgen*, also offer information on events and exhibitions.

**Magazines on sale in Brussels**

# SURVIVAL GUIDE

# PRACTICAL INFORMATION

Although comfortable with its status as a major political and business centre, Brussels has sometimes struggled with its role as a tourist destination. It can be hard to find all but the most obvious sights: the same goes for inexpensive hotels. Both the Upper and Lower Town can easily be negotiated on foot, which might be a relief to those visitors reluctant to take

**Guided tour walking group**

on the challenging Belgian drivers and roads. Brussels is a very cosmopolitan city, and its residents, many of whom are foreigners themselves, are usually charming and friendly, with most speaking English. The tourist office goes out of its way to help travellers enjoy the city and provides help with everything from finding hidden sights to medical and financial information.

## CUSTOMS AND IMMIGRATION

Belgium is one of the 11 EU countries to have signed the 1985 Schengen agreement, which means travellers moving from one Schengen country to another are not subject to border controls. If you enter Belgium from France, Luxembourg, Germany or the Netherlands, you will not have to show your passport, although it is wise to carry it in case of trouble. Bear in mind that it is a legal requirement in Belgium to carry ID on the person at all times. Britain does not belong to Schengen, so travellers coming from the UK must present a valid passport and hold proof of onward passage when entering Belgium. This also applies to US, Australian, Canadian and other Commonwealth citizens.

British travellers no longer benefit from duty-free goods on their journey. Travellers from non-EU countries are still entitled to refunds of VAT (21 per cent on most products) if they spend more than €127 in a single transaction.

## TOURIST INFORMATION

Brussels is rarely crowded, so you should not expect to queue at major attractions and museums unless a special event or show is taking place. If you are planning to do extensive sightseeing, the one-day tram and bus pass *(see pp168–9)* is a must. Better still, pick up a Brussels Card from the tourist office *(see below)*. Drivers should avoid rush hour (Monday to Friday

from 8am to 9:30am and 5pm to 7pm), although public transport is manageable throughout the day. Many of the city's prestige hotels slash their rates at weekends, when business custom slacks off, so it can be worthwhile timing a short visit around this. Although Brussels' reputation as a rainy city is overplayed, bring a raincoat or waterproof jacket in summer and warm clothing for winter.

The Tourist and Information Office publishes a variety of maps, guides and suggested tours. It offers discount coupons for a number of major attractions at a cost of €15.62, as well as the Brussels Card for €30, which includes a three-day travel pass, free access to 30 museums and a colour guide to the city.

## OPENING HOURS

Most shops and businesses are open Mondays to Saturdays from 10am to 6pm, with some local shops closing for an hour during the day.

Supermarkets are usually open from 9am to 8pm. For late-night essentials and alcohol, "night shops" stay open to 1am or 2am. Banking hours usually run on weekdays from 9am to 1pm and 2 to 4pm. Most branches have 24-hour ATMs, and many have Visa or Euro points with Maestro, where foreign cashcards can be used. Many sights are closed on Mondays. Public museums are usually open on Tuesdays to Sundays from 10am to 5pm.

## MUSEUM ADMISSION CHARGES

There was much controversy when the city's major museums, including the Musées des Beaux-Arts and the Musées Royaux d'art et d'histoire introduced a €3.70 admission charge in the mid-1990s, but so far the money seems to have been well spent, with the Cinquantenaire Museum in particular undergoing much-needed layout improvements. Elsewhere, admission charges

**The sculpture court in the Musées Royaux des Beaux-Arts in summer**

Visitors taking a break from sightseeing in a pavement café

range from free entry to a daily tariff starting at €5. Reductions for students, children, the unemployed and senior citizens are always given.

## TIPPING

A SERVICE CHARGE OF 16 per cent as well as VAT of 21 per cent are included in restaurant bills (this is marked on the menu as "*Service et TVA compris*"), but most diners round up the bill or add about 10 per cent if the service has been particularly good. Service is also included in taxi fares, although a 10 per cent tip is customary. Some theatre and cinema ushers expect €0.25 per person. You should pay nightclub doormen around €1 if you plan to go back. In hotels, a small tip for the chambermaid and porter should be given personally to them or left in your vacated room, and expect to pay railway porters €1 per bag. Finally, many public toilets – including those in bars, restaurants and even cinemas – have attendants who should be given €0.25.

## DISABLED TRAVELLERS

B RUSSELS IS NOT the easiest city for the disabled traveller, but the authorities are beginning to recognize that there is room for improvement. Most of the more expensive hotels have some rooms designed for people with disabilities, and most metro stations have lifts.

There are designated parking spaces for disabled drivers, and newer trams have wheelchair access. The Tourist Office provides information and advice about facilities within the city.

Façade of the Sterling bookshop

## NEWSPAPERS, TV AND RADIO

M OST BRITISH AND American daily newspapers produce international editions, which are on sale at major newsstands. The *Financial Times*, the *International Herald Tribune* and the *Wall Street Journal* are widely available. **Librairie de Rome, Waterstone's** or **Sterling Books** sell English magazines.

Belgium has one of the world's most advanced cable TV networks, with access to more than 40 channels, including BBC 1 and 2, CNN, NBC, MTV and Arte. Belgian channels include RTL and RTBF 1 and 2 (French-speaking) and VTM and Ketnet/Canvas (Flemish-speaking). TV listings are in the English-language magazine *The Bulletin*. Classical music stations include Musique 3 (91.2 FM) and Studio Brussel (100.6 FM).

# Personal Security and Health, Banking and Communications

BRUSSELS IS ONE OF Europe's safest capitals, with street crime against visitors a relatively rare occurrence. The poorer areas west and north of the city centre, including Anderlecht, Molenbeek and parts of Schaerbeek and St-Josse, have quite a bad reputation, but these areas are perfectly safe during the daytime for everyone except those who flaunt their wealth. After dark, it is sensible not to walk around on your own in these areas. Public transport is usually safe at all hours. Banking follows the European system and is straightforward. In addition, there are hundreds of 24-hour cashpoints located around the city.

## LAW ENFORCEMENT

BELGIUM HAS A complex policing system, whose overlapping and often contradictory mandates have been criticized in the past. Calls have been made to simplify the judicial structure, a process that is still slowly taking place. Major crimes and motorway offences are handled by the national gendarmerie. However, visitors are most likely to encounter the communal police, who are responsible for law and order in each of the capital's 19 administrative districts. All Brussels police officers must speak French and Flemish.

The main police station for central Brussels is on Rue du Marché au Charbon, close to the Grand Place. If stopped by the police visitors will be asked for identification, so carry your passport at all times. Belgian law classes as a vagrant anyone carrying less than €15 cash. Not using road crossings correctly is also illegal here.

**Female police officer**

## SAFETY GUIDELINES

MOST OF Brussels' principal tourist attractions are located in safe areas where few precautions are necessary. When driving, make sure car doors are locked and any valuables are kept out of sight. If you are sightseeing on foot, limit the amount of cash you carry and never leave bags unattended. Women should wear handbags with the strap across the shoulder and the clasp facing towards the body. Wallets should be kept in a front, not back, pocket. Hotel guests should keep rooms and suitcases locked and avoid leaving cash or valuables lying around. Rooms often come with a safe; if not, there should be one at reception.

At night, avoid the city's parks, especially at Botanique and Parc Josaphat in Schaerbeek, both of which are favoured haunts of drug-dealers.

## LOST PROPERTY

CHANCES OF retrieving property are minimal if it was lost in the street. However, it is worth contacting the police station for the commune in which the article disappeared. (If you are not sure where that is, contact the central police station on Rue du Marché au Charbon.) Public transport authority **STIB/MIVB** operates a lost-and-found service for the metro, trams and buses. Report items lost in a taxi to the police station nearest your point of departure; quote registration details and the taxi licence number.

## TRAVEL AND HEALTH INSURANCE

TRAVELLERS FROM Britain and Ireland are entitled to free healthcare under reciprocal agreements within the EU. British citizens need an E111 form from a post office, which should be validated before their trip. Europeans should make it clear that they have state insurance, or they may end up with a large bill. While generous, state healthcare subsidies do not cover all problems and it is worth taking out full travel insurance. This can also cover lost property.

---

| **DIRECTORY** | | | |
|---|---|---|---|
| **CRISIS INFORMATION** | **Medigard Private Doctor Bureau** ( (02) 479 1818. | **Hôpital Universitaire Saint Luc** Ave Hippocrate 10, 1200 Brussels. ( (02) 764 1602. | **STIB/MIVB** Avenue de la Toison d'Or 15, 1050 Brussels. **Map** 2 D5. ( (02) 515 2000. |
| **Police** ( 101. | **Medigard Private Dentist Bureau** ( (02) 426 1026. | | w www.stib.be w www.mivb.be |
| **Ambulance and fire services** ( 100. | **EMERGENCY DEPARTMENTS** | **Community Help Service** ( (02) 648 4014. | **LOST CREDIT CARDS** |
| **Central police station** Rue du Marché au Charbon 30, 1000 Brussels. **Map** 1 C3. ( (02) 279 7979. | **Institut Edith Cavell** Rue Edith Cavell 32, 1180 Brussels. ( (02) 340 4001. | **LOST PROPERTY** **Central police station** ( (02) 517 9611. | **American Express** ( (02) 676 2111. **MasterCard** ( (02) 205 8585. **Visa** ( (02) 205 8585. |

## MEDICAL MATTERS

WHETHER OR not you have insurance, doctors in Belgium will usually expect you to settle the bill on the spot – and in cash. Arrange to make a payment by bank transfer (most doctors will accept this if you insist).

Pharmacies are generally open Mondays to Saturdays from 8:30am to 6:30pm, with each commune operating a rota system for late-night, Sunday and national holiday cover. All pharmacies display information about where to find a 24-hour chemist.

Assistants at pharmacies may not speak good English, so when receiving a prescription, make sure the doctor goes through the details before you leave the surgery.

## EMERGENCIES

FOR EMERGENCIES requiring police assistance, call 101, for medical or fire services, phone 100. Hospitals with emergency departments include **Institut Edith Cavell** and **Hôpital Universitaire Saint-Luc**. The Community Help Service's (CHS) 24-hour English-language help line is for expatriates, but it may be able to assist tourists.

## CURRENCY

BELGIUM, together with 11 other countries, has replaced its traditional currency with the euro. Austria, Finland, France, Germany, Greece, Ireland, Italy, Luxembourg, Netherlands, Portugal and Spain also chose to join the new currency.

The euro came into circulation in Belgium on 1 January 2002. There followed a transition period during which euros and Belgian francs (BF) could be used together, with the franc finally being phased out by mid-2002.

The Euro bank notes have seven denominations. The 5-euro note (grey) is the smallest, followed by the 10-euro note (pink), 20-euro note (blue), 50-euro note (orange), 100-euro note (green), 200-euro note (yellow) and the 500-euro note (purple). The euro has eight coin denominations: the 1 euro and 2 euros are both silver and gold in colour; the 50-, 20- and 10-cent coins are gold; and the 5-, 2- and 1-cent coins are bronze.

## BANKING

MOST BANKS IN Brussels are open from 9am–1pm and 2–4pm; some open late on Friday until 4:30 or 5pm, and a few on Saturday mornings.

Banks often offer very competitive exchange rates, and most will happily serve non-clients. Many transactions (especially money transfers) are liable to banking fees, so ask in advance what these rates might be. Most banks will be able to cash traveller's cheques with the signatory's passport or other form of photographic identification. Visitors are usually able to exchange foreign currency, again with valid ID. Many bank attendants speak good English.

## CREDIT CARDS

AMERICAN EXPRESS, Diners Club, Mastercard and Visa are widely accepted in Brussels, although it is wise to check in advance if booking a hotel or restaurant. Most hotels will accept a credit card booking. The cardholder may be asked for a credit card imprint at check-in.

## POST AND COMMUNICATIONS

BRUSSELS' PUBLIC payphones are run by former state operator Belgacom. Public phone booths are plentiful but the service information can be difficult to understand; the operator can be contacted by dialling 1380 or directory enquiries in English on 1405. Payphones accept Belgacom phonecards, and both €5 and €10 cards are sold at newsagents, post offices and train stations. Payphones in metro stations accept cash. When using the postal service, addresses should be written in capital letters. A blue "A prior" sticker should ensure swifter delivery on international mail.

**ATM machine in Brussels**

## AUTOMATED TELLER MACHINES

MOST BANK branches have 24-hour cashpoint facilities. Often you will find that there is one machine located in a lobby reserved for members of the bank, while a second ATM on the wall outside is available to everyone. Most ATMs will accept a wide range of cards including those belonging to the Cirrus, Plus, Maestro and Star systems, as well as those from MasterCard and Visa.

## BUREAUX DE CHANGE

IF YOU ARE unable to change money at a bank or to use one of the many cashpoint machines around the city, you may be forced to rely on bureaux de change to obtain euros. These often charge a commission of 3 to 4 per cent and on top of that may have uncompetitive exchange rates. It is therefore worth comparing prices between different bureaux or looking for an alternative. There is a 24-hour automated exchange machine at Grand Place 7, while in the streets around the square there are several bureaux open until 7pm or later. You will also find exchange booths at the city's major stations.

**Red Belgian postbox**

# GETTING TO BRUSSELS

**High-speed Thalys train**

Brussels is well suited to both casual and business travellers, with abundant and excellent connections by air, rail and road. The increasing political significance of Brussels in its new role as the heart of Europe has led to greater competition between airlines, with many operators offering a variety of discounted fares. The Eurostar and Thalys high-speed trains link the city with London, Paris, Amsterdam and Germany, and compare favourably with flying in terms of time. British travellers can use the Channel Tunnel to bring their car with them.

**An aeroplane from Belgian carrier SN Brussels Airlines' fleet**

## ARRIVING BY AIR

Situated 14 km (8¾ miles) northeast of the city centre, Brussels National Airport is in the Flemish commune of Zaventem (the name by which it is known to most citizens, including taxi drivers). A centre for Belgian carrier SN Brussels Airlines, the airport is also served by major carriers such as British Airways, American Airlines, Air Canada, Delta, Lufthansa and Air France. Among the low-cost operators flying to and from Zaventem are Virgin Express (for London and Europe) and City Bird (for US destinations). A typical journey from London takes 45 minutes. Costs for UK flights range from £60 for a student flight to £270 for a scheduled return flight.

Reaching Brussels from the US can be more expensive than reaching other European cities. Return flights average US $700 for a charter return from New York. Prices from Canada are comparable.

The best-value flights from Australia and New Zealand include Alitalia, Lauda-air, and KLM, with fares from A$2,100.

Brussels South-Charleroi Airport has become a second hub, since Ryanair has been operating scheduled flights from various European destinations, including the UK. This is now under review due to a dispute over discounted landing fees. The airport is 55 km (34 miles) from the centre of Brussels and can be reached by train or coach.

## AIRPORT FACILITIES

Brussels National Airport has been extensively renovated over the past decade, with a new concourse for intra-EU travel recently completed. Brussels airport features baggage reclaim, customs, car-hire booths, tourist information and ground transport on the lower level. The departure lounge has check-in facilities, ticket and insurance counters and restaurants, bars and shops, before and after the security checkpoints. In addition, there are special lounges for business or first-class SN Brussels Airlines passengers, and a corporate meeting centre. On arrival, passengers will also find ATMs, foreign exchange booths and coin- and card-operated payphones.

## GETTING INTO TOWN

The cheapest way of getting from Zaventem to the city centre is the express train from the airport to Gare du Nord, Gare Centrale or Gare du Midi. Tickets (about €2.50) are on sale in the airport complex or, for a small supplementary fee, on the train itself. Three trains run each hour, between 5am and midnight; the journey to Gare Centrale takes 20 minutes.

There is a taxi rank outside the arrivals hall. A one-way fare to the centre of Brussels will cost €30–€35 and should take around 20 minutes (longer at rush hour). If you plan to return by taxi, ask the driver about deals as some companies offer discounts on return fares.

An SNCB/NMBS train runs from Charleroi to Gare du Midi. It takes about 45 minutes to/from the station.

## ARRIVING BY TRAIN

Brussels is at the heart of Europe's high-speed train networks, connected to London by the Eurostar service and to Paris, Amsterdam and Cologne by the Thalys network. These trains have a top speed of 300 kph (186 mph) and have slashed journey times between northern Europe's major cities, making them a challenge to the supremacy of the airlines.

Eurostar passengers should book their tickets at least a week in advance, especially to take advantage of reduced

**SN Brussels Airlines**

**Logo for SN Brussels Airlines**

fares; they should also arrive at the terminal at least 20 minutes before departure to go through check-in and customs before boarding. You may be refused access to the train if you arrive after this, although you can often be transferred to the next service at no extra charge.

Trains run hourly between London's Waterloo station and Brussels via the Channel Tunnel; the journey takes 2 hours 20 minutes, arriving at the Gare du Midi. Return fares start at around £79/€112. The trains are comfortable, with plenty of legroom, and have two buffet cars, one of which is licensed; first-class passengers receive a meal, free drinks and the day's international newspapers.

Many visitors to Brussels arrive from mainland Europe. The high-speed train company Thalys offers a comfortable journey, with Paris accessible in 1 hour 25 minutes, Amsterdam in around two hours and Cologne in under three.

**Eurostar train arriving at the Gare du Midi, Brussels**

## ARRIVING BY SEA

B ELGIUM CAN easily be reached from the UK several times daily. Cross-Channel ferries run frequently from Dover to Calais and Dunkirk, Felixstowe to Ostend and Hull to Zeebrugge. Foot passengers do not usually need to book, but those with cars should always reserve a space and arrive promptly.

Visitors with children should be aware that ferry companies have good child discounts, often with children under 14 years old travelling free. Hoverspeed operates a catamaran service, the SeaCat, from Dover to Calais, but no longer direct to Ostend.

## ARRIVING BY CAR

T HE OPENING of the Channel Tunnel has given drivers from Britain a new option for reaching mainland Europe: Le Shuttle. This is a car train that takes vehicles from the Tunnel entrance near Folkestone to Calais, with the journey taking around 35 minutes. From there, Brussels is a two-hour drive via the A16 motorway, which becomes the E40 when you cross the Franco Belgian border. Follow signs to Brugge (Bruges), then Brussels. Those planning to ride Le Shuttle should book tickets in advance and try to arrive early. Three trains per hour run between 6:30am and midnight, with one train hourly from midnight to 6:30am. Standard fares start at around £170 return per vehicle, but rise for stays over five days and at popular times.

## PASSPORTS AND ENTRY REQUIREMENTS

V ISITORS FROM Britain will find that a passport is the only documentation required for a stay of up to 90 days. For a visit of the same length, European nationals should be prepared to produce their identity card. Travellers from the US and Canada need a full passport. All visitors should, if asked, be able to produce enough money, or proof of access to money, on arrival to pay for their entire stay as well as a return ticket to their home country.

The Hoverspeed catamaran SeaCat crossing the Channel

# Getting around Brussels

**Metro station street sign**

A LTHOUGH ITS public transport system is clean, modern and efficient, Brussels is a city best explored on foot. Most of the key attractions for first-time visitors are within a short walk of the Grand Place, and the Art Nouveau architecture in Ixelles and Saint-Gilles is also best enjoyed on a leisurely stroll. For those anxious to see the main sights in limited time, the tram and metro network covers most of the city at speed, while buses are useful for reaching more out-of-the-way areas. Although expensive, taxis are recommended for late-night journeys. Cycling can be hazardous for the inexperienced.

## PLANNING YOUR JOURNEY

I F YOU ARE seeing Brussels by car, avoid its major roads during rush hours, which run on weekdays from 8–9:30am and 5–7pm as well as Wednesday lunchtimes during the school year, when there is a half day. Tram and bus services run frequently at peak time and are usually not too crowded. However, the small size of Brussels means that walking is usually a viable option.

## WALKING IN BRUSSELS

T HE SHORT distance between sights and the interest in every corner make central Brussels easy to negotiate on foot. Outside the city centre, walking is the only way to appreciate the concentration of Art Nouveau buildings on and around Square Ambiorix, around the district of Ixelles and near St-Gilles Town Hall.

Drivers in Brussels have a bad reputation, and it is important to be alert to traffic while crossing roads. Until 1996, motorists were not obliged to stop at pedestrian crossings: the laws came into effect on April 1 of that year and many drivers still treat them as a seasonal pleasantry. At traffic lights, motorists turning right or left may ignore the walkers' priority. It is essential to be careful even in residential areas.

Blue or white street signs are placed on the walls of buildings at one corner of a street, and can be somewhat hard to locate. Street names

are always in French first, then Flemish, with the name in capital letters and the street type in small letters to the top left and bottom right corners (for example, Rue STEVIN straat).

**Mother and child seeing Brussels' historic architecture by bicycle**

## CYCLING

C OMPARED TO THE cyclist-friendly cities of Flanders, Brussels can be a frustrating place for pushbike-riders. Car-free zones are few, but the

number of cycle lanes is on the increase. However, on a trip to the suburbs or the Fôret de Soignes, bicycles are the best option and can be cheaply hired from most railway stations (non-Belgians must leave a small deposit).

## TRAVELLING BY BUS, TRAM AND METRO

T HE AUTHORITY governing Brussels' public transport is the bilingual **STIB/MIVB**, which runs buses, trams and metro services in the capital. Tickets are valid on all three services, which run between 5:30am and 12:30am on weekdays with shorter hours on Sundays and public holidays.

A single ticket, which allows the passenger an unlimited number of changes within one hour (excluding the Nato-Brussels Airport line 12), costs €1.40. You can also buy a ten-ticket card at €9.20 or a one-day pass costing €3.70. The five-ticket card, for €6, is not competitively priced but it can be convenient for avoiding repeated queues. There are also combined "STIB/MIVB + Taxi" tickets, a single ticket that offers a reduction on taxi rides.

Single tickets can be bought on buses and trams, and should be stamped in the orange machines next to the exits; you must restamp your ticket if the journey involves a change. On the metro, tickets must be bought and stamped before you reach the platform. Metro ticket offices and most private newsagents sell 10-ticket cards and one-day passes.

**Bus at a stop in Brussels city centre**

**A city tram travelling down Rue Royale towards the city centre**

Most stops have clear, comprehensible maps of the city's public transport system, with metros in orange, trams in blue and buses in red (see endpaper), and timetables mark all the stops on each route. Metro stations in the city centre have electronic displays showing where each train is in the system. Those unfamiliar with the tram system will notice the lack of on-board information; there is no indication of what the upcoming stop is, of which many are request stops. Request stops can be made by pressing the yellow buttons by each of the vehicle's exits. Ask the driver to call the relevant stop. Smoking is banned, as is playing music, although dogs are allowed on trams and buses.

A few bus services in the capital are run by the Walloon transport group (TEC) or the Flemish operator De Lijn. These services have lettered rather than numbered codes (for instance, the 60 bus is run by STIB/MIVB, the W by De Lijn), but most tickets are valid on all the services.

## BRUSSELS BY CAR

IT MAY BE A small city, but Brussels has been known to reduce motorists to tears. The seemingly perverse one-way system in many sections of the city centre can swiftly confuse newcomers, while the network of tunnels that bisect the city are notoriously difficult to navigate even for city-dwellers. Belgian drivers, too, have been the butt of jokes from their fellow Europeans for decades. Nonetheless the city's systems are not difficult to learn, and a car is handy for planning day trips around the rest of Belgium.

Most international rental agencies have branches here, many at the National Airport in Zaventem or at the Gare du Midi, where the Eurostar and train offices arrive. Like the rest of mainland Europe, Belgium drives on the right, and the "priorité à droite" rule – which means that the driver coming from the right at junctions has absolute priority to pull out unless otherwise indicated – is enforced with sometimes startling regularity. Always watch for vehicles coming from the right, no matter how small the road; some drivers have been known to take their priority even though it means a crash, secure in the knowledge that they are legally correct. Verve and confidence are helpful when driving in a city where

**One-day travel pass**

many motorists take a flexible approach to road rules. Essential safety precautions, however, should be adhered to at all times. Safety belts are obligatory in all seats, and children under 12 years old are not allowed in the front when other seats are free.

**Cars and taxis threading their way through the main streets**

Drink-driving is illegal (the limit in Belgium is currently 0.5g/l). Speed limits are 50 kph (30 mph) in built-up areas, 120 kph (75 mph) on motorways and dual carriageways and 90 kph (55 mph) on all other roads. Always give way to trams, who will ring their bells should a car be in the way. Street parking, usually by meters, is becoming increasingly difficult in the city centre.

## TAKING A TAXI

BRUSSELS' TAXIS are among Europe's more expensive, but most journeys are short and cabs are the city's only 24-hour transport service. Service is generally efficient with most drivers speaking at least a little English, although some people may be surprised at many drivers' lack of familiarity with sections of the city. All taxis have a rooftop sign which is illuminated when the vehicle is vacant. Most cars are either black or white, with Mercedes the make of choice for most companies. It is advisable to find a taxi rank or order a cab by phone, although occasionally drivers will stop if hailed on the street. Passengers ride in the back seat, with the fare met on the dashboard or just behind the gear-stick. Fares should be posted inside the vehicle. Tips are included in the price, but an extra is usually expected.

To make a complaint to the **CCN-Service des Taxis et Limousines**, Rue du Progrès 80. Give the taxi's number, its ... when making ...

# Getting around Belgium

As you might expect from a country that is small, modern and predominantly flat, Belgium is an extremely easy place in which to travel. The toll-free motorways compare favourably with any in France, train travel is swift and competitively priced and there are good bus services in those areas not covered by the railway network. Public transport is clean and efficient and the range of touring tickets allows a great deal of freedom and the ability to see the whole country inexpensively. In the level Flemish countryside to the north, hiking and cycling are highly pleasant ways to get around.

**Cyclists on a tour of the scenery of Durbuy in the Ardennes**

## TRAVELLING BY CAR

After the rather enervating traffic in Brussels, driving in the rest of Belgium comes a something of a relief. The motorways are fast, reason-ably well maintained and toll-free, while major roads are also excellent. Drivers in cities outside the capital tend to be more relaxed, although the trend in Flanders for car-free city centres can make navigation demanding. The only difficulty most drivers encounter is an occasional absence of clear signs for motorway exits and junctions, which can necessitate taking care when approaching ···ons (in Flanders, many ··· are confused by signs ···it". It means exit).
··· rules detailed in ··· Around Brussels ···169) hold good ··· the country, with ··· 50 kph (30 mph) ··· 120 kph (75 ··· ays and dual ··· 00 kph (55 ··· nal roads.

If you break down, three motoring organizations should be able to provide assistance: **Touring Club de Belgique, Royal Automobile Club de Belgique** and **Vlaamse Automobilistenbond** in Flanders. It is worth getting breakdown coverage before you leave, and you must have a valid driving licence (from the EU, US, Australia or Canada) or an International Driving Licence on your person. It is also essential to have comprehensive insurance and/or a Green card, and visitors are expected to carry a first-aid kit and a warning triangle at all times.

All the major rental agencies operate in Belgium, although renting a car can be an expensive business. To rent a vehicle, you must be 21 or over, with a year's driving experience, and have a credit card. A week's rental with unlimited mileage will cost €370 or more but might be reduced on the regular special deals at the big firms. Local agencies may also be cheaper, but be sure to check the terms and conditions. Bicycle hire is available in most Flemish towns with a modest deposit of €15.

## TRAVELLING BY TRAIN

Belgium's train network is a more than adequate means of getting to and from major towns and cities. From Brussels, there are direct links to Antwerp, Ghent, Bruges, Ostend, Liège, Mons, Namur and the Ardennes, and even journeys involving a change rarely take more than two hours in total.

Run by **Belgian National Railways** (Société Nationale Chemins de Fer Belges/ Belgische Spoorwegen), the system is clean, modern and efficient, although the quality of rolling stock varies some-what: older carriages have a slightly drab feel, but new

---

### FRENCH/FLEMISH PLACE NAMES

One of the most confusing aspects of travel in Belgium is the variation between French and Flemish spellings of town names. On road signs in Brussels, both names are given, while in Flanders only the Flemish and in Wallonia only the French are shown. The following list gives main towns:

| French | Flemish | French | Flemish |
|---|---|---|---|
| Anvers | Antwerpen | Malines | Mechelen |
| Ath | Aat | Mons | Bergen |
| Bruges | Brugge | Namur | Namen |
| Bruxelles | Brussel | Ostende | Oostende |
| Courtrai | Kortrijk | Saint-Trond | Sint-Truiden |
| Gand | Gent | Tongrès | Tongeren |
| Liège | Luik | Tournai | Doornik |
| Louvain | Leuven | Ypres | Ieper |

**Train travelling through Belgium on a spring evening**

models are spacious, very comfortable, and, typically Belgian, offer fine meals and light refreshments.

Fares for standard second-class tickets are calculated by distance, with 100 km (63 miles) costing around €9.40; first-class fares will set you back around 50 per cent more. Because distance is the determining factor in price, return tickets generally offer no saving and are valid only until midnight. Children aged under six travel free, with a maximum of four children allowed per adult, and those aged between six and 11 receive a 50 per cent discount. Several special tariffs are available, including discounts for young adults aged under 26, with weekend tickets and day returns

**Train and motor tour logos**

reducing the price by up to 40 per cent. The more people travelling, the larger the discount; family members may be eligible for discounts of up to 60 per cent.

A variety of rail passes are on offer for extensive travel. The Belgian Tourrail pass (approximately €68) allows unlimited travel on any five days within one month of purchase, while the Carte de réduction à prix fixe (at approximately €16) offers 50 per cent off all first- and second-class tickets for one month.

## TRAVELLING BY BUS

WHILE SLOWER and less comfortable for travelling between major cities, buses come into their own in the more remote or rural areas of the rest of Belgium, as well as in city suburbs. In Flanders, buses are run by the **De Lijn** group; in Wallonia, the network is operated by **TEC**.

Fares are calculated according to distance, and are bought from the driver. Bus stops and terminals are generally close to railway stations. Buses have priority on public roads, so journeys are often swift.

## SPECIALIST TOURS

TOURING CAN BE be a journey full of cultural variety in both Brussels and the rest of the country. In the capital, the Tourist Information Centre

(see p162) runs a series of over 40 walking and car day tours that cover all the capital and its 19 districts with topics as diverse as "Humanist Brussels" and "Industrial Belgium". The focus is largely on the city's exceptional range of art and architecture, but many diverse themes are covered.

In each major regional city, detailed, multi-lingual private tours are available in the historic town centre; contact the town's main tourist booth for full information.

Away from cities, Belgium also offers hiking and cycling excursions, ranging from one-day adventures to five-day hikes. The Ardennes is a popular destination for hikers, who can appreciate the area's flora and fauna as well as its dramatic history. Tours can be arranged through the Rambler's Association (08 422 3397).

**A coach full of passengers travelling on a main bus route in Belgium**

# BRUSSELS STREET FINDER

T HE PAGE GRID superimposed on the area by area grid below shows which parts of Brussels are covered in this *Street Finder*. The central Upper and Lower Town areas are marked in the colours that are also the thumbtab colours throughout the book. The map references for all sights, hotels, restaurants, shopping and entertainment

**Nymph in Parc de Bruxelles**

venues described in this guide refer to the maps in this section. A street index follows on pp178–81. The key, set out below, indicates the scales of the maps and shows what other features are marked on them, including transport terminals, emergency services and information centres. All the major sights are clearly marked so they are easy to locate. The map on the inside back cover shows public transport routes.

## KEY TO STREET FINDER

| | |
|---|---|
| | Major sight |
| | Other sight |
| | Other building |
| M | Metro station |
| | Train station |
| | Tram route |
| | Bus station |
| | Taxi rank |
| P | Parking |
| i | Tourist information |
| | Hospital |
| | Police station |
| | Church |
| ⊠ | Post office |
| = | Railway line |
| → | One-way street |
| | Pedestrian street |

### SCALE OF MAPS          1:16,000

| 0 metres | 250 |
|---|---|
| 0 yards | 250 |

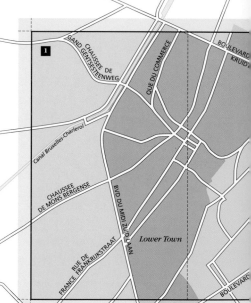

**Façade of La Maison des Ducs de Brabant, Grand Place** *(see pp42–3)*

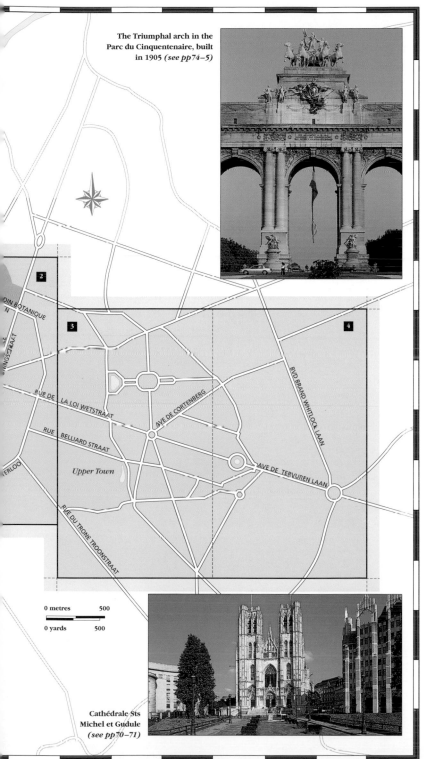

The Triumphal arch in the
Parc du Cinquentenaire, built
in 1905 *(see pp74–5)*

**2**

**3**

**4**

DIN BOTANIQUE
N

INGSTRAAT

RUE DE LA LOI WETSTRAAT

RUE BELLIARD STRAAT

ERLOO

*Upper Town*

RUE DU TRONE TROONSTRAAT

AVE DE CORTENBERG

BVD BRAND WHITLOCK LAAN

AVE DE TERVUREN LAAN

| 0 metres | 500 |
| 0 yards | 500 |

Cathédrale Sts
Michel et Gudule
*(see pp70–71)*

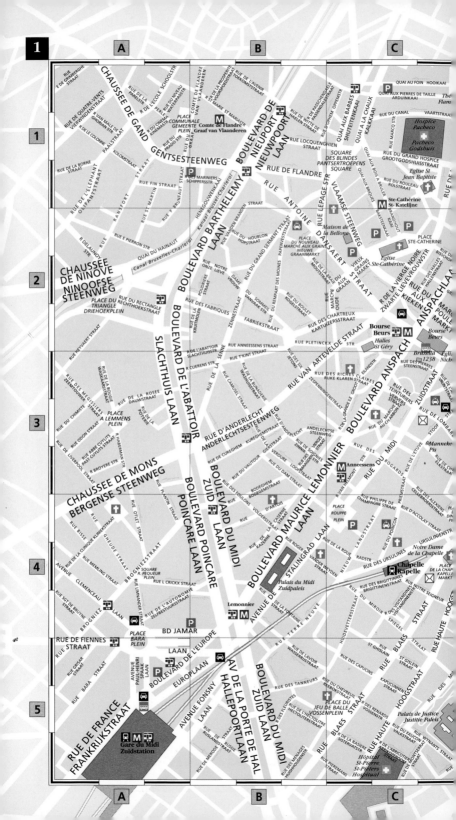

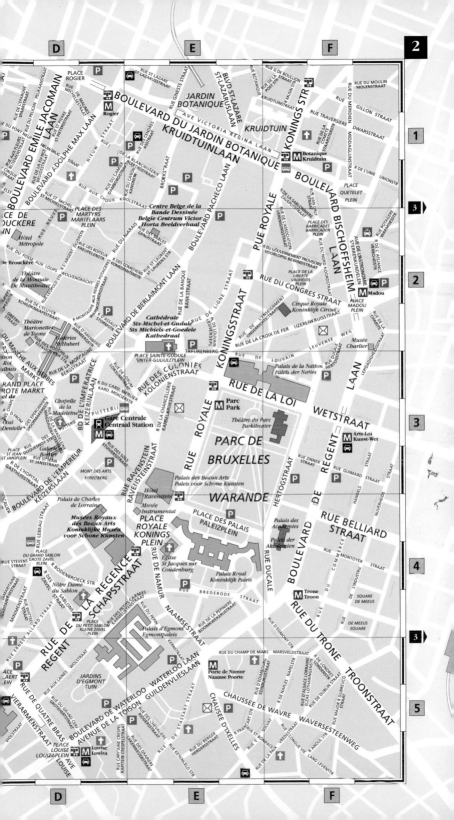

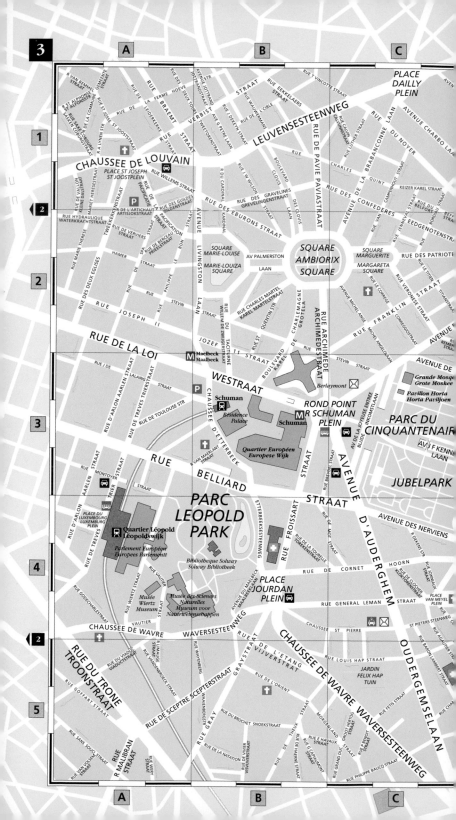

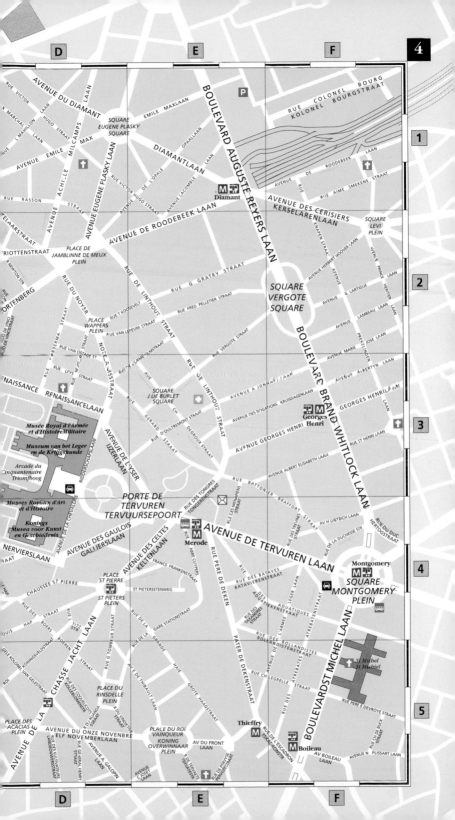

# Street Finder Index

# General Index

# Acknowledgments

DORLING KINDERSLEY would like to thank the following people whose assistance contributed to the preparation of this book:

## MAIN CONTRIBUTORS

ZOË HEWETSON is based in London but works in Brussels as a simultaneous translator for the European Commission. She is also a keen walker and has recently published a guide to walking in Turkey.

PHILIP LEE lives and works in Nottingham. A veteran travel writer, he has contributed to numerous *Rough Guide* and *Dorling Kindersley Travel Guide* publications, including the *Rough Guide to Belgium*. He frequently writes on travel for British newspapers and magazines.

ZOË ROSS is a London-based writer and editor. She has worked on several Dorling Kindersley travel guides, and is now a freelance author.

SARAH WOLFF has lived and worked in Brussels for several years. An editor and journalist, she is currently working for *The Bulletin*, Brussels' English-language newsweekly magazine.

TIMOTHY WRIGHT lived in Brussels for most of the 1990s. A successful journalist, he contributed to several English-language magazines published in Brussels and elsewhere in the Benelux countries.

JULIA ZYRIANOVA is a freelance journalist and translator. She lived in Brussels and Paris for several years and is now based in London.

## FOR DORLING KINDERSLEY

Gillian Allan; Douglas Amrine; Louise Bostock Lang; Vivien Crump; Donald Greig, Marie Ingledew; Lee Redmond; Marisa Renzullo.

## PROOFREADER

Sam Merrell.

## INDEXER

Hilary Bird.

## ADDITIONAL PHOTOGRAPHY

Steve Gorton, Ian O'Leary, Neil Mersh, David Murray, Tim Ridely, Jules Selmes, Clive Streeter, Matthew Ward.

## SPECIAL ASSISTANCE

Many thanks for the invaluable help of the following individuals: Joanna at Belgo; Derek Blyth; Christiana Ceulemans at Institut Royal Du Patrimonie Artistique; Charles Dierick at Centre Belge de la Bande Dessinée; Anne at Gaspard de Wit; Elsge Ganssen and Georges Delcart at Rubenshuis; Doctor Janssens at the Domaine de Laeken; Leen de Jong at Koninklijk Museum Voor Schone Kunsten; Antwerpen; Noel at Leonidas; Chantal Pauwert at Stad Brugge Stedelijke Musea; Marie-Hélène van Schonbroek at Cathédrale Sts Michel et Gudule; Elaine de Wilde and Sophie van Vliet at Musées Royaux des Beaux-Arts.

## PHOTOGRAPHY PERMISSIONS

Dorling Kindersley would like to thank all the cathedrals, churches, museums, hotels, restaurants, shops, galleries and sights too numerous to thank individually for their assistance and kind permission to photograph at their establishments.

Placement Key - t=top; tl=top left; tlc= top left centre; tc= top centre; trc= top right centre; tr= top right; cla= centre left above; ca= centre above; cra= centre right above; cl = centre left; c= centre; cr= centre right; clb= centre left below; cb = centre below; crb = centre right below; bl= bottom left; blc= bottom left centre; bc= bottom centre; bcl= bottom centre left; br= bottom right; d = detail.

Works of art have been produced with the permission of the following copyright holders: ©Casterman 19 br, Ted Benoit Berceuse Electrique 50clb; ©DACS 2000 16bl, 51t/cra/crb/b, 78tr/cl/cr; ©Dupuis 1999 18tr, 19ca; Sofa Kandissy ©Alessandro Medini 111c; Lucky Luke Licensing ©MORRIS 18br; @Moulinsart SA 4, 18tl/cr/cl/bl, 50tl/tr/cra/crb, 51cla/clb; ©Peyo 1999 - Licensed through I.M.P.S. (Brussels) 19bc; 50cla;

The publishers would like to thank the following individuals, companies, and picture libraries for their kind permission to reproduce their photographs:

AKG, LONDON: 31b, 34t, 36b, 37bl, 37br, 142tr; Galleria Nazdi Cupodimonte 20-1; Erich Lessing 28,/ Kunsthistoriches Museum 31t; Musée du Louvre 29b; Musée Royaux d'Arts et d'Histoire, Brussels 35c; Museo de Santa Cruz, Toledo 29t; Museum Deutsche Geschichte, Berlin 31c; Private Collection 142tl; Pushkin Museum 30c; Victoria and Albert Museum, London 32c.

DUNCAN BAIRD PUBLISHERS: Alan Williams 143br. CH. BASTIN & J. EVRARD: 16tr/cb/bc, 17tr/br, 82bl/br; 91t, 99t, 112b, 115br; BRIDGEMAN ART LIBRARY, LONDON: Christie's Images, London Peter Paul Rubens (1557–1640) *Self Portrait* 15t; Musée Crozatier, Le Puy-en-Velay, France designed by Berain (c.1725–1730) *Dawn*, Brussels lace 21bl; Private Collection/ Marie-Victoire Jaquotot (1778–1855) *Portrait of the Duke of Wellington* 35h /Max Silbert (b.1871) *The Lacemakers of Ghent* 1913 21t; Private Collection French School (19th century) Louis XIV (1638–1715) *of France in the costume of the Sun King in the ballet 'La Nuit'* c.1665 (litho) 32br; Private Collection/Bonhams, London/Robert Alexander Hillingford (1825–1904) *The Turning Point at Waterloo* (oil on canvas) 34bl; STAD BRUGGE STEDELIJKE MUSEA: Groeninge-museum 118ca/cb/b, 119c/bl; Paul Delveaux *Serenity*, 1970 ©Foundation P. Delveaux – St Idesbald, Belgium 118t; Gruithuis 116t/cb/b, 117c; Gruuthusemuseum 30t.

CAFÉ COULEUR: 25t; CEPHAS: Nigel Blythe 122 3;.TOP/A. Riviere-Lecoeur 142bl; CHIMAY: 142cr; DEMETRIO CARRASCO: 13/b; ALAN LOPBONI 13bl, 3/c; CORBIE: David Bartrutt 19cb, 140tr; Wolfgang Kaehler 167c; Patrick Ward 25b.

DAS PHOTO: 158c, 164c, 166t, 170.

ECRAN TOTAL©CINEDIT: 158t; ET ARCHIVE: Imperial War Museum, London 107b; EUROPEAN COMMISSION: 22b.

ROBERT HARDING PICTURE LIBRARY: Julian Pottage 77t, 169b; Roger Somvi 15b, 24t/c; HOVERSPEED: 167b; HULTON GETTY COLLECTION: 22c, 33t, 34c, 36c, 91b; Keytone 37t.

INSTITUT ROYAL DU PATRIMOINE ARTISTIQUE/KONINKLIJK INSTITUUT VOOR HET KUNSTPATRIMONIUM: 20tr, Societé des Expositions du Palais des Beaux-Arts de Bruxelles 53tr.

KONINKLIJK MUSEUM VOOR SCHONE KUNSTEN, ANTWERP: P. Delvaux *Pink's Row* ©Foundation P. Delveaux – St Idesbald, Brussels/DACS, London 2000 95c; J. Jordaens *As the old sang, the young ones play pipes* 95tr; R. Magritte *Madame Recamier*©ADAGP, Paris and DACS, London 2000 95b; P.P. Rubens *Adoration of the Magi* 95tl; J. Van Eyck *Saint Barbara* 94c; R. Wouters *Woman Ironing* 94b.

MUSÉE DE L'ART WALLON DE LA VILLE DE LIÈGE: Legs M. Aristide Cralle (1884) 35tl; MUSÉES ROYAUX DES BEAUX-ARTS DE BELGIQUE, BRUXELLES-KONINKLIJKE MUSEA VOOR SCHONE KUNSTEN VAN BELGIË, BRUSSEL: photo Cussac 6–7, 14t, 34–5, 62clb, 63crb/bl, 64ca/b, 65tl/tr, 66t, 67b, /©ADAGP, Paris and DACS, London 2000 65br, /© The Henry Moore Foundation 65c; photo Speltdoorn 14b, 15c, 20c, 63cr, 66b,/©ADAGP, Paris James Ensor *Skeletons Fighting Over a Pickled Herring*, 1891 ©DACS 2000 64t; and DACS, London 2000 67t.

Document OPT: Alain Mathieu 171t.

Pictor: 89t; Robbie Polley: 112b, 116ca, 117b, 118tr, 162t, 163c, 165t, 168c/b, 171b; Private Collection: 7, 34, 39, 85, 123, 161.

Rex Features: 22, 24b, 26c, Action Press 36t; Sipa Press/Vincent Kessler 23t.

Sabena: 166clb; Science Photo Library: CNES 1992 Distribution Spot Image 8; ©Standaard Strips: 19bl; Neil Setchfield: 20tl, 88t, 140c, 157t/c; Sundancer: © Moulinsart 18cl.

Telegraph Colour Library: Ian McKinnell 84-5; Archives du Theatre Royal de la Monnaie: 35tr; Tony Stone Images:

Richard Elliott 27; Hideo Kurihara 2–3; ©Toerisme Ooost-Vlaanderen: 99br; Service Relations Exterieures City of Tournai: 20b.

Roger Viollet: 32t; Musee San Martino, Naples 33b.

World Pictures: 26b, 101b.

Jacket
Front - DK Picture Library: Pinkus Muller Brewery, Germany cr; Demetrio Carrasco bc, cl; Powerstock: A. Gin main image. Back - DK Picture Library: Demetrio Carrasco tl, br. Spine -Powerstock: A. Gin.

**All other images ©Dorling Kindersley.**
**For further information see: www.dkimages.com**

## Dorling Kindersley Special Editions

Dorling Kindersley books can be purchased in bulk quantities at discounted prices for use in promotions or as premiums.
We are also able to offer special editions and personalized jackets, corporate imprints, and excerpts from all of our books, tailored specifically to meet your own needs.

To find out more, please contact:
(in the United Kingdom) –
Sarah.Burgess@dk.com or Special Sales, Dorling Kindersley Limited, 80 Strand, London WC2R ORL;

(in the United States) – Special Markets Dept., DK Publishing, Inc., 375 Hudson Street, New York, NY 10014.

# Phrase Book

## TIPS FOR PRONOUNCING FRENCH

French-speaking Belgians, or Walloons, have a throaty, deep accent noticeably different from French spoken in France. Despite this, there are few changes in the vocabulary used in spoken and written language.

Consonants at the end of words are mostly silent and not pronounced. *Ch* is pronounced *sh*; *th* is *t*; *w* is *v*; and *r* is rolled gutturally. *Ç* is pronounced *s*.

## IN EMERGENCY

| | | |
|---|---|---|
| Help! | **Au secours!** | oh se**koor** |
| Stop! | **Arrêtez!** | aret-**ay** |
| Call a doctor! | **Appelez un medecin** | apuh-**lay** uñ med**sañ** |
| Call the police! | **Appelez la police** | apuh-**lay** lah pol-**ees** |
| Call the fire brigade! | **Appelez les pompiers** | apuh-**lay** leh poñ-**peeyay** |
| Where is the nearest telephone? | **Ou est le téléphone le plus proche** | oo ay luh tehleh**fon** luh ploo **prosh** |
| Where is the nearest hospital? | **Ou est l'hôpital le plus proche** | oo ay l'opee**tal** luh ploo **prosh** |

## COMMUNICATION ESSENTIALS

| | | |
|---|---|---|
| Yes | **Oui** | wee |
| No | **Non** | noñ |
| Please | **S'il vous plait** | seel voo **play** |
| Thank you | **Merci** | mer-**see** |
| Excuse me | **Excusez-moi** | exkoo-**zay** mwah |
| Hello | **Bonjour** | boñzhoor |
| Goodbye | **Au revoir** | oh ruh-**vwar** |
| Good night | **Bonne nuit** | boñ-**swar** |
| morning | **Le matin** | matañ |
| afternoon | **L'apres-midi** | l'apreh-**meedee** |
| evening | **Le soir** | swah |
| yesterday | **Hier** | eeyehr |
| today | **Aujourd'hui** | oh-zhoor-**dwee** |
| tomorrow | **Demain** | duhmañ |
| here | **Ici** | ee-**see** |
| there | **Là bas** | lah bah |
| What? | **Quel/quelle?** | kel, kel |
| When? | **Quand?** | koñ |
| Why? | **Pourquoi?** | poor-**kwah** |
| Where? | **Où?** | oo |
| How? | **Comment?** | kom-**moñ** |

## USEFUL PHRASES

| | | |
|---|---|---|
| How are you? | **Comment allez vous?** | kom-moñ talay voo |
| Very well, thank you. | **Très bien, merci.** | treh byañ, mer-**see** |
| How do you do? | **Comment ça va?** | kom-moñ sah **vah** |
| See you soon | **A bientôt.** | byañ-toh |
| That's fine | **Ça va bien.** | Sah vah byañ |
| Where is/are...? | **Où est/sont...?** | ooh ay/soñ |
| How far is it to...? | **Combien de kilomètres d'ici à...?** | kom-**byañ** duh keelo-**metr** d'ee-**see** ah |
| Which way to ? | **Quelle est la direction pour...?** | kel ay lah deer-ek-**syoñ** poor |
| Do you speak English? | **Parlez-vous Anglais?** | par-**lay** voo oñg-**lay** |
| I don't understand. | **Je ne comprends pas.** | zhuh nuh kom-**proñ** pah |
| Could you speak slowly? | **Vous puissez parlez plus lentement?** | voo pwee-say par-lay ploos **loñ**tuh-moñ |
| I'm sorry. | **Excusez-moi.** | exkoo-**zay** mwah |

## USEFUL WORDS

| | | |
|---|---|---|
| big | **grand** | groñ |
| small | **petit** | puh-**tee** |
| hot | **chaud** | show |
| cold | **froid** | frwah |
| good | **bon** | boñ |
| bad | **mauvais** | moh-**veh** |
| enough | **assez** | assay |
| well | **bien** | byañ |
| open | **ouvert** | oo-**ver** |
| closed | **fermé** | fer-**meh** |
| left | **gauche** | gohsh |
| right | **droite** | drawh |
| straight on | **tout droit** | too drwah |
| near | **près** | preh |
| far | **loin** | lwañ |
| up | **en haut** | oñ oh |
| down | **en bas** | oñ bah |
| early | **tôt** | toh |

| | | |
|---|---|---|
| late | **tard** | tar |
| entrance | **l'entrée** | l'on-**tray** |
| exit | **la sortie** | sor-**tee** |
| toilet | **toilette** | **twah**-let |
| occupied | **occupé** | o-koo-**pay** |
| free (vacant) | **libre** | leebr |
| free (no charge) | **gratuit** | grah-**twee** |

## MAKING A TELEPHONE CALL

| | | |
|---|---|---|
| I would like to place a long-distance telephone call | **Je voudrais faire un interurbain** | zhuh voo-**dreh** faire uñ añter-oorbañ |
| I'd like to call collect | **Je voudrais faire un communication PCV** | zhuh voo-**dreh** faire oon kom-oonikah-**syoñ** peh-seh-veh |
| I will try again later | **Je vais essayer plus tard** | zhuh vay ess-ay-eh ploo tar |
| Can I leave a message? | **Est-ce que je peux laisser un message?** | es-**keh** zhuh puh less-**ay** uñ meh-sazh |
| Could you speak up a little please? | **Pouvez-vous parler un peu plus fort?** | poo-**vay** voo par-**lay** uñ puh ploo for |
| Local call | **Communication local** | komoonikah-**syoñ** low-**kal** |

## SHOPPING

| | | |
|---|---|---|
| How much does this cost? | **C'est combien?** | say kom-**byañ** |
| I would like.... | **Je voudrais** | zhuh voo-**dray** |
| Do you have... | **Est-ce que vous avez...** | es-**kuh** voo zavay |
| I'm just looking | **Je regarde seulement** | zhuh ruh**gar** suhl-**moñ** |
| Do you take credit cards? | **Est-ce que vous acceptez les cartes de crédit** | es **kuh** voo zaksept-**ay** leh kart duh kreh-**dee** |
| Do you take travellers' cheques? | **Est-ce que vous acceptez les chèques de voyage** | es-**kuh** voo zak-sept-ay lay shek duh vwayazh |
| What time do you open? | **A quelle heure vous êtes ouvert** | ah kel urr voo zet oo-**ver** |
| What time do you close? | **A quelle heure vous êtes fermé** | ah kel urr voo zet fer-**may** |
| This one | **Celui ci** | suhl-wee **see** |
| That one | **Celui-là** | suhl-wee **lah** |
| expensive | **cher** | shehr |
| cheap | **pas cher, bon marché** | pah shehr, boñ mar-shay |
| size, clothes | **la taille** | tye |
| white | **blanc** | bloñ |
| black | **noir** | nwahr |
| red | **rouge** | roozh |
| yellow | **jaune** | zhownh |
| green | **vert** | vehr |
| blue | **bleu** | bluh |

## TYPES OF SHOPS

| | | |
|---|---|---|
| shop | **le magasin** | le maga-**zañ** |
| bakery | **la boulangerie** | booloñ-**zhuree** |
| bank | **la banque** | boñk |
| bookshop | **la librairie** | lee-**brehree** |
| butcher | **la boucherie** | boo-**shehree** |
| cake shop | **la pâtisserie** | patee-**sree** |
| chocolate shop | **la chocolatier** | shok-oh-lah-tyeh |
| chip stop/stand | **la friterie** | free-tuh-ree |
| chemist | **la pharmacie** | farmah-**see** |
| delicatessen | **la charcuterie** | shah-koo-tuh-ree |
| department store | **le grand magasin** | groñ maga-**zañ** |
| fishmonger | **la poissonerie** | pwasson-ree |
| greengrocer | **le marchand des légumes** | mar-**shoñ** duh lay-**goom** |
| hairdresser | **le coiffeur** | kwafuhr |
| market | **le marché** | marsh ay |
| newsagent | **le magasin de journaux/tabac** | maga-**zañ** duh zhoor-**no**/ta-bak |
| post office | **le bureau de poste** | boo-**roh** duh pohst |
| supermarket | **le supermarché** | soo-pehr-**marshay** |
| travel agent | **l'agence de voyage** | azhons duh vwayazh |

## SIGHTSEEING

| | | |
|---|---|---|
| art gallery | **le galérie d'art** | galer-**ree** dart |
| bus station | **la gare routière** | gahr roo-tee-yehr |

| cathedral | la cathédrale | katay-**dral** |
| church | l'église | aygleez |
| closed on public holidays | fermeture jour ferié | fehrmeh-tur zhoor fehree-ay |
| garden | le jardin | zhah-**dañ** |
| library | la bibliothèque | beeb**leeo**-tek |
| museum | le musée | moo-**zay** |
| railway station | la gare (SNCF) | gahr (es-en-say-ef) |
| tourist office | les informations | layz uñ-for-mah-syoñ |
| town hall | l'hôtel de ville | ohtel duh vil |
| train | le train | trañ |

## STAYING IN A HOTEL

| Do you have a vacant room? | est-ce que vous avez une chambre? | es-kuh voo zavay oon shambr |
| double room with double bed | la chambre à deux personnes, avec un grand lit | la shambr uh duh per-**son** uh-vek uñ groñ lee |
| twin room | la chambre à deux lits | la shambr ah duh lee |
| single room | la chambre à une personne | la shambr ah oon pehr-**son** |
| room with a bath | la chambre avec salle de bain | shambr ah-vek sal duh bañ |
| shower | une douche | doosh |
| I have a reservation | J'ai fait une reservation | zhay fay oon ray-zehrva-**syoñ** |

## EATING OUT

| Have you got a table? | Avez vous une table libre? | avay-**voo** oon tahbl leebr |
| I would like to reserve a table. | Je voudrais réserver une table. | zhuh voo-dray rayzehr-**vay** oon tahbl |
| The bill, please. | L'addition, s'il vous plait. | l'adee-**syoñ**, seel voo **play** |
| I am a vegetarian. | Je suis végétarien. | zhuh swet vezhay-**tehryañ** |
| waitress/waiter | Monsieur, Mademoiselle | gah-sohn/ mad-uh-mwah-zel |
| menu | le menu | men-**oo** |
| cover charge | le couvert | luh koo-**vehr** |
| wine list | la carte des vins | lah **kart**-deh vañ |
| glass | verre | vehr |
| bottle | la bouteille | boo-**tay** |
| knife | le couteau | koo-**toh** |
| fork | la fourchette | for-**shet** |
| spoon | la cuillère | kwee-**yehr** |
| breakfast | le petit déjeuner | puh-**tee** day-**zhuh-nay** |
| lunch | le déjeuner | day-**zhuh-nay** |
| dinner | le dîner | dee-**nay** |
| main course | le grand plat | groñ plah |
| starter | l'hors d'oeuvres | or duhvr |
| dessert | la dessert | duh-zehrt |
| dish of the day | le plat du jour | plah doo joor |
| bar | le bar | bah |
| cafe | le café | ka-**fay** |
| rare | saignant | say-nyoñ |
| medium | à point | ah **pwañ** |
| well done | bien cuit | byañ **kwee** |

## NUMBERS

| 0 | zero | zeh-**roh** |
| 1 | un | uñ, oon |
| 2 | deux | duh |
| 3 | trois | trwah |
| 4 | quatre | katr |
| 5 | cinq | sañk |
| 6 | six | sees |
| 7 | sept | set |
| 8 | huit | weet |
| 9 | neuf | nerf |
| 10 | dix | dees |
| 11 | onze | oñz |
| 12 | douze | dooz |
| 13 | treize | trehz |
| 14 | quatorze | katorz |
| 15 | quinze | kañz |
| 16 | seize | sehz |
| 17 | dix-sept | dees-**set** |
| 18 | dix-huit | dees-**zweet** |
| 19 | dix-neuf | dees-**znerf** |
| 20 | vingt | vañ |
| 21 | vingt-et-un | vañ ay uhn |
| 30 | trente | tront |
| 40 | quarante | karoñt |
| 50 | cinquante | sañkoñt |

| 60 | soixante | swahsoñt |
| 70 | soixante-dix | swahsoñt-dees |
| 80 | quatre-vingt | katr-**vañ** |
| 90 | quatre-vingt-dix/ nonante | katr vañ dees/ nonañ |
| 100 | cent | soñ |
| 1000 | mille | meel |
| 1,000,000 | million | miyoñ |

## TIME

| What is the time? | Quelle heure? | kel uhr |
| one minute | une minute | oon mee-**noot** |
| one hour | une heure | oon uhr |
| half an hour | une demi-heure | oon duh-mee uhr |
| half past one | une heure et demi | uhr ay duh-mee |
| a day | un jour | zhuhr |
| a week | une semaine | suh-mehn |
| a month | un mois | mwah |
| a year | une année | annay |
| Monday | lundi | luñ-**dee** |
| Tuesday | mardi | mah-**dee** |
| Wednesday | mercredi | mehrkruh-**dee** |
| Thursday | jeudi | zhuh-**dee** |
| Friday | vendredi | voñdruh-**dee** |
| Saturday | samedi | sam-**dee** |
| Sunday | dimanche | dee-**moñsh** |

## BELGIAN BEER AND FOOD

| fish | poisson | pwah-**ssoñ** |
| bass | bar/loup de mer | bah/loo duh mare |
| herring | hareng | ah-**roñ** |
| lobster | homard | oh-ma |
| monkfish | lotte | lot |
| mussel | moule | mool |
| oyster | huitre | weetr |
| pike | brochet | brosh-ay |
| salmon | saumon | soh-moñ |
| scallop | coquille Saint-Jacques | kok-eel sañ jak |
| sea bream | dorade/daurade | doh-rad |
| prawn | crevette | kreh-vet |
| skate | raie | ray |
| trout | truite | trweet |
| tuna | thon | toñ |

## MEAT

| meat | viande | vee-**yand** |
| beef | boeuf | buhf |
| chicken | poulet | poo-**lay** |
| duck | canard | kanar |
| lamb | agneau | ahyoh |
| pheasant | faisant | feh-zoñ |
| pork | porc | por |
| veal | veau | voh |
| venison | cerf/chevreuil | surf/shev-roy |

## VEGETABLES

| vegetables | légumes | lay-**goom** |
| asparagus | asperges | ahs-pehrj |
| Belgian endive /chicory | chicon | shee-koñ |
| Brussels sprouts | choux de bruxelles | shoo duh broocksell |
| garlic | ail | eye |
| green beans | haricots verts | arrykoh vehr |
| haricot beans | haricots | arrykoh |
| potatoes | pommes de terre | pom-duh **tehr** |
| spinach | epinard | aypeenar |
| truffle | truffe | troof |

## DESSERTS

| pancake | crêpe | crayp |
| waffle | gauffre | gohfr |
| fruit | fruits | frwee |

## DRINKS

| coffee | café | kah-**fay** |
| white coffee | café au lait | kah-**fay** oh lay |
| milky coffee | caffe latte | kah-**fay** lat-uh |
| hot chocolate | chocolat chaud | shok-oh-lah shoh |
| tea | thé | tay |
| water | l'eau | oh |
| mineral water | l'eau minérale | l'oh meenay-ral |
| lemonade | limonade | lee-moh-nad |
| orange juice | jus d'orange | zhoo doh-ronj |
| wine | le vin | vañ |
| house wine | vin maison | vañ may-sañ |
| beer | un bière | byahr |

## TIPS FOR PRONOUNCING FLEMISH

Flemish is a dialect of Dutch, with most of the language remaining the same, bar some regional differences. The language is pronounced in largely the same way as English, although many vowels, particularly double vowels, are pronounced as long sounds. *J* is the equivalent of the English *y*, *v* is pronounced *f*, and *w* is *v*.

## IN EMERGENCY

| | | |
|---|---|---|
| Help! | **Help!** | help |
| Stop! | **Stop!** | stop |
| Call a doctor! | **Haal een dokter!** | Haal uhn **dok**-tur |
| Call the police! | **Roep de politie!** | Roep duh poe-**leet**-see |
| Call the fire brigade! | **Roep de brandweer!** | Roop duh **brahnt**-vheer |
| Where is the nearest telephone? | **Waar ist de dichtsbijzijnde telefoon?** | Vhaar iss duh **dikst**-baiy-zaiyn-duh-tay-luh-**foan** |
| Where is the nearest hospital? | **Waar ist het dichtsbijzijnde ziekenhuis** | Vhaar iss het **dikst**-baiy-zaiyn-duh **zee**-kuh-huws |

## COMMUNICATION ESSENTIALS

| | | |
|---|---|---|
| Yes | **Ja** | yaa |
| No | **Nee** | nay |
| Please | **Alstublieft** | ahls-tew-**bleeft** |
| Thank you | **Dank u** or | dhank-ew |
| Excuse me | **Pardon** | pah-**don** |
| Hello | **Bedankt** | be-dunk |
| Goodbye | **Dag** | dahgh |
| Good night | **Slaap lekker** | slap **lek**-kah |
| morning | **Morgen** | **mor**-ghugh |
| afternoon | **Middag** | **mid**-dahgh |
| evening | **Avond** | **av**-vohnd |
| yesterday | **Gisteren** | **ghis**-tern |
| today | **Vandaag** | van-**daagh** |
| tomorrow | **Morgen** | **mor**-ghugh |
| here | **Hier** | heer |
| there | **Daar** | daar |
| What? | **Wat?** | vhat |
| When? | **Wanneer?** | vhan-**eer** |
| Why? | **Waarom?** | vhaar-**om** |
| Where? | **Waar?** | vhaar |
| How? | **Hoe?** | hoo |

## USEFUL PHRASES

| | | |
|---|---|---|
| How are you? | **Hoe gaat het ermee?** | Hoo ghaat het er-**may** |
| Very well, thank you | **Heel goed, dank u** | Hayl ghoot, dhank ew |
| How do you do? | **Hoe maakt u het?** | Hoo maakt ew het |
| See you soon | **Tot ziens** | Tot zeens |
| That's fine | **Prima** | Pree-mah |
| Where is/are...? | **Waar is/zijn...?** | vhaar iss/zayn |
| How far is it to...? | **Hoe ver is het naar...?** | Hoo vehr iss het nar |
| How do I get to...? | **Hoe kom ik naar...?** | Hoo kom ik nar |
| Do you speak English? | **Spreekt u engels?** | Spraykt uw **eng**-uhls |
| I don't understand | **Ik snap het niet** | Ik snahp het neet |
| Could you speak slowly? | **Kunt u langzamer praten?** | Kuhnt ew lahng-zarmer-praat-tuh |
| I'm sorry | **Sorry** | sorry |

## USEFUL WORDS

| | | |
|---|---|---|
| big | **groot** | ghroat |
| small | **klein** | klaiyn |
| hot | **warm** | vharm |
| cold | **koud** | khowt |
| good | **goed** | ghoot |
| bad | **slecht** | slekht |
| enough | **genoeg** | ghuh-**noohkh** |
| well | **goed** | ghoot |
| open | **open** | open |
| closed | **gesloten** | ghuh-**slow**-tuh |
| left | **links** | links |
| right | **rechts** | rekhts |
| straight on | **rechtdoor** | rehkht dohr |
| near | **dightbij** | dikht baiy |
| far | **ver weg** | vehr vhekh |
| up | **omhoog** | om-**hoakh** |
| down | **naar beneden** | naar buh **nay**-duh |
| early | **vroeg** | vrookh |

| | | |
|---|---|---|
| late | **laat** | laat |
| entrance | **ingang** | **in**-ghang |
| exit | **uitgang** | **ouht**-ghang |
| toilet | **wc** | vhay-say |
| occupied | **bezet** | buh-**zett** |
| free (vacant) | **vrij** | vraiy |
| free (no charge) | **gratis** | **ghraah**-tiss |

## MAKING A TELEPHONE CALL

| | | |
|---|---|---|
| I'd like to place a long-distance telephone call | **Ik wil graag interlokal telefoneren** | ik vhil ghraakh **inter**-loh-kaal tay-luh-foh-**neh**-ruh |
| I'd like to call collect | **Ik wil "collect call" bellen** | ik vhil "collect call" **bel**-luh |
| I will try again later | **Ik probeer het later nog wel eens** | ik pro-**beer** het laater nokh vhel ayns |
| Can I leave a message? | **Kunt u een boodschap doorgeven?** | kuhnt ew uhn **boat**-skhahp **dohr**-ghay-vuh |
| Could you speak up a little please? | **Wilt u vat harder praten?** | vhilt ew vhat **hahr**-der **praat**-ew |
| Local call | **Lokaal gesprek** | low-**kaahl** ghuh-**sprek** |

## SHOPPING

| | | |
|---|---|---|
| How much does this cost? | **Hoeveel kost dit?** | hoo-**vayl** kost dit |
| I would like... | **Ik wil graag...** | ik vhil ghraakh |
| Do you have...? | **Heeft u...?** | hayft ew |
| I'm just looking | **Ik kijk alleen even** | ik kaiyk alleyn **ay**-vuh |
| Do you take credit cards? | **Neemt u credit cards aan?** | naymt ew credit cards aan? |
| Do you take travellers' cheques? | **Neemt u reischeques aan?** | naymt ew **raiys**-sheks aan |
| What time do you open? | **Hoe laat gaat u open?** | hoo laat ghaat ew opuh |
| What time do you close? | **Hoe laat gaat u dicht?** | hoo laat ghaat ew dikht |
| This one | **Deze** | **day**-zuh |
| That one | **Die** | dee |
| expensive | **duur** | dewr |
| cheap | **goedkoop** | ghoot-**koap** |
| size | **maat** | maat |
| white | **wit** | vhit |
| black | **zwart** | zvhahrt |
| red | **rood** | roat |
| yellow | **geel** | ghayl |
| green | **groen** | ghroon |
| blue | **blauw** | blah-ew |

## TYPES OF SHOPS

| | | |
|---|---|---|
| antique shop | **antiekwinkel** | ahn-**teek**-vhin-kul |
| bakery | **bakker** | **bah**-ker |
| bank | **bank** | bahnk |
| bookshop | **boekwinkel** | **book**-vhin-kul |
| butcher | **slager** | slaakh-er |
| cake shop | **banketbakkerij** | bahnk-**et**-bahk-er-aiy |
| chip stop/stand | **patatzaak** | pah-**taht**-zak |
| chemist/drugstore | **apotheek** | ah-poc-**taiyk** |
| delicatessen | **delicatessen** | daylee-kah-**tes**-suh |
| department store | **warenhuis** | **vhaah**-uh-houws |
| fishmonger | **viswinkel** | **viss**-vhin-kul |
| greengrocer | **groenteboer** | **ghroon**-tuh-boor |
| hairdresser | **kapper** | **kah**-per |
| market | **markt** | mahrkt |
| newsagent | **krantenwinkel** | **krahn**-tuh-vhin-kul |
| post office | **postkantoor** | **pohst**-kahn-tor |
| supermarket | **supermarkt** | **sew**-per-mahrkt |
| tobacconist | **sigarenwinkel** | see-**ghaa**-ruh-vhin-kul |
| travel agent | **reisburo** | **raiys**-bew-roa |

## SIGHTSEEING

| | | |
|---|---|---|
| art gallery | **gallerie** | ghaller-ee |
| bus station | **busstation** | **buhs**-stah-shown |
| bus ticket | **strippenkaart** | **strip**-puh-kaart |
| cathedral | **kathedraal** | kah-tuh-**draal** |
| church | **kerk** | kehrk |
| closed on public holidays | **op feestdagen gesloten** | op **fayst**-daa-ghuh ghuh slow **tuh** |
| day return | **dagretour** | **dahgh**-ruh-tour |
| garden | **tuin** | touwn |
| library | **bibliotheek** | bee-bee-yo-**tayk** |
| museum | **museum** | mew-**zay**-um |

| English | Flemish | Pronunciation |
|---|---|---|
| railway station | **station** | stah-**shown** |
| return ticket | **retourtje** | ruh-**tour**-tyuh |
| single journey | **enkeltje** | eng-**kuhl**-tyuh |
| tourist information | **dienst voor tourisme** | deenst vor **tor**-ism |
| town hall | **stadhuis** | **staht**-houws |
| train | **trein** | traiyn |

### STAYING IN A HOTEL

| English | Flemish | Pronunciation |
|---|---|---|
| Do you have a vacant room? | **Zijn er nog kamers vrij?** | zaiyn er nokh **kaa**-mers vray |
| double room with double bed | **een twees persoons-kamer met een twee persoonsbed** | uhn **tvhay** per-soans-ka-mer met uhn **tvhay** per-**soans** beht |
| twin room | **een kamer met een lits-jumeaux** | uhn **kaa**-mer met uhn lee-zjoo-**moh** |
| single room | **eenpersoons-kamer** | ayn-per-**soans** kaa-mer |
| room with a bath/shower | **kaamer met bad/ douche** | **kaa**-mer met baht/doosh |
| I have a reservation | **Ik heb gereserveerd** | ik hehp ghuh-ray-sehr-**veert** |

### EATING OUT

| English | Flemish | Pronunciation |
|---|---|---|
| Have you got table? | **Is er een tafel vrij?** | iss ehr uhn **tah**-fuhl vraiy |
| I would like to reserve a table | **Ik wil een tafel reserveren** | ik vhil uhn **tah**-fel ray sehr-**veer**-uh |
| The bill, please | **Mag ik afrekenen** | muhk ik **ahf**-ray-kuh-nuh |
| I am a vegetarian | **Ik ben vegetariër** | ik ben fay-ghuh-**taahr**-ee-er |
| waitress/waiter | **serveerster/ober** | schr-**veer**-ster/**oh**-ber |
| menu | **de kaart** | duh kaahrt |
| cover charge | **het couvert** | het koo-**vehr** |
| wine list | **de wijnkaart** | duh **vhaiyn**-kart |
| glass | **het glass** | het ghlahss |
| bottle | **de fles** | duh fless |
| knife | **het mes** | het mess |
| fork | **de vork** | duh fork |
| spoon | **de lepel** | duh **lay**-pul |
| breakfast | **het ontbijt** | het ont-**baiyt** |
| lunch | **de lunch** | duh lernsh |
| dinner | **het diner** | het dee-**nay** |
| main course | **het hoofdgerecht** | het **hoaft**-ghuh-rekht |
| starter, first course | **het voorgerecht** | het **vhor**-ghuh-rekht |
| dessert | **het nagerecht** | het **naa**-ghuh-rekht |
| dish of the day | **het dagmenu** | het **dahg**-munh-ew |
| bar | **het cafe** | het kaa-**fay** |
| café | **het eetcafe** | het **ayt**-kaa-**fay** |
| rare | **rare** | 'rare' |
| medium | **medium** | 'medium' |
| well done | **doorbakken** | door-**bah**-kuh |

### NUMBERS

| | Flemish | Pronunciation |
|---|---|---|
| 1 | **een** | ayn |
| 2 | **twee** | tvhay |
| 3 | **drie** | dree |
| 4 | **vier** | feer |
| 5 | **vijf** | faiyf |
| 6 | **zes** | zess |
| 7 | **zeven** | **zay**-vuh |
| 8 | **acht** | ahkht |
| 9 | **negen** | **nay**-guh |
| 10 | **tien** | teen |
| 11 | **elf** | elf |
| 12 | **twaalf** | tvhaalf |
| 13 | **dertien** | **dehr**-teen |
| 14 | **veertien** | **feer**-teen |
| 15 | **vijftien** | **faiyf**-teen |
| 16 | **zestien** | **zess**-teen |
| 17 | **zeventien** | **zayvuh**-teen |
| 18 | **achtien** | **ahkh**-teen |
| 19 | **negentien** | **nay-ghuh**-tien |
| 20 | **twintig** | **tvhin**-tukh |
| 21 | **eenentwintig** | **aynuh**-tvhin-tukh |
| 30 | **dertig** | **dehr**-tukh |
| 40 | **veertig** | **feer**-tukh |
| 50 | **vijftig** | **faiyf**-tukh |
| 60 | **zestig** | **zess**-tukh |
| 70 | **zeventig** | **zay**-vuh-tukh |
| 80 | **tachtig** | **tahkh**-tukh |
| 90 | **negentig** | **nayguh**-tukh |
| 100 | **honderd** | **hohn**-durt |
| 1000 | **duizend** | **douw**-zuhnt |
| 1,000,000 | **miljoen** | mill-**yoon** |

### TIME

| English | Flemish | Pronunciation |
|---|---|---|
| one minute | **een minuut** | uhn meen-**ewt** |
| one hour | **een uur** | uhn ewr |
| half an hour | **een half uur** | een hahlf uhr |
| half past one | **half twee** | hahlf twee |
| a day | **een dag** | uhn dahgh |
| a week | **een week** | uhn vhayk |
| a month | **een maand** | uhn maant |
| a year | **een jaar** | uhn jaar |
| Monday | **maandag** | **maan**-dahgh |
| Tuesday | **dinsdag** | **dins**-dahgh |
| Wednesday | **woensdag** | **vhoons**-dahgh |
| Thursday | **donderdag** | **donder**-dahgh |
| Friday | **vrijdag** | **vraiy**-dahgh |
| Saturday | **zaterdag** | **zaater**-dahgh |
| Sunday | **zondag** | **zon**-dahgh |

### BELGIAN BEER AND FOOD
#### FISH

| English | Flemish | Pronunciation |
|---|---|---|
| fish | **vis** | fiss |
| bass | **zeebars** | see-buhr |
| herring | **haring** | **haa**-ring |
| lobster | **kreeft** | krayft |
| monkfish | **lotte/zeeduivel** | lot/seafuhdul |
| mussel | **mossel** | **moss**-uhl |
| oyster | **oester** | **ouhs**-tuh |
| pike | **snoek** | snook |
| prawn | **garnaal** | gar-nall |
| salmon | **zalm** | sahlm |
| scallop | **Sint-Jacobsoester/ Jacobsschelp** | **sind**-yakob-ouhs-tuh/yakob-schuhlp |
| sea bream | **dorade/zeebrasem** | doh-rard |
| skate | **rog** | rog |
| trout | **forel** | foh-ruhl |
| tuna | **tonijn** | tuhn-een |

#### MEAT

| English | Flemish | Pronunciation |
|---|---|---|
| meat | **vlees** | flayss |
| beef | **rundvlees** | **ruhnt**-flayss |
| chicken | **kip** | kip |
| duck | **eend** | aynt |
| lamb | **lamsvlees** | **lahms**-flayss |
| pheasant | **fazant** | **fay**-zanh |
| pork | **varkensvlees** | **vahr**-kuhns-flayss |
| veal | **kalfsvlees** | **karfs**-flayss |
| venison | **ree (bok)** | ray |

#### VEGETABLES

| English | Flemish | Pronunciation |
|---|---|---|
| vegetables | **groenten** | **ghroon**-tuh |
| asparagus | **asperges** | as-puhj |
| Belgian endive/ chicory | **witloof** | vit-lurf |
| Brussels sprouts | **spruitjes** | spruhr-tyuhs |
| garlic | **knoflook** | **knoff**-loak |
| green beans | **princesbonen** | prins-ess-buh-nun |
| haricot beans | **snijbonen** | snee-buh-nun |
| potatoes | **aardappels** | **aard**-uppuhls |
| spinach | **spinazie** | spin-a-jee |
| truffle | **truffel** | truh-fuhl |

#### DESSERTS

| English | Flemish | Pronunciation |
|---|---|---|
| fruit | **fruit/vruchten** | vroot/vrooh-tuh |
| pancake | **pannekoek** | **pah**-nuh-kook |
| waffle | **wafel** | vaff-uhl |

#### DRINKS

| English | Flemish | Pronunciation |
|---|---|---|
| beer | **bier** | beeh |
| coffee | **koffie** | coffee |
| fresh orange juice | **verse jus** | **vehr**-suh zjhew |
| hot chocolate | **chocola** | sho-koh-**laa** |
| mineral water | **mineraalwater** | meener-**aahl**-vhaater |
| tea | **thee** | tay |
| water | **water** | **vhaa**-ter |
| wine | **wijn** | vhaiyn |

# FOR PEACE OF MIND ABROAD,
## WE'VE GOT IT COVERED

VIDES YOU

LDWIDE

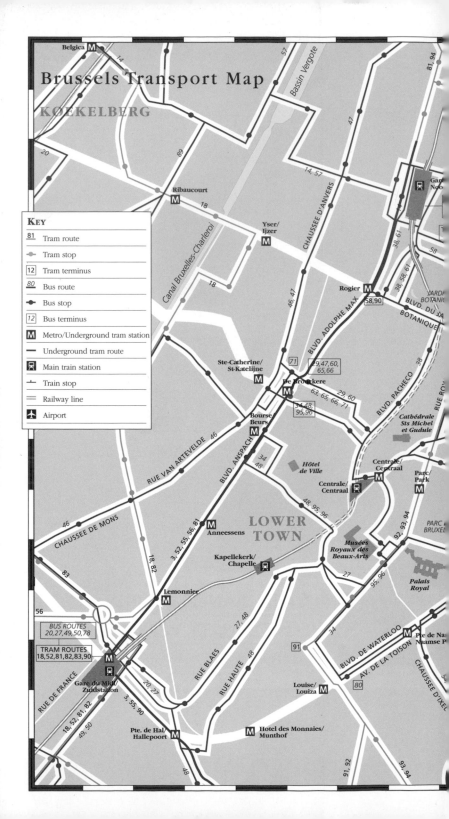